Diversity Itself

Essays in Australian Arts and Culture

[handwritten signature]
2. April 1997
[handwritten signature]

Diversity Itself

Essays in
Australian Arts
and Culture

Edited by
Peter Quartermaine

Exeter Studies in American and Commonwealth Arts
No. 1
Published by the University of Exeter for AmCAS

First published 1986 by the University of Exeter

© 1986 University of Exeter and the several authors,
each in respect of the paper contributed

ISBN 0 85989 282 4

Exeter Studies in American and Commonwealth Arts
General Editor: Richard Maltby

Exeter University Publications
Reed Hall
Streatham Drive
Exeter
Devon EX4 4QR

Printed in Great Britain by A. Wheaton and Co. Ltd, Exeter

This book is dedicated
by the Authors to

*Nelson and Winnie
Mandela*

Contents

List of Illustrations

Acknowledgements

An apparent bias towards Western Australia in the geographical location of contributors (Graeme Turner moved from Perth to Queensland during publication on the editor's orders) reflects the two fruitful months I spent there in 1984 researching in the English departments of the University of Western Australia and the Western Australian Institute of Technology. For this I am specially grateful to Bruce Bennett and Don Grant.

A wise old Australian historian once observed that academics research most of those areas which feed their own paranoias, and as hapless daily victims here my Exeter undergraduates deserve a mention. It is reassuring to have a former student contributing to this volume as both colleague and friend. My greatest debt, though, is to colleagues in American & Commonwealth Arts at Exeter, past and present – not least the many Australian visitors over the years.

My thanks go to the Publications Committee of the University of Exeter for their support in producing this volume, and especially to Barbara Mennell. For invaluable help in different ways I am grateful to Mervyn Bennun, Tamsin Donaldson, Alastair Niven and Michael Wood, though none is to be held responsible for any failings in the book. Tony Clayden, Head of Graphic Design at Exeter College of Art and Design gave invaluable advice on layout and design, and Carol Kemp, a second-year student in the section, designed the book.

A grant from the Literature Board of the Australia Council, for my earlier collection *Readings in Australian Arts* (Exeter 1978), has enabled the modest profits from that volume to offset somewhat the much greater costs of this.

Finally, David and Mary Alice Lowenthal have provided a base for my London forays over many years; this book is small recompense for their hospitality and inspiration.

Peter Quartermaine
Exeter 1986

Introduction

Although their immediate focus is 'Australian studies', I hope these essays will provoke discussion of wider issues. With this in mind, contributors were left completely free to write on what they felt important within the overall concept of a non-specialist book on Australian arts and culture. As editor I have tampered very little with the papers, and then only with the writer's agreement.

To write an introduction for essays on Australian arts and culture by colleagues from Glasgow to Perth can only be a pleasure. An editor's role here is to enhance the complementary discussions of the various authors, for it is their book. My own principles are set out in my contribution to the volume, but the very appearance of this collection, drawn as it is from Australia, Denmark, England, Scotland and Switzerland, confirms the value of the twenty years I have spent teaching Australian arts at Exeter University. Like other interests, 'Australian studies' can have its narrow and self-regarding side, but for me it has meant introducing British students to authors and artists of whom usually they have not heard (and on whom, often, there has been little available in print). This has posed a healthy challenge to teacher and student alike.

Neither the Nobel Prize nor the America's Cup has changed the fact that to teach Australian culture in Britain is to be an outsider. Australia is the place to which we sent our convicts, in which we tested our atomic bombs. It is a blank on the map, though many Britons still assume that Australia is very much 'part' of Britain in some curious way. (British business executives apparently sometimes arrive at Heathrow airport without visas for Australia, assuming that a British passport is quite sufficient for their return trip.) But Australia is only one blank among many on the world map, and can usefully be studied as representative rather than unique in the cultural questions that its history and culture pose. Exactly such questioning is stimulated by teaching and research in Commonwealth areas.

1

This collection is not intended as a comprehensive coverage of Australian arts and culture. Music, sculpture, drama, architecture and photography are obvious gaps. It seemed sensible not to aspire to any representative (let alone comprehensive) coverage, but rather to point up the diversity of the field while exploring in some depth selected aspects of it. Now that the papers are gathered in, the extent to which they offer a pattern of cross-references in their concerns and approaches is striking (at least to a hopeful editor's eye).

To see a commitment to marginalized cultures as a characteristic of several papers in the collection is to invite accusations of several kinds (most obviously of Eurocentric assumptions on my part, perhaps). Yet, as my own chapter argues, Australian culture is inevitably marginal seen from Britain – but that very marginality can be seized upon and used as a way of challenging the marginalizing assumptions of British cultural self-definition. In this sense the 'margins' have something to offer that the 'centre' lacks, a belief which has always informed the American & Commonwealth Arts course within which I teach at Exeter (though in what sense – and by whom – Irish history, North American Indians, Les Murray or Hollywood can be seen as 'marginal' will be established only through that wide-ranging debate that is the essence of any university course).

All teachers spend much time and energy fighting institutional battles which inevitably seem irrelevant at times. Brighter moments bring the realization that such disagreements are not 'merely' bureaucratic or administrative, but are themselves part of the culture within which intellectual initiatives must be pursued. Ian Craven writes that, to be available as a cultural discourse, a text must be 're-inserted into an active context, not simply set against, and at a remove from, its "background"', and Delys Bird stresses that 'ideology enters into literary discourse in indirect, subtle ways, but necessarily . . . by way of the writer's historical and cultural situation'. These writers here draw upon, and refer to, not just the experience of teaching Film in Glasgow or Women's Studies in Perth, but the crucial sense in which these 'academic' concerns (as some would see them) define their own position and interests in culture and society at large. For women, 'writing from a place unrecognized (and therefore unnamed . . .)' within social and academic traditions, the issue is specific, but its implications are widespread and profound.

In the visual arts, Sam Smiles notes that even the landscape itself, once 'shot through with expressionist excess and heroic potential', has become 'a fragile environment needing protection'; the conclusion of Fay Gale and Jane Jacobs is that the preservation of Aboriginal rock art has a special urgency here, if questions of national self-perception, as well as Australian art history, are to be properly understood. David

Bromfield draws attention to artist Keith Looby's shrewd (and witty) insistence that 'establishment exhibitions and public tastes and attitudes to the arts as part of Australian life, do matter'. Tastes and attitudes, moreover, are not formed entirely by chance, and Graeme Turner traces how 'one's training as a literary critic provides "a range of attitudes which accompany a respect for the literary and a discomfort with the popular"' – an outlook which sits uneasily alongside some cherished stereotypes of Australian populism, and is totally wrong for the fruitful study of film.

Henry Reynolds assesses the breaking of 'The Great Australian Silence' about Aboriginal history ('We have to admit and accept the past', in Federal Minister Clyde Holding's words) and Sneja Gunew argues the centrality of multiculturalism in demonstrating that it is 'impossible to speak any longer of an aesthetics which transcends the political'. They thereby place teaching, research and writing in the arts at the very centre of human activity. In truth it has always been there, but too many politicians – and some teachers, more's the pity – believe that today the arts have little of 'relevance' to offer.

Bruce Clunies-Ross praises Les Murray's poetry for creating 'a richly-defined world; the Australia we always knew, yet revealed with a depth and clarity which enlarges understanding and fosters love'. Such terms are little used today, whether in the arts or more widely, but unless space is found for them we shall all be the poorer. As Werner Senn rightly concludes, in exploring ways of seeing Australia 'we may also find fresh ways of seeing ourselves'. At this late hour it seems important to try.

1 Teaching by example: Australian studies and a British education

Peter Quartermaine

'progress is not a comfortable bettering of what we have, in which we might look for an indolent repose, but a succession of adventures, partings of the way, and constant shocks . . . it is not enough to nurture local traditions and to save the past for a short period longer. It is diversity itself which must be saved . . .'.
(Claude Lévi-Strauss, *Race and History*, UNESCO Paris 1958, p. 46.)

The teaching of literature has lost for ever any sure sense of purpose it might once have had, and is in crisis. The insufficiency of 'literary values' to sustain what was thought to be a 'discipline' has been eloquently proven, but has left the status of texts and critics alike (not to mention authors) in a state of some uncertainty. This essay deals only with some specific issues relating to the teaching of Commonwealth literature in Britain, and offers no comprehensive solutions. If diversity is indeed to be saved, it must embrace diversity in critical opinions as well as diversity of texts. Which is not to deny that some critical attitudes are strongly to be preferred to others.

My own preferences, and their justifications, reflect a profound shift during the 1980s in my own perceptions of what I was about in teaching Australian arts and culture in Britain. Some references are inevitably topical, but there seemed no way to remove these without impairing what I needed to say.

Those who teach, and research in, Commonwealth arts and cultures in Britain today bear a special responsibility, for the very essence of their work should inevitably involve questioning that consensus of social and racial attitudes formed in, or inherited from, the nation's imperial past. Such teaching and research reveals the insularity of 'Western' (let alone British) values for understanding the history and aspirations of different cultures. It should also pursue the implications of such shortcomings for relations not only with those proverbial 'foreigners' (ie. the rest of the world) but also between Britons of diverse ethnic origin within the nation itself. It must take to heart Roy Sawh's

5

advice, 'Never forget, you people in England, that the West Indies are your Southern States'.[1] Accepting these implications of teaching Commonwealth arts and cultures (equivalent considerations hold for 'science' topics) entails also that 'Commonwealth' must include South Africa.[2] No responsible teaching or research in any Commonwealth area can be unaffected by those events which illustrate with such terrible clarity the historical consequences of ruthless imperial exploitation executed through institutionalized racist oppression.

Literature is here especially inextricable from historical issues, and a comment made in 1974 of historians in the States and their attitudes to Black history has special relevance:

although they may have succeeded in ridding themselves of preconceptions, and opening their minds to reassessing their sources, they are still subject to some nagging doubts. Many historians have a built-in skepticism concerning innovation, particularly when it comes to a new field of inquiry or a new viewpoint about a low-status minority. The instinct for disciplinary tidiness can be especially strong in a field that is preoccupied with the past.[3]

The final chapter title of Terry Eagleton's *Literary Theory: An Introduction*,[4] is 'Political Criticism'. Eagleton explains that he means by the political 'no more than the way we organize our social life together, and the power-relations which this involves', adding that 'the history of modern literary theory is part of the political and ideological history of our epoch'. (p. 194) In this sense, as he rightly says, there is 'no need to drag politics into literary theory: as with South African sport, it has been there from the beginning'. (p. 194)

Not only is it impossible to avoid politics in academic life any more than in 'real life', but misguided to try. In constructing a supposed defence based on the 'apolitical' nature of their concerns the humanities undermine the very basis of their importance, and allow others to determine the politics of their role. Abnegation of one's political responsibility does not bring freedom from politics (whatever this might mean). Not to vote is a political act, with specific political consequences. These consequences (typically, maintenance of the *status quo*) are, of course, often well understood by those who so virtuously adopt an 'apolitical' stance. Not surprisingly, this position is usually held by people whose ready access to power, whether through colour, birth, education or talent, obviates any need to understand, let alone question, its working.[5] It has yet to be understood that to discuss imperialism, racism, slavery and apartheid is no more (and certainly no less) political than to discuss free enterprise, colonial policy, merchant venturers and separate development.

Since Eagleton coined his title, others have contributed to discussion of literature and politics in Britain. The Secretary of State for

Education, Sir Keith Joseph, stated in his 1985 Green Paper, *Planning for the late 1980s*, that 'The Government is convinced of the importance of providing adequately for the arts . . . for the sake of scholarship, and to give students with true potential to benefit from such study the opportunity to do so and to acquire the associated intellectual skills which are widely valued by employers'. (p. 9) It is difficult, though, to be entirely reassured by the Green Paper's statement that 'Higher education's output of able, skilled and well-motivated graduates is vital to the country's economic performance'. (p. 6) And it is not just governmental insistence on such narrow 'profit and loss' accounting that makes these such dark days for education in Britain. Even more destructive is that attitude of mind among some teachers which sees such political decisions as a god-given opportunity to 'tighten up standards'. Images of weeding and pruning prevail in the talk of such people, and we can all put faces to our local green-fingered educationalists.

The problem for all those involved with arts subjects as they perform bizarre exercises in 'productivity' and 'cost-effectiveness' is that their contribution to the country's economic performance is difficult to assess, to say the least. There is even the real possibility that some areas of academic enquiry damage national economic performance by alerting students to moral ('political') issues of which they might otherwise remain unaware. Learning can be a complex and unsettling experience, a fact ignored by a vision of education as a purely financial investment whose 'value' can be assessed by monitoring the increased financial returns it should bring. Is the student whose South African studies lead to support for a complete economic boycott – in disagreement with official Government policy – a financial liability to the country? And do those teaching such a course deserve state support, especially when compared, say, with a technology transfer project which could result in valuable exports to South Africa?

Such questions were always political, and the crudity with which the Green Paper assesses arts courses lays bare what once the ivy of academe concealed, by chance if not by design. The Thatcher government has done no more than make explicit what was implicit all along; that education is about making and encouraging choices, whether openly or tacitly. We all have different ideologies, in which we sincerely believe, and regard education as the business of explaining and imparting these ideologies to as many students as possible. And lest the word 'ideology' encourage anyone to sit back with a sense of thankful exclusion, we might note Eagleton's contention that '"ideology" is always a way of describing other people's interests rather than one's own'. (p. 210)

In 1967 George Steiner contended that 'whoever teaches or interprets literature . . . must ask of himself what he is about', adding that nothing was more worrying about the present state of English studies in the universities 'than the fact that such an inquiry should be deemed bizarre or subversive'. On the contrary, asserted Steiner, it was 'of the essence'.[6] Ten years later, in 1977, John Docker contended that one value of Australian, and more generally Commonwealth, literature was that it challenged the defenders and controllers of traditional English departments to 'make their anglocentric assumptions explicit'.[7] The suggested reforms that Docker listed were remarkably similar to those drawn up by the Kenyan writer Ngugi wa Thiong'o in his essay 'On the Abolition of the English Department' (included in his 1972 book *Homecoming*),[8] the original text of which had been presented to the Acting Head of the English Department at the University of Nairobi in October 1968. That some academics in centres as different as Nairobi and Canberra were voicing similar frustrations was but one aspect of the shared problem they perceived in asking themselves 'what they were about'; that of imposed courses in 'English' literature.

In 1974 the Nigerian writer Chinua Achebe (who had himself lectured in Australia the previous year) observed that 'the European critic of African literature must cultivate the habit of humility appropriate to his limited experience of the African world and purged of the superiority and arrogance which history so insidiously makes him heir to'.[9] Today, as Chris Tiffin argued in the Introduction to his 1978 book *South Pacific Images*, 'the cultural imperialism of the superpowers seems much more directly related to their political and economic goals – a buffer of sentiment and perhaps idealism has been lost – and it now seems fatuous to discuss modern cultural manipulation independently of those goals'.[10]

Britain is hardly a superpower, more (and increasingly so) a neocolony of the United States, even if Mrs Thatcher cherishes delusions that the Falklands War proved that we are still 'the nation that had ruled a quarter of the world'.[11] Increasingly, though, it is indeed fatuous to ignore the political dimension of teaching. How, for example, could the facts of Britain's 400-year lucrative participation in the slave trade be reconciled with pride in being still the same nation that once 'ruled' a quarter of the world, especially in a racially mixed classroom? How should teachers approach the recent history of Argentina (including Britain's massive investments there for some 200 years) – or of Cyprus, Gibraltar, Northern Ireland?

Such problems of balancing supposed historical objectivity (concentrating on 'the facts') with the realities of political pressure (and, often, control of basic sources), have always been present. What is different is the openness with which assumptions are now made as to what is educationally appropriate or not. A research unit devoted to peace studies would seem unlikely at present to receive government funding, no matter how distinguished the staff it assembled. Military-oriented research, though, forms an increasingly large part of scientific research in universities in the United Kingdom (greater, I believe, than in any other EEC country). But then, war helps economic performance so much more than peace.

Australian literature might seem remote from such considerations, but Eagleton's definition entails that nothing which affects 'the way we organize our social life together' can be *that* remote, however desirable that might be for some schools of criticism. The Australian government has itself set up a committee to examine the teaching of 'Australian studies' in tertiary education both within Australia and abroad.[12] Given that the committee is composed of only three people, each of them with considerable and varied experience in the field of Australian studies, its report is unlikely to be bland, and for the government to act on it will undoubtedly please some and upset others. The greatest worry I heard voiced in Australia in 1984 was that government concern to promote a certain definition of 'Australian studies' (one that emphasised national identity and achievement in the run-up to the bicentennial, say) might result in selective funding for centres perceived to be furthering research along such lines, and a corresponding starving of institutions or individuals who were seen as following 'irrelevant' paths of inquiry. Senator Susan Ryan, the Australian Minister for Education, seemed, on brief acquaintance, very different from Sir Keith Joseph, but there are dangers in their respective intentions to shape education in the humanities for too specific ends.

To explore, and to articulate one's understanding of, another culture in the widest sense (and with a small 'c') is to acquire familiarity, however partial, with another view of the world. And if such familiarity does not lead to an essentially humbling interest in the people who make cultural artifacts (whether machines, legends, songs, films or paintings) then scholarship degenerates into academic triviality on the one hand or cultural exploitation on the other. In many ways the two are closely related in maintaining what Edward Said has termed 'the approved practice of high culture' as 'marginal to the serious political concerns of society':

This has given rise to a cult of professional expertise whose effect in general is pernicious. For the intellectual class, expertise has usually been a service rendered, and sold, to the central authority of society. . . . We tell our students and our general constituency that we defend the classics, the virtues of a liberal education, and precious pleasures of literature even as we show ourselves to be silent (perhaps incompetent) about the historical and social world in which all these things take place.[13]

A lawyer from South Africa assured me in 1983 that Johannesburg was the best place in the world to study law. No one in Rome or

London, apparently, pursues the finer points of Roman law with such precise insight and consummate style as those judges and lawyers among whom he moved on his regular visits to South Africa. I suggested to him that, given the problems of South Africa, there were more pressing issues for a lawyer. He disagreed. 'Let me tell you something', he offered, 'I've always kept out of politics, and I'll take anyone's case – black or white. I'm just interested in law'. (A brief aside: he was white, and admitted in reply to a direct question that no black person had ever approached him with a case.)

South Africa exemplifies principles and actions so destructive of human life and dignity that we can all, perhaps, feel at least moderately virtuous (I write this in March 1986). The point of my anecdote, though, is precisely the reverse; that the same kind of choice faces all teachers everywhere. In social terms the results of our choice in Britain may be less immediately apparent, but educationally and morally the choice itself is just as fundamental.

A student of mine once expressed her preference for 'pure literature' as opposed to the extensive 'background material' encountered on my Commonwealth course. Such a preference for pure literature may seem less contradictory than the white South African's interest in pure law, but in its assumptions and effects it is just as exclusive and repressive, just as culturally arrogant. Such an approach to literature poses as 'common sense' while at the same time seeking privileged access (through the good offices of that cultivated minority of experts whose 'established authority' it naturally bolsters) to an equally 'pure' world of supposedly universal verities and values. Other cultural and political contexts could demand different stances, but in my own I hold it to be self-indulgent and sterile, in that it transfers emotion provoked by the work 'from the plane of lived experience to that of disinterested "art appreciation"'. My terms here are Peter Fuller's, from his excellent little book *Seeing Berger*,[14] and I would like to keep in play his distinction between 'lived experience' and 'art appreciation' in the firm conviction that Australian studies can have no independent life – 'pure Australian studies' has (I trust) a strange ring to it. As a topic it becomes interesting, worth fighting for, only when, far from having a life of its own, it becomes part of ours.

Germaine Greer has argued that art is not for art's sake but 'for life's sake', and as the epigraph to *The Obstacle Race* she quotes Gough Whitlam on this topic. His words bear directly upon the complex relationship between excellence (a term much-beloved by Sir Keith Joseph) and education in a wider and wiser sense. They are words profoundly relevant for all those in the humanities:

A healthy artistic climate does not depend solely on the work of a handful of supremely gifted individuals. It demands the cultivation of talent and ability at all levels. It demands that everyday work, run-of-the-mill work, esoteric and unpopular work should be given a chance; not so much in the hope that genius may one day spring from it, but because, for those who make the arts their life and work, even modest accomplishment is an end in itself and a value worth encouraging. The pursuit of excellence is a proper goal, but it is not the race itself . . . .[15]

Lest this seem rather remote, though, let us approach this question (which forms the nub of my argument) via topics more familiar in time and space, at least to Britons; *The Pelican Guide to English Literature*, Ireland, colonial wars.

In a 1983 review for the *Irish Times* of volumes 5 and 6 of the *Pelican Guide*, Aidan Mathews touched on the question of lived experience and art appreciation in very specific terms. He even raised the old chestnut of why the Napoleonic wars do not feature in Jane Austen's novels, a question which he (looking from Dublin) saw as expressing 'the outsider's pique at the clannishness of nineteenth-century English fiction, its quality of being uninvaded and self-absorbed'. He found this same quality characteristic of the *Guide* itself:

When the *Guide* speaks of 'here' and 'us', using pronouns that indicate the native reader, but subtly exclude the English-speaking foreigner, it seeks to recreate what Jane Austen and George Eliot loved: the sense of a culture at one with itself.[16]

I have written elsewhere of why it should be impossible to see contemporary British culture as at one with itself, and of the dangers of writing as though it were.[17] The Scarman Report[18] on the 1981 inner city riots both identified, and was a symptom of, tensions within British society as serious as any in the past. Those who have personal, professional or community links with Commonwealth and/or Black British and Asian centres around the United Kingdom know this already. The Irish know it too, for different reasons.

In a seminar paper at the London Australian Studies Centre in 1985, Dr Paul Reynolds from the University of Queensland defined one of the important questions for all those teaching Australian studies as 'to whom is our work addressed?' The question intrigued me at the time because I held it to have a very straightforward answer, namely that given by the Black British poet Linton Kwesi Johnson after a reading at Exeter, in reply to a (loaded) question as to *his* intended audience: 'My poetry is for anyone who wants to listen', he said. I talked along these lines in discussion after Reynolds's paper, but thinking further now I am aware of other possible answers. Moreover, the information relevant to framing an answer depends very much upon context, location, point of view. Working as I do at Exeter alongside colleagues (all White British) who teach American film, Native American and

Anglo-Irish culture (not to mention my own work on Australian painting and photography, as well as selected African, Canadian and Caribbean teaching) my interest in Australian culture grows within a particular space, assumes a specific shape. 'Australian studies' in Exeter cannot be the same as 'Australian studies' in Brisbane, any more than 'English studies' can be. Geography plays its part in defining what any work 'means'.

Politics plays a part, too. Teaching in areas felt to be largely irrelevant by the academic majority can induce a dangerously obsessive and defensive attitude, but (to quote a remark I have heard attributed variously to Henry Kissinger and Johnny Rotten) 'Just because you're paranoid, don't mean they're not out to get you'. Working on what most people see as the edge does bring acute consciousness of the power wielded by the centre, a power of which most people (because the force is with them) are unaware. In this sense, to have had since 1983 an Australian Studies Centre in London – in the heart of darkness – has been an invaluable asset in academic political terms, as well as a real pleasure in human terms. (More of this Conradian reference later).

What should the role of such a Centre be, though? It is easy to cast this question in the form of one which the Centre itself should answer, but each of us must make of it what we wish. The attraction, and the challenge, of Australian studies is that so little can be taken for granted, and that so much depends upon individual initiative, personal belief and on perseverance. The answers that each of us gives to the question 'what is Australian studies?' will be largely determined, however, by sharply practical considerations.

Bluntly, given the problems of fitting it into the syllabus, what do Australian studies have to offer that is unique and valuable? Large issues lurk behind this seemingly innocent question: how 'fixed' should a syllabus be (and who fixes it)? Does something have to be 'unique' to be on the syllabus? What kind(s) of 'value' are we talking about? Such fundamental theoretical issues are liable to surface, though, as the 'merely practical' question of how to adjust the established 'core' courses in order to make room for 'option' courses (under which, it is automatically assumed, Australian studies will come). The common sense approach, yet again.

No one would dispute, I take it, that a representative sampling of one's own culture is something that education should aim to provide. This seems simple enough in spirit, if daunting in scope. In literature, for example, might not the *Pelican Guide* act as a basic map for our children, as it undoubtedly did for many British 'O' and 'A' level candidates of my generation? (I still have my own well-thumbed and underlined school copies.) After all, the literary terrain is well known, and the landmarks ever more clearly defined, or so the traditionalists, with their trust in 'established values', would have us believe. Aidan Mathews, though, has some unsettling suggestions on the cultural significance of the *Guide* in his *Irish Times* review. 'It may seem strange,' he admits, 'to recall that the *Guide* made its first appearance shortly after the Suez crisis. Few of us feel that a state's foreign conflicts and a book's publishing history have much to do with each other'. Perhaps the majority of readers here think the same. If so, as Mathews notes, 'the *Guide* agrees with us: it nowhere suggests the remotest relation between English literature and the British Empire'. We can all draw our own conclusions as to the usefulness of the *Guide* for our children in the light of this omission.

What Mathews suggests is that in important respects the *Guide* provides not so much carefully considered assessments of British culture in the 1850s as raw evidence of British culture in the 1950s. 'The first edition was', he argues, 'an attempt at self-definition, at a time when the affairs of the Empire were in disarray, and the concept of Englishness – a concept that relies heavily upon a sense of continuity – had to be reaffirmed'. Events in the South Atlantic in 1982 showed just how strong that sense of continuity is in Britain: Trafalgar, Dunkirk and Suez – not to mention Drake and his bowls – were variously (and oddly) invoked in the media, and by politicians, during the Falklands War.

Amid such imperial images it is worth remembering that to consider their culture 'uninvaded', as Mathews puts it, is a delusion that writers and artists in Commonwealth countries cannot easily suffer from. From their perspective that English culture which seems so self-contained (and yet so 'universal') to the writers of the *Pelican Guide* is, to a greater or lesser extent, that of an invader, a colonizer – a foreigner. This clearly applies to Africa, India and the Caribbean, for example, but also to Australia when Aboriginal history and culture is properly included in 'Australian'. Yet to think that all must inevitably be loss and lament is pessimistic. In a seminar held at The Commonwealth Institute in London in 1982, the writer Salman Rushdie (who describes himself as 'British Indian') referred to his own people in the following manner: 'Having been borne across the world, we are the translated men. It is normally supposed that something always gets lost in translation; I cling, obstinately, to the notion that something can also be gained'.[19]

As migrant cultures play an increasingly prominent part in Australia, and as the neglected Aboriginal dimension of the nation's history is recovered, it may well be that such a sense of 'translation' will prove a key term in applying the richness of diverse cultures to Australian self-definition and (not the same thing) foreigners' definitions of Australia. All non-Aboriginal Australians are, to some degree, 'translated' people in Rushdie's terms.

Viewed from Britain, there is the danger that nostalgic and irrelevant perceptions of what the empire was (or is thought to have been) may obscure the very different expectations of the Commonwealth shared by the majority members, which are inevitably non-Eurocentric in focus. If Conrad's *Heart of Darkness* (1902) is arguably a classic literary text for understanding Europe's scramble for Africa, it is also limited in its failure to give any role to Africans themselves, except as dancing savages on the river bank – part of the threatening darkness. Protected and isolated on the moving island of the river steamer, the reader travels with Conrad's narrator, Marlow, through but not into the landscape. 'We were cut off from the comprehension of our surroundings', says Marlow, 'we glided past like phantoms'.[20] 'Comprehension of surroundings' for the reader of Conrad's work is at least partly dependent upon greater awareness of its historical, economic and political context; what can we know of what actually happened in the Belgian Congo at this time? How close to fact is Conrad's Kurtz, for example, no matter how symbolic we readily see him to be? His letters and journals reveal Conrad himself to have been deeply affected by what he experienced in Africa, yet this context for the reading of his works is rarely invoked.

Such questions cannot be answered from within the book itself, but if we are uninterested in the answers, thrilling to the symbolism will hardly compensate for our political and moral bankruptcy.[21] Significantly, the story opens and closes on the Thames (location of the ivory wharves and gateway to empire) but though alert to the horrors of imperialism, Conrad's narrative structure still assumes a view of Africa as distant, dangerous, other. It is still that blank space on the map into which a host of historical and fictional European heroes have ventured, and at which we know the young Conrad himself had gazed as part of his love of maps.[22] Just such blank spaces feature large in books by Commonwealth writers as diverse as (for example) Jean Rhys, Alice Munro, V.S. Naipaul, Patrick White and Buchi Emecheta. In their writings, though, as often as not such spaces are located in that unknown country of Britain as in heartland regions closer to home.

Patrick White's German explorer laconically commented: ' "The map?" . . . I will first make it'.[23] Maps are instruments of power, and when the power centre shifts, they become baffling. Studying application forms for research grants from the British Academy, I see that the world is divided (at least for the purpose of the grants) into 'European and American' and 'Oriental and African'. Discussing with a colleague where to locate Australia on such a map, we agree that it must be 'East of Suez'; equally, that it cannot be 'Oriental'. Beyond that we are lost. This exact cosmology is, of course, echoed in stone on many of the University of London buildings, to which a small brass plate saying 'Australian Studies Centre' is but a recent addition. Australia and Canada are, in fact, anomalies in this particular *A to Z*. Technologically advanced, and enjoying the complex infrastructure of general government funding of social needs, both maintain a comparatively recent (but nevertheless conspicuous) profile in London. With the establishment of the Studies Centre, Australia has gone some way to matching the imaginative programme of cultural events that Canada has long staged at Canada House and elsewhere in London.

Australia and Canada are anomalies in the 'African and Oriental' cosmology not least because they are both part of what a London publisher once oddly termed 'the old white Commonwealth'. They have *bought* their place on this map, rather than being identified by Britain as interestingly exotic areas to study (initially for commercial exploitation, later for their art, too). Australian initiative in the creation of the Studies Centre is an example of this. To trace the interests that led to the founding of the large London-based schools for 'Commonwealth studies' and, at a later period, the relation between the growth of interest in 'Commonwealth Literature' and the return to Britain of a whole generation of English literature teachers from universities in Africa and the Middle and Far East, would indeed be a fascinating sidelight on 'the political and ideological history of our epoch'.

In many ways Australia and Canada, like New Zealand, share economic problems with those Commonwealth countries often included within the Third World. They depend largely for their income upon the export of cash crops and raw materials, such trade often being handled by multinational corporations. The motor industry is the clearest example of this: iron ore is extracted by RTZ from (say) Western Australia, shipped to Japan for processing, and sent back to Australia as shiny Toyotas. 'Proudly printed in Australia' reads the small print on a colour advertisement for just such a 'fully imported' Japanese car in 1984 Perth magazine. Any such naive nationalistic claims are liable to prove similarly embarrassing.

Among the things that we can learn from both arts and sciences is that national boundaries have often very little relevance for understanding the workings of the creative imagination, no matter how convenient some critics, politicians (and advertisers) may find them. The 'proper' understanding of British history would illuminate that truth.

The 'example' I have in mind in the title of this essay is twofold. Firstly, that Australian topics can illustrate aspects of culture more usually taught from examples nearer home. Such an approach to Australian studies is modest and non-nationalistic, emphasising less what is unique about Australia than what Australia shares with cultures elsewhere. But the principle of choosing examples of social patterns, music, economics, geography, science or art from a distant and largely unknown country would in itself be an educative experience for both pupils and teachers.

There are problems, and local considerations can be crucial. 'All literatures are regional', as V.S. Naipaul has observed.[24] Nevertheless, provided the 'pure literature' fallacy is avoided, much could be gained by reading English-language literary works as part of 'literature in English' (not to be confused with 'English literature') rather than pigeon-holing them as 'Commonwealth'. This applies to the tendencies of publishers, critics and teachers. Such a shift can only work, though, if all idea of some objective, qualitative hierarchy of 'classic texts' on the one hand (the 'core') and 'emergent literatures' on the other (the 'options') is dropped. *All* texts must be there to be read as examples of the local literatures from which they come. Positive discrimination will have to be practised if Commonwealth texts are to get a fair showing, for the whole weight of publishing finance, reviewing policy, conservative opinion and sheer inertia (plus downright prejudice) is against them. Professor Arthur Pollard argued in 1982, in response to a suggestion that there should be more Afro-Caribbean options in 'A' Level examination papers:

The fact remains that, with the possible exception of Naipaul, there really is nothing in African and Caribbean literature to match in quality those works which are normally found within the substantive body of texts set at Advanced Level.

As Ken Parker (who quotes this remark in a perceptive essay on the 'black presence' in the British classroom) has observed of this statement, whereas he himself believes education to be 'about liberation from ignorance and prejudice, for preparation for living in and contributing to society', Professor Pollard 'appears to believe that it is about "texts"'.[25]

In this context teaching by example will involve the teacher not only selecting texts, but also setting an example in attitude and action, both in class and out. Too often the routine teaching of set texts on the one hand and animated discussions over coffee on the other seem to have nothing in common, whether for students or staff, but the same concerns and enthusiasms should inform both. (Where there are no animated discussions, all is already lost.)

My title uses the phrase 'a British education' with the intention of redefining it. Today's young need not a narrow pride in Britain's 'imperial achievements', but a broad understanding of the complex reasons for the growth and decline of an empire which the *Pelican Guide* may contrive to ignore, but whose story can alone make sense of Britain as it is today. As Bernard Porter observed in 1975, a multi-racial Britain has been 'one of the main results of empire, but one for which the empire, despite all its high multi-racial pretensions' has 'very poorly prepared her people'.[26] In the comparative brevity of its 'European' history, yet its overall complexity of racial and cultural relations, Australian pre-history, history, geography and sociology have many insights to offer. Above all, Australia was first the land of the Aborigines, and their story runs as a strong undertow beneath any superficial excitement at European exploration and expansion. The lessons to be learnt here are hard, and may take more time than our generation has, but learnt they will have to be.

My enthusiasm for Australian studies rests on the belief that a better understanding of Australia can bring a better understanding of ourselves. In this respect, of course, Australia has no special claim on our attention, and engagement with any other culture should equally foster the wisdom I have in mind. But interest in Australia is a worthwhile starting point. Where this interest leads will depend upon the maps we draw, and how we read them. What we can all share, and what must be defended against those (oh-so-reasonable) voices which will preach 'purity', 'traditional values' and 'assimilation', is that very diversity of Australian culture itself, and of the questions and responses this provokes.

The humanities perform a vital function in raising questions to which there are often no straightforward answers. Whether the wide-ranging debate they encourage gives 'value for money' is one such question. We live, still, in a world where the humanities themselves can be seen as both useless and dangerous. Maybe it will always be so. Worldwide the shadows of intolerance fall ever longer, but Australia perhaps still has the chance to achieve an integration which can serve as an example to us all. Only if it is remembered, though, that at 'the heart of true integration' must lie the provision for each individual and group 'to rise and attain the envisioned self'.[27]

NOTES

1. Quoted in Ann Dummett, *A Portrait of British Racism*, CARAF Publications, Manchester, 1984 (first published Penguin, Harmondsworth, 1973), p. 267. Dummett's book is a moving – and disturbing – documentation of the foundations and effects of British racism. It is an ideal teaching text of wide relevance.
2. This is the case with 'Commonwealth' courses at Exeter. The term has its unhelpful political overtones, but is briefer (if less exact) than alternatives such as 'world literature written in English'.
3. Benjamin Quarles, 'Black History Unbound' in *Slavery, Colonialism, and Racism*, Edited by Sidney W. Mintz, Norton & Co, New York, 1974, pp. 163–78. Reference on page 165.
4. Terry Eagleton, *Literary Theory: An Introduction*, Oxford, 1983.
5. I hope it is unnecessary to emphasise how directly this often applies to the ranks of university teachers (especially in the arts) in Britain today. As Ann Dummett observes: 'Education has two functions, to impart information and to inculcate values; one cannot, in fact, do one of these things without the other, for the provision of

information, being selective, itself suggests values of what is good and desirable and what is not, and the inculcation of values can only proceed by the giving of examples'. *A Portrait of British Racism*, p. 279.

6. George Steiner, *Language and Silence: Essays 1958–1966*, Faber and Faber, London 1967, pp. 21–2. Quoted in Harry Heseltine '*A Centre at the Edge*': *On Professing English in Townsville*, Inaugural Lecture Presented at the James Cook University of North Queensland on 7 June 1978. See also Ian Donaldson, 'Centres and Circumferences: Australian Studies and European perspective' in *Australian and New Zealand Studies, Papers presented at a colloquium at the British Library 7–9 February 1984*, Edited Patricia McLaren-Turner, The British Library, London, 1985 pp. 194–202.

7. John Docker, 'Commonwealth Literature and the Universities' in *New Literature Review*, No.1, Canberra 1977, p. 7.

8. Ngugi wa Thiongo, 'On the Abolition of the English Department' in *Homecoming: Essays on African and Caribbean Literature, Culture and Politics*, Heinemann, London, 1972, pp. 145–50.

9. 'Colonialist Criticism' in *Morning Yet on Creation Day*, Heinemann, London, 1975. Reference on p. 6.

10. Chris Tiffin (editor), *South Pacific Images*, South Pacific Association for Commonwealth Literature and Language Studies, Brisbane, 1978, p. 6.

11. This extraordinary claim appears in Mrs Thatcher's speech at Cheltenham racecourse, 3 July 1982. The speech is reprinted in full in *Iron Britannia: Why Parliament waged its Falklands War*, Anthony Burnett (editor), Allison and Busby, London, 1982, pp. 149–53. Reference on p. 150.

12. The Committee to review Australian studies consisted of Dr Kay Daniels (chairperson), Associate Professor Bruce Bennett and Mr Humphrey McQueen.

13. Edward Said, 'Secular Criticism' in *The World, the Text, and the Critic*, Faber and Faber, London, 1984 (first published Harvard University Press, 1983), p. 2.

14. Peter Fuller, *Seeing Berger: A Revaluation*, Writers and Readers Publishing Cooperative, London, 1981, p. 8.

15. Germaine Greer, *The Obstacle Race*, Secker & Warburg, London, 1979.

16. Aidan Carl Mathews, 'Grand Tour', *Irish Times*, 9 July 1983, p. 12.

17. See my article 'The Commonwealth Comeback' in *The Times Higher Education Supplement*, 12 February 1982, p. 11. Some thoughts originally written (and delivered) very much in the wake of the Falklands War are expressed in my paper '"On Albion's Shore": Australian literature and National Consciousness' in *Australian Papers: Yugoslavia, Europe and Australia*, edited Mirko Jurak, University of Ljubljana, 1983, pp. 295–301. For full historical and cultural context for the issues I touch on see Peter Fryer, *Staying Power: The History of Black People in Britain*, Pluto Press, London and Sydney, 1984, and David Dabydeen *The Black Presence in English Literature*, Manchester University Press, 1985.

18. Lord Scarman, *The Scarman Report*, Penguin Books, Harmondsworth, 1982.

19. Salman Rushdie, 'The Indian Writer in English', in *The Eye of the Beholder: Indian Writing in English*, edited Maggie Butcher, Commonwealth Institute, London, 1983, pp. 75–83. Reference on p. 80.

20. Joseph Conrad, 'Heart of Darkness', in *Heart of Darkness and The Secret Sharer*, Bantam Books, New York, 1971, p. 59.

21. The shortcomings of some recent criticism of Conrad are explored in the review 'Seeing through the story' by Edward S. Said in *The Times Literary Supplement*, 12 October 1984, p. 1149.

22. See Jocelyn Baines, *Joseph Conrad: A Critical Biography*, Pelican Books, Harmondsworth, 1971 (first published Weidenfeld and Nicolson, London, 1960), p. 135.

23. Patrick White, *Voss*, Penguin Books, Harmondsworth, 1963 (first published Eyre and Spottiswoode, London, 1957), p. 23.

24. V.S. Naipaul, 'Jasmine', *The Times Literary Supplement*, 4 June, 1964. Reprinted in Robert D. Hamner (editor) *Critical Perspectives on V.S. Naipaul*, Heinemann, London, 1979 (first published Three Continents Press, 1977), pp. 16–22. Reference on p. 21.
25. Kenneth Parker, 'The revelation of Caliban: "the black presence" in the classroom' in Dabydeen op.cit. pp. 186–206. Reference on pp. 197–8.
26. Bernard Porter, *The Lion's Share: A Short History of British Imperialism* 1850–1970, Longman, London and New York, 1975, p. 351.
27. Steve Biko, 'Black Souls in White Skins' in *Steve Biko, I Write What I Like: A Selection of his Writings*, edited Aelred Stubbs C.R., Heinemann, London, 1979, pp. 19–26. Reference on p. 21.

2 Les Murray's Vernacular Republic

Bruce Clunies Ross

Les Murray has published seven books of poetry, including the novel sequence *The Boys Who Stole the Funeral*, as well as a chapbook and a *Selected Poems* which has now been superseded by a collection of all the poems he so far wishes to preserve. In addition there are two collections of prose, and a book on the seasons in Australia.[1] It is a rich and varied achievement in ideas, language and the perspectives which it takes on a surprising range of subjects. Yet for all its variety it is remarkably even in quality and coherent in style. Murray has brought under control a large repertoire of poetic resources so that everything he writes – though it may range as widely in idiom or voice as the first and last poems in *Ethnic Radio* (1977),[2] or touch upon quite unexpected subjects – bears his unmistakable stamp.

There are two main reasons for this. Firstly, Murray's work is informed by a comprehensive vision which he has continued to unfold in a succession of characteristic meditative poems. This vision is at the same time integrated and capable of extensive development, and its possibilities are richly explored in the recent books *Ethnic Radio, The Boys Who Stole the Funeral* (1980) and *The People's Otherworld* (1983), where it is deepened and refined but never exhausted. It clearly has the power to sustain a lifetime's major work. Secondly, Murray has developed a flexible poetic language which is rooted in the rhythms, inflections, idioms and diction of Australian speech, without in any way being constrained by them. His language is continuous with English in the widest sense and adds a new dimension to it. It serves equally the full range of poetic functions from philosophical exposition to the expression of delicate nuances of feeling, and is capable of fine gradations of tone, from humour and irony to commemoration and celebration. Above all, it meshes exactly with his imagination. Murray's poetry has always been marked by the richness and aptness of its figurative language; by the way in which his ideas and insights are unfolded through images. At the heart of all his major poems there is

21

an imagined conception enacted in language, and as his poetry has
developed, the interconnections between language, theme and imagery
have become more subtle and intricate. Some of his recent poems are
extended conceits, embodied in Murray's characteristic Australian
idiom.

Murray's vision is centred on Australia, and expresses an intense
feeling for the country. It relates to the central themes and preoccupations of Australian poetry, like those explored in Judith Wright's
book on the subject,[3] but it is a deeper and more complex image of
Australia than we have seen before. Murray re-examines things which
have slipped out of sight; he sees Australia in long historical and broad
geographical perspectives; he questions and revises common and fash-
ionable assumptions about the country and sharpens his readers'
perceptions of place and time.

An early poem, 'Noonday Axeman',[4] introduces some of the themes
which Murray has continued to recapitulate and develop. In its opening
stanza, modern civilization is set against the silence of the bush:

> Axe-fall, echo and silence. Noonday silence.
> Two miles from here, it is the twentieth century:
> cars on the bitumen, powerlines vaulting the farms.
> Here, with my axe, I am chopping into the stillness.

It is a poem about nature and civilization; about country and city, and
in the context of these topics, about Australia. Towards the end of the
poem, the poet speculates that

> It will be centuries
> before many men are truly at home in this country

foreshadowing a thought developed some fifteen years later in 'The
Gallery':[5]

> to be here with your country, that will waken when it wakens,
> that won't be awakened by contempt or love:
> to know you may live and die in colonial times.

'Noonday Axeman' is typical of Murray's work in several ways. It is
a poem in which observations about nature and rural work give rise to
philosophical reflections; activity is given an historical dimension and
geographically placed, and as in many of Murray's meditative poems,
ideas are developed through elaborating the central images. For example, the axeman working on the edge of civilization, in a silence which
a hundred years of settlement have made

> human and familiar
> no further than where the farms rise into the foothills

is an analogy for the poet, looking back at the tide of civilization, but
also beyond and around it, and cutting into the silence with language.

The poem touches, implicitly or explicitly, a cluster of related concepts which are central to Murray's philosophy: nature and culture; environment and inherited tradition; Australia (or the New World) and Europe; geography and history; the country and the city. These pairs are potentially opposed, and in some poems that is how they appear. In 'Visiting Anzac in the Year of Metrication', for example, there is a stanza which suggests an opposition between geography and history:

> Our continent is uncrowded space,
> a subtler thing than history.
> The Day of our peace will need a native
> herb that outsavours rosemary.

but it would be wrong to suppose that in Murray's vision of things these pairs form stark or simple contrasts. They inter-relate throughout his work in different ways. History, for example, and a sense of the past which reaches back beyond the historical dimensions in which Australian is usually regarded, is equally important with geography, or place, in some of his poems. In the closing lines of 'Elegy for Angus MacDonald of Cnoclinn' Murray perceives a connection between them, made possible by the settlement of Australia: exile – geographical displacement – is

> . . . a rampart, sometimes to the past
> a distiller of spirit from bruised grains;
> this is a meaning of the New World.

This is a typical example of the way implied pairs operate in Murray's poetry. They are grounded on observation of things as they are[6] in Australia, and guide the reader to insights into the way the world being created by white Australians commutes between them. Murray's vision incorporates a set of concepts which are both elenctic and mediating. If there is a tendency throughout his work to emphasize the left-hand terms of the pairs I have mentioned, this is to counterbalance the dominance in contemporary Western thought of attitudes bounded by those on the right. These are particularly inappropriate in Australia and lead to misconceptions about its true nature. However, it would be a mistake to see Murray as supporting one side while completely dismissing the other. His work constantly reveals a dislike of divisive thought and an inclination towards reconciliation, based on a candid examination of things as they are. This is apparent from his attitude to city and country in the closing lines of 'Noonday Axeman' and throughout his work right up to 'The Sydney High-Rise Variations'. A preoccupation with the urban geography (or demography) of Australia – a metropolitan and surburban strip along perhaps a third of the littoral of a continent otherwise 'set aside for mystic poetry'[7] – is central to his thought. It is a misconception to regard him as a 'rural poet'.

'Noonday Axeman' is certainly not simply a rural poem. Its title may recall a colonial theme and some of the outback paintings of the Heidelberg School – Streeton's *The Selector's Hut* (*Whelan on the Log*) and Condor's matching *Under a Southern Sun* (both 1890) or Roberts' *The Splitters* (*c.* 1886) and *Dogging a Log* (undated) – and Murray's work does have links with the nationalist art of the 1890s, but his perspective is different for obvious reasons. The axeman is now on the frontier of the twentieth century, and the metropolitan attitudes which have attained dominance during that period have relegated him. He is no longer a typical pioneer-hero, yet Murray *centres* the poem on him working at the *edge* of things. He looks both ways; towards the wilderness and back at the cities, and is precisely located to realize the slender hold which civilization has on the Australian continent.

When Murray, therefore, claims to speak for relegated rural Australians[8] it is not only to take up the cudgels on their behalf. It is also because they see things as they are. Though they may be victims of metropolitan arrogance they are in a position to know the true geography of Australia and understand its implications. There is, of course, no reason why one cannot live in the cities with this view; indeed it is precisely Murray's point that it would be delusory to do otherwise, but urban life makes it easy to disregard the fact that large stretches of the continent remain untamed.

From the beginning, Murray's poetry has worked against the common assumption that because most of its population lives in cities, Australia is essentially a metropolitan civilization. As well as ignoring the position of the cities on the whole island-continent Australians claim as their own, this assumption enlarges the split in Australian life described in 'Sydney and the Bush':

> When Sydney rules without the Bush
> she is a warder's shop
> with heavy dancing overhead
> the music will not stop
>
> and when the drummers want a laugh
> Australians are sent up.
> When Sydney and the Bush meet now
> there is no common ground.

In Murray's vision of things, this is a harmful division which has to be healed, and it can be, in the imagination, through art. Murray's work therefore offers his readers a truer and more comprehensive imaginary map of Australia. Although poems like 'Noonday Axeman', 'Blood', 'Toward the Imminent Days' and others return to certain traditional Australian themes, like country life and the force of nature, they do not recommend anything as simple and escapist as a retreat to the country or the past. On the contrary, they suggest that withdrawal into metropolitan culture, with the denial it entails of whatever is inconsistent with modernity, is partial and spiritually damaging.

Murray developed some of these ideas explicitly in an essay he wrote on Peter Porter's 'On First Looking Into Chapman's Hesiod'.[9] Instead of an Athenian model of civilization, centred on the city, Murray proposes a Boeotian model, rooted in the country. Where the Athenian model emphasizes the role of the city in civilization and fosters urbanity, style and wit, the Boeotian model emphasizes nature and community and fosters the rites of commemoration and celebration. The Athenian model, which has been predominant for most of Western civilization, and is now in the ascendant, is hierarchical and elitist. By placing the city at the centre and apex of civilization, it has an inbuilt tendency to rate things in relation to the city: urbanity becomes a positive value; provincialism a negative one. Athenianism runs the danger of disregarding anything outside itself; a typical metropolitan delusion.

Boeotia is not *centred* in this way, and is therefore not potentially exclusive. Though it involves a 'refusal of relegation' as Murray puts it in 'The Euchre Game', one of his 'genre' poems of Boeotian life, it does not discount the city but includes it. It aims to sustain a balance between the two, as we see the axeman doing in the closing stanzas of 'Noonday Axeman'. The question at issue is not *where* people live, but the attitudes and presumptions instilled by two different views of civilization. It is possible to be a Boeotian in the cities by avoiding those tendencies in metropolitan life which instil the sense that the cities are the centres, and even the whole of culture, and by remembering the 'larger' geography of the cities (at least in Australia). However, Murray's poems constantly suggest that in order to sustain this outlook it is necessary to return periodically to the country and to nature, like the axeman at the end of the poem, and many other figures in later books. Returning to the country is, in fact, a major theme in Murray's work.

The Boeotian strain is present in Murray's poetry in a variety of ways. In 'Walking to the Cattle Place', the long cycle where it was first made explicit, it is suggested by the very title. Place, and the naming of places in the manner of rural people, is an aspect of the idea which Murray takes up here and develops extensively in later poems. Moreover, the whole cycle of sixteen poems is framed by a Boeotian day. After a prelude – 'Sanskrit' – it begins with hard work – milking on a frosty morning – and ends with an evening festival in which people mingle with their cattle. In between, Murray unfolds an enormous range of associations with cattle, exploring the way the very word implies a link between human beings and domesticated animals, and bridging a variety of cattle cultures: Indo-European, its Australian offshoot and Bantu, for example.

At the heart of the sequence is an idea of Boeotian history which Murray made explicit in a recent slightly provocative note on the poem:

> Western civilization itself has so far been the
> biggest cattle drive known to history, though
> other, ephemeral features tend to overlie this
> and obscure it.[10]

Along with its broad range of cultural and geographical reference, the sequence reaches back to

> the glimmering ice
> from the north returning world

and the culture of the Australian settlers is included in this context:

> Far back as I can glimpse with descendant sight
> beyond roads or the stave-plough, there is a boy on cold upland
> gentle tapper of veins, a blood-porridge eater
> his ringlets new-dressed with dung, a spear in his fist,
>
> it is thousands of moons to the cattle-raid of Cooley
>
> but we could still find common knowledge, verb-roots
> and noun-bark enough for an evening of sharing
> cattle wisdom.[11]

'Walking to the Cattle Place' thus charts intersections between the moment-to-moment passage of time – the common experience of living in a continuous present – with phenomena which appear to be timeless, or change only slowly, or cyclically. This complex sense of time is central to Murray's work; it is already embodied in 'Noonday Axeman' and is implicit in the idea of Boeotian civilization. It is denied by Athenian civilization which, with its emphasis on the present moment, fashion and modernity, has only a simple time dimension. At the recent end of its time scale, the sequence extends beyond the culture of white Australians to include the Aboriginals who have adapted to the presence of cattle in their country by becoming stockmen, a point Murray would probably consider strengthens the case for a Boeotian Australia, as well as exemplifying his idea of convergence.[12] The 'Stockman Songs' in 'Walking to the Cattle Place' are therefore cast in the rhythms of Aboriginal song, something Murray was to elaborate later in a major poem.

Murray does not idealize Boeotia: he specifically sets it against Arcadian notions of country life:

> We'll suffer culture for some of our devilry yet
> as Athens comes for our hide, or sends Arcadia.
> Consequences hurt worse, but impoverish less
> being Nature.[13]

Boeotian life is hard. The advantages of its communal patterns of life, centred on rural work and seasonal festivals are impaired by gossip and a lack of privacy:

> I'm thinking of aunts who had telescopes to spot
> pregnancies, inside wedlock or out.[14]

but it sustains a sense of wholeness and balance.

Boeotia is often rendered in terms of the place Murray would call 'Up Home'; specifically the region around Bunyah on the north coast of New South Wales and, by extension, rural Australia. Its localities and activities are commemorated or celebrated in 'Evening Alone at Bunyah', 'Blood', the splendid epithalamium 'Toward the Imminent Days', 'Thinking About Aboriginal Land Rights I Visit the Farm I will not Inherit', 'The Euchre Game', 'Laconics: The Forty Acres', 'The Gallery', 'The Grassfire Stanzas' and many others. Often in these, and in poems like 'The Action', 'S.M.L.E.' or 'The Returnees', the evocation of place, life and work leads to philosophical meditation, generally developed through an implicit or explicit colloquy, like the dialogue between the poet and his cousin in 'Blood', so that these poems convey the country voice, and open up a region not only rich in images, but also in perspectives on life.

In none of these poems is the country simply set against the city, or Boeotia against Athens. 'Things are what they are...', and Murray faces them. His aim is always to hold the two in balance. Three examples will illustrate this:

> He sees hope
> in asking me about cities. How can I tell him
> the cities are debris driven by explosions
>
> whose regulation takes a merciless cunning?
> I love my cities too well not to start at least there.
>   ('Toward the Imminent Days')

On a swimming snake in 'The Returnees':

> we
> kept up with the blunt, heat-tasting head
> debating its life, and sparing it,
>
> which is the good of Athens.

In 'The Mitchells' the two men, judging by their speech and dress are Boeotians, and they are envisaged setting up a pole in the countryside. Yet 'Sometimes the scene is an Avenue'. The importance of communion between city and country is evident from the fine poems about returning 'Up Home', like 'Troop Train Returning', 'Escaping Out There' or 'The Returnees', and this is the main theme of two of Murray's major works, 'The Buladelah-Taree Holiday Song Cycle' and *The Boys Who Stole the Funeral*.

'The Buladelah-Taree Holiday Song Cycle' discovers a convergence between urban and rural white Australians and the Aborigines. An ordinary Australian activity – driving out into the country on week-ends and holidays – is linked to the Boeotian theme and to the Aboriginal custom of revisiting spirit places, and its significance is revealed through extended images and associations. The holiday traffic is seen as both the 'Long Narrow City' and as the Rainbow Snake of Aboriginal mythology, for example. Through this process, white Australians, like the Aborigines, gain spiritual health by returning to the land; using it, enjoying it, naming it and communing with its past associations. The poem is a vast expansion of an idea touched on in the concluding stanzas of 'Noonday Axeman', 'Blood' and other earlier pieces. Murray has himself provided a fairly detailed account of its composition which is useful,[15] though explanation is hardly necessary for this lucid poem.

It was inspired by Murray's reading of R.M. Berndt's version of the 'Wonguri-Mandjikai Song Cycle of the Moon Bone', and its form is founded upon the line Professor Berndt used for translating the Aboriginal couplets. The long lines which Murray devised on this basis capture the idioms of Australian English while retaining underlying hints of the original source: instead of constraining the rhythms of speech it releases them.

> The people are eating dinner in that country north of Legge's Lake:
> behind flywire and venetians, in the dimmed cool, town people eat
>   Lunch.
> Plying knives and forks with a peek-in sound, with a tuck-in sound
> they are thinking about relatives and inventory, they are talking about
>   customers and visitors.
> In the country of memorial iron, on the creek-facing hills there, they are
>   thinking about bean plants, and rings of tank water, of growing a
>   pumpkin by Christmas;
> rolling a cigarette, they say thoughtfully Yes, and their companion nods,
>   considering.

Murray has taken certain characteristics of Berndt's translation and refined them for his own purposes. Since he is an accomplished linguist, he may also have been able to appreciate two of them in the original: development through varied repetition, a fairly typical quality of oral poetry, and the naming of places, more apparent in the lines following those just quoted.

> to the place of Bingham's Ghost, of the Old Timber Wharf, of the Big
>   Flood That Time,
>   . . .
> the places of sitting down near ferns, the snake fear places, the cattle-
>   crossing-long-ago places.

The third is a structure and rhythm built around a syntax using -*ing* forms. These are prominent in Berndt's translation, and in Murray's poem occur in almost every line, mainly in verbal constructions, but subtly varied for their potential as nouns and adjectives. On this predominant syntax, Murray suspends long lines of six, seven or eight stresses, broken by two or three caesuras. They are intricately patterned in sound and rhythm, and reinforced through assonance and alliteration, which occasionally results in phrases like Old English half-lines: 'the fumes of fun hanging above ferns', 'to the grinners under grass'. These, incidentally, are consistent with the use elsewhere of kennings like 'roof-water drinker' or 'worm-ocean'. Mostly, however, the traditional effects of alliterative poetry are hinted at, or elaborated, rather than imitated:

> Cars pass with a rational zoom, panning quickly towards Wingham,
> through the thronged and glittering, the shale-topped ridges, and the
>   cattlecamps,
> towards Wingham for the cricket, the ball knocked hard in front of
>   smoked-glass ranges, and for the drinking.

Throughout the poem, the weight and lift of each line; the way it picks up or leans into the surrounding context, is controlled by playing off the effect of clusters of short, stressed words – 'the ball knocked hard' – against cadences with more evenly distributed stresses. In the opening lines, already quoted, the weight of three pairs of stressed words in the second part of a line – 'in the dimmed cool, town people eat Lunch' – is suspended and released two lines later, where six stresses are spread across the line.

'The Buladelah-Taree Holiday Song Cycle' is a celebration of place, and in it Murray elaborates an element which has always been present in his poetry. Compare, for example, the opening lines of 'Visiting Anzac in the Year of Metrication':

> Gelibolu, Chanakkale –
> there's no place called Gallipoli

with a passage from 'Escaping Out There':

> Farm people step down
> at Howards and Scobies and Where The Old School Got Burnt.
> At All The Blackwoods
> and at the Flying-Fox Cooking-Place
> timber people step down.
> There are no people now at Praising White Mothe Larvae
> and no one gets off Where The Big Red Bull Went Over.

The second foreshadows the mode of the Song Cycle, especially by establishing parallels between the way country people name places and

Aboriginal place names. However, in the Song Cycle Murray develops a characteristic place-name grammar, using possessive constructions like 'the place of Bingham's Ghost . . .', into a kind of leitmotif, thus extending a construction which is prominent throughout his work, and is apparent in typical metaphors like 'the tea-pot of calm' or 'the hung pots of self expression'.

With the Song Cycle Murray reversed the treatment of Australian English by most post-war writers except Bruce Dawe, who also created his poetic language out of the vernacular. Other poets, like A.D. Hope and even Judith Wright pruned or flattened some of its distinctive features to make it more accommodating to poetic conventions, themes or ideas. The Australian idiom only seemed to be available for literature in an exaggerated form, for broad characterisation or mockery, which quickly became a kind of stage Australian, but Murray strips away the burlesque connotations and discovers in the Australian vernacular a potential for the full range of poetic effects. Without diminishing its regional distinction, he reveals its continuity with, rather than difference from, the rest of the English language. The process began with his earliest poems, but by his fifth book, *Ethnic Radio* he had extended its range and refined its expressive power to produce pieces as varied as 'The Euchre Game', 'Sydney and the Bush', 'The Returnees', 'Laconics: The Forty Acres', 'Immigrant Voyage' and 'The Figures in Quoniam'. However, it was in the big poem in that book, 'The Buladelah-Taree Holiday Song Cycle' that his creation of an Australian poetic language culminated. There are few, if any, Australian poems to match it.

Murray's next book, *The Boys Who Stole the Funeral*, was another formal innovation: a verse novel which succeeds brilliantly, partly as a result of casting it in sonnets (or at least, in a sequence of fourteen-line poems) and partly because of the richness and variety of its language. Because it is a more capacious form than the stanzas usually employed in narrative poetry, the sonnet could accommodate a complete action, and a sequence of sonnets thus facilitated the interweaving of story-lines through the cuts, overlappings and flashbacks characteristic of the novel. Where free verse might have had a tendency to spread, the necessity of making each sonnet somehow complete in itself, even if also part of a subsidiary sequence, drives the novel forward. Moreover, Murray was able to exploit the potential for extreme variation in the loose sonnet form. Each unit of the book retains some residual property of the sonnet, not always just its line length, but also its capacity for multiple subdivision; for containing and balancing material in various ways, as well as, at other points, its use of rhyme and metrical regularity.[16]

Like the Song Cycle, *The Boys Who Stole the Funeral* fuses a number of themes. It is, firstly, Murray's fullest elaboration of the theme of returning 'Up Home'. It is also a funeral journey, a common theme of folk-lore and urban legend, notably used by Faulkner.[17] The journey of the two boys is also a quest, and the survivor, Kevin Forbutt, undergoes an initiation and sups from the Common Dish, Murray's version, or rather inversion, of the Holy Grail. Finally, the novel, like the Song Cycle, explores the idea of convergence between Aboriginal and white ways of life in Australia. The Whistlecock Man who appears and disappears near the beginning of the journey is presumably a Man of High Degree, and he may have something to do with Athol Dunn's prophetic dream which occurs just before his appearance. Certainly his remarks on the subject of blood foreshadow Kevin's dream-like initiation according to Aboriginal rites at the end of the book. In addition, the whole story is centred on the return of the body of Clarrie Dunn to his spirit place, in the manner of the Aboriginal dead. This idea is linked to Murray's Boeotian philosophy, which pervades the whole sequence. In returning Clarrie's body from city to country, Kevin Forbutt and Cameron Reeby travel from Athens to Boeotia. Various incidents en route bring out this significance in the journey and the rites of passage which Kevin undergoes confirm it. Balance is restored when he accepts the whole of life as it is symbolised in the Common Dish, and he is able to enjoy this sense of wholeness through helping Jim Dunn build his patent passion-fruit trellis. Kevin's difficult enlightenment is accompanied by a deeper understanding of Australia – in sonnets 127 and 128 he is shown a vision of 'the great land' and its blood history is revealed. *The Boys Who Stole the Funeral* is not only about personal salvation, but about coming to terms with the *country* in every sense of the word.

It is in relation to the Boeotian theme that the advantages of a novel over a narrative poem are apparent. The novel, with its quality of verisimilitude or formal realism is a kind of imagined history, and this historical dimension was necessary to connect Murray's analysis of civilization with modern Australia. *The Boys Who Stole the Funeral* therefore introduces the reader to credibly-developed characters who belong to a specific time. Stacey Forbutt, the political intellectual, Noeline Kampff, the radical feminist and the two boys are shaped, or warped, by the events and attitudes of recent times. They encounter country people who seem to embody more timeless attitudes and values, but the country is also infected with Athenianism. This is reflected in the sense of relegation felt by some of the country characters and expressed by the Burning Man, in the centralised regulation of farming which necessitates the meat smuggling episode leading to the death of Reeby and in such things as Burning Man Powell's campaign for a residence test on farm tax concessions. Indeed, Murray's story convinces the reader of the correctness of his analysis by presenting a completely credible picture of the disjunction and hostility between country and city attitudes and values. In this novel 'there is no common ground'.

However, underlying the novel (with its convincing characterisation and credible action) there is a fable, and where the novel culminates in violence with the death of Reeby, the fable reaches a resolution in the following sonnets with the initiation of Forbutt. There is a complete change of mode at this point. Time stops; the formally realistic manner of the novel is suspended and a dreamlike passage supervenes. Forbutt is lost for five days to the world while he is taken by two guides through a series of rites, shown the great land from above and below, and presented with the Common Dish. After this passage of mythic narrative with its analogies to Aboriginal lore and quest stories, the book closes with a resolution of novel and fable. Forbutt is restored to the world with deeper powers of perception which enable him to experience dimensions of reality he still does not fully understand. It is perhaps his spiritual renewal which gives the closing sonnets an harmonious tone, elegaic at first, because of the loss of Jenny to the country, but finally resolved on the note of 'wry laughter'.

To have woven all these themes and modes into an intricately seamless narrative in only 140 sonnets is an amazing achievement. Murray brings it off because by the time he wrote *The Boys Who Stole the Funeral* he had delicate control over a wide tonal range and a skill for matching the rhythms of poetry with the rhythms of narrative. This is obvious in passages where whole scenes are neatly fitted into a single sonnet, like the encounter with the motor-cycle toughs in sonnet 13[18] which is both self-contained and dramatically linked to the following sonnet where the boys flee. These foreshadow and balance sonnets 117 and 118 which contain a major climax; the encounter with the policeman and Reeby's death. Here Murray manages to render a scene of dramatic violence in two sonnets, giving full value to each detail while controlling the pathos – for the reader has built up an identification with Reeby – as well as the action.

More subtle, perhaps, because it is less dramatic, is the exactly timed beginning in the midst of the action, where the fluently shifting rhythms of the two opening sonnets reflect the car driving through the Sydney suburbs and the fluctuations in mood of the two boys inside it. Murray is sharply alert to the effects of transition throughout the book, and at this point the flowing rhythms of the opening sonnets are set against the closed periods of the third which introduces Kevin Forbutt's father, the counterforce in the story. An even more striking transition occurs when the body of Clarence James Dunn is introduced in the sixth sonnet, with its long lines balanced around the mid-point. The first half is developed through images associated with the farmer and soldier; the second half through cold details of the mortuary. It marks the first still point in the book, and underlines by contrast the narrative flow of the beginning.

The creation of an easy narrative voice, with the use of the vernacular and dialogue in a loose sonnet form is a remarkable attribute of the book considered as a novel, but it also preserves the possibilities of the sonnet sequence. For example, an ironic note is emphasized in the opening passage just discussed by matching the exactly balanced fourth sonnet, with its theory of the Anzacs, with the exactly balanced sixth sonnet on Clarence Dunn, the dead Anzac. An indication of the way Murray can control tone, meeting the requirements of fictional language while preserving the potential of poetry can be gained from the Arcadian passage (sonnets 93 and 94). The ninety-third sonnet opens with a passage of dialogue contained in a pentameter which captures its inflections precisely:

> '*Gooday.*/*Ah. Kevin. Chicken? Glass of Wine?*'

Murray departs from the pentameter for the rest of the octave, which contains a three-way conversation; the father trying to impress the boy with his appreciation of the landscape, the radical feminist interrupting with angry slogans about country people ('*Fucking patriarchal Bjelke incest cretins? –* ') and Kevin trying to remain politely distant. Murray uses the turn into the sestet to emphasize that this Arcadian picnic is not harmonious, but an 'image of the nation torn apart'. The father's chicken, wine and observations on idyllic scenery are at odds with the setting. This qualifies the next sonnet, a delicately-rhymed pastoral depicting the burgeoning love between Reeby and Jenny:

> Hibbertia with blossoms yellow as a Teach Yourself book
> is knotted on the hilltop where two stand and look
> all down at impending forests and cleared farms;

The sonnet is exactly divided into balancing sections in which the rhymed verses frame snatches of awkward dialogue. The language tempts us into pathos, but its formality, infected by the tone on the preceding sonnet, leaves us slightly disturbed. The Arcadian associations are offered in these sonnets only because they represent an imposition on the country which must be rejected; as Murray makes clear in a recent poem 'there is only love; there are no Arcadias'.[19]

'The Buladelah-Taree Holiday Song Cycle' and *The Boys Who Stole the Funeral* are major achievements in Australian literature in which Murray unfolds the enormous riches he has discovered in the country and its language. In his latest book, *The People's Other-world* (1983), he produced their counterpart, revealing his command of austere means in the 'Three Poems in Memory of My Mother, Miriam Murray, née

Arnall'. The book picks up an idea which has always been present in his work, and is explicit in a couple of passages in the previous collection:

> Intelligence here
> is interest and the refusal of relegation.
>
> ('The Euchre Game')

> the Otherworld
> becomes ancestral, a code of history,
> a style of fingering, an echo of vowels,
> honey that comes to us from the lost world.
>
> ('Elegy for Angus MacDonald of Cnoclinn')

The collection includes a number of poems which explore various associations of the 'Otherworld' and trace those clues – the codes, styles and echoes – suggested in the closing lines of the Elegy. There is a pervasive idea throughout that unnoticed, or barely noticed, states of experience betray the existence of continuous 'otherworlds'. Equanimity is one – or rather the little noticed grace in things in a state of balance; interest is another, or more precisely, the state which interest induces:

> our intake of that non-physical breath
> which our lungs mimic sharply, to cancel the gap in pressure
> left by our self vanishing into its own alert.
>
> ('First Essay on Interest').

The idea is developed both seriously and wittily. In 'Homage to the Launching Place', for example, the 'mattrassphere' seems to be an 'otherworld'. This poem is a reminder that Murray has always been interested in material culture; in the tools – often machines – which human beings have developed. The latest book includes a number of poems on such subjects, notably the five 'Sydney High-Rise Variations' which chart the transformation of Sydney during Murray's writing life from a spreading five-storey city to a cluster of steel and glass towers, and develop his ideas about cities. However, it is the three poems on his mother which are at the centre of the book and give it its title:

> Justice is the people's otherworld.

This is the last line of Murray's most explicitly personal sequence; a new departure for a writer whose work from the beginning has shown a powerful fictionalising imagination. The third poem, 'The Steel' has the kind of direct simplicity which could probably only have been achieved after building up the rich resources of language which culminated in the Song Cycle and the novel sequence. By contrast, 'The Steel' is a poem with nothing to spare. Murray limits himself to a plain relation of his mother's death in a tone of subdued ordinary speech. The art of this kind of poem is a matter of finding the precise idioms and ordering them so exactly that the whole thing will appear artless. Murray does this by employing some of the off-hand flatness of low-keyed Australian talk in a poem of short lines organized in stanzas – or paragraphs – of three to six lines, occasionally shaped by unobtrusive rhyme:

> I was in the town at school
> the afternoon my mother
> collapsed, and was carried from the dairy.
> The car was out of order.
>
> The ambulance was available
> but it took a doctor's say-so
> to come. This was refused.
> My father pleaded. Was refused.

The way the flatly idiomatic 'say-so/to come' is bent around the turn of the line so that its tone is preserved but its flatness controlled is characteristic, but the real art of these lines is in the acceptance and exploitation of such a simple detail as the repeated, unstressed past tense 'was . . .'. It occurs in six of the eight lines; is avoided only in the second lines of each stanza, which run on, to produce third lines punctuated near the head of each. The only other marked caesura, towards the end of the last line, serves to emphasize just slightly the repetition 'Was refused', so that we hear in it an echo of the syntax which has been running through both stanzas. This suggests the pattern underlying the unadorned narrative which centres around the alternation 'was available': 'Was refused'.

These lines also illustrate another accomplishment in the poem; the gift for narrative which has been noticed in Murray's other work is here revealed in its plainest form. The story is told the way it would be told 'Up Home', without flourishes, and without artful re-arrangement, nor indeed, by subordinating some parts of it to others. The details accumulate with equal weight, into a narrative where 'nothing is diminished by perspective'. Once again, there is the precise matching of narrative and poetic rhythms, but here Murray has nothing to help him like the loose sonnet form of *The Boys Who Stole the Funeral*. The irregular short lines of 'The Steel' are shaped by the rhythms of quiet talk, yet at the same time Murray manages to maintain a tight connection between line length and narrative flow; a detail to every line, or pair of lines, with a sparse use of broken or run-on lines:

> I am older than my mother.
> Cold steel hurried me from her womb.
> I haven't got a star.

What hour I followed
the waters into this world
no one living can now say.
My zodiac got washed away.

Altogether, Les Murray has created a richly defined world; the
Australia we always knew, yet revealed with a depth and clarity which
enlarges understanding and fosters love. Above all, he has evolved an
Australian poetic language capable of comprehending and expressing
every facet of experience. He builds on the work of his predecessors, and
his vision touches theirs – in his concern with nature, and particularly
in his justification of the Jindyworobak insights, which the originators
failed to transform into verse. However, his work transcends theirs and
re-orients us to the whole Australian tradition. In its variety of forms,
range of tones and imaginative insights it is an achievement unmatched
by any Australian poet.

NOTES

1. *The Ilex Tree* (with Geoffrey Lehmann), Canberra, 1965; *The Weatherboard Cathe-dral*, Sydney, 1969; *Poems Against Economics*, Sydney, 1972; *Lunch and Counterlunch*, Sydney, 1974; *Ethnic Radio*, Sydney, 1977; *The Boys Who Stole the Funeral*, Sydney, 1980; *The People's Otherworld*, Sydney, 1983; *Selected Poems: The Vernacular Republic*, Sydney, 1976; *The Vernacular Republic, Poems 1961–1981*, Sydney and Edinburgh, 1982; *Selected Poems*, Manchester, 1986; *The Peasant Mandarin*, St Lucia, 1978; *Persistence in Folly*, Sydney, 1984; *The Australian Year*, North Ryde (N.S.W.) and London, 1985. For information on Murray's recent work, and for general help with this essay, I am indebted to Mr Martin Leer, of the Australian Studies Centre at the University of Queensland.
2. 'The Euchre Game' and 'The Figures in Quoniam'.
3. *Preoccupations in Australian Poetry*, Melbourne, 1965.
4. Included in *The Ilex Tree*.
5. In *Ethnic Radio*.
6. 'Things are what they are, and that is frightening
   they require obedience, if they are to be mastered
   and so many have tried to force their dreams on this planet'.
   ('Noonday Axeman': the lines have since been cancelled.)
7. From 'Louvres', 1984, *Selected Poems*, 1986, 133–4.
8. 'Notes on Writing a Novel Sequence' in *Persistence in Folly*, p. 108.
9. First published in P.K. Elkin, (ed.) *Australian Poems in Perspective*, St Lucia, 1978; reprinted in *The Peasant Mandarin* as 'On Sitting Back and Thinking About Porter's Boeotia'.
10. *The Vernacular Republic*, p. 215.
11. 'The Names of the Humble'.
12. Explained in the latest version of 'The Human Hair Thread', in *Persistence in Folly*, pp. 29.
13. 'Gōloka'.
14. 'Birds In Their Title Work Freeholds of Straw'.
15. In 'The Human Hair Thread' loc. cit.

16. See Murray's own account in 'Notes on Writing A Novel Sequence', loc. cit.
17. *As I Lay Dying*, New York, 1930.
18. Numbers in brackets refer to sonnets in *The Boys Who Stole the Funeral*.
19. 'Equanimity', in *The People's Otherworld*.

3 The Breaking of the Great Australian Silence: Aborigines in Australian Historiography 1955–1983*

Henry Reynolds

Most books written about the Australian colonies in the nineteenth century contained a chapter or two about the Aborigines and their relations with the European settlers. The few major historical works written before 1900 like West's *History of Tasmania* and Rusden's *History of Australia* paid considerable attention to the great tragedy of destruction and dispossession. But during the first half of the twentieth century the Aborigines were dispersed from the pages of Australian history as effectively as the frontier squatters had dispersed them from the inland plains a century before. Little attention was given to the Aboriginal occupation of the continent in the millennia before the appearance of the white men. Most books began with the voyages of assorted European explorers or with the decision to send an English expedition to Botany Bay. This is true even of the most recent comprehensive academic history – Crowley's *A New History of Australia* – published ten years ago and still widely used. The book opens with the sentence:

Australia was conceived officially when King George III announced to parliament, on 22 January 1787, that a plan had been made 'to remove the inconvenience which arose from the crowded state of the gaols in the different parts of the Kingdom'.[1]

Australia's beginnings, then, were Georgian, British, official. There is not a word about the ancient societies in occupation of almost every corner of the vast continent in question.

Having begun the saga of settlement with the planting of the flag at Sydney Cove the typical mid-century history made fleeting mention of the blacks around the pin-points of European settlement while a few individuals like Bennelong were given walk-on parts in the drama of early Sydney. Inland clans met and sometimes harassed intrepid

---

* This paper was delivered as the First Trevor Reese Memorial Lecture at the University of London, 30 January 1984, under the auspices of the Institute of Commonwealth Studies and the Australian Studies Centre.

DI-D

explorers and hardy pioneers; black spears symbolizing the hostility of an alien environment there to be mastered. Many writers discussed and deplored the fate of the Tasmanian Aborigines but after the mid-nineteenth century interest faltered and there was little further mention of the blacks at all. Racial conflict was portrayed as a feature of the earliest period of Australian history with little relevance to the present.

Why were the Aborigines written out of the historical record early this century? Many influences were probably at work. Some of the major ones can be noted here. Until the 1940s the overwhelming opinion – both popular and scientific – was that the blacks were 'dying out', condemned by the iron laws of evolution to eventual extinction. With only a minor black role in the present, and none in the future, the Aboriginal past could be discounted. Early twentieth-century history was selfconsciously nationalistic and written to foster patriotism in the present, pride in the past. Racial violence was an embarrassment best forgotten, especially as the heroes of the pioneer legend – squatters, prospectors, explorers, overlanders – had helped to bloody the billa-bongs. To create doubts about the means of European occupation was to question the morality of settlement, even the right to the continent. Such questions had no place in works which celebrated steady material progress, the creation of free institutions and the evolution of a happy, hedonistic life style.

The last fifteen years have seen dramatic changes in the attention devoted both to the Aborigines and to the whole character of Australian historiography. Stimulus for change came from many sources. Australia has been influenced by the world-wide re-assessment of European imperialism which followed in the wake of decolonization and Third World assertiveness. Indigenous minorities embedded in European settler societies – American Indians, Maoris, Aborigines – have linked arms, assessments and aspirations. Aboriginal political activism has challenged assumptions about the past as surely as it has questioned contemporary attitudes and current policies. The establishment of the Tent Embassy on the lawns of Parliament house in Canberra in 1972 and the unfurling of the Aboriginal flag were events resonant with historical as well as political significance. The pivotal issue of land-rights is above all about history. Its roots go back to the first days at Sydney Cove when the colonists, adopting the view that Australia was *terra nullius*, – a land without legitimate owners – annexed a continent of which they knew less than one hundredth part. The Aborigines and their supporters are not only struggling for land but for a radical re-interpretation of the past as well. On the other hand the results of the new historical scholarship reach far beyond the study and the conference room, feeding both political and cultural springs of the Aboriginal Renaissance.

Australian pre-history has been transformed in the last twenty years. What archaeology existed before the 1960s was old-world archaeology. The first university appointment in Australian pre-history was not made until 1961, at which time the Aborigines were thought to have been in the continent for 10,000 years. Since then our view of ancient Australia has been totally re-shaped. Pre-history has become a field of intense activity, of intellectual excitement, of popular interest. These developments were summarized in a recent article published in the journal *World Archaeology*:

In 1961 the oldest date was some 9,000 years, by 1968 four sites older than 20,000 years were known and by the early 1970's at least two sites older than 30,000 years were accepted. For the last five years, 50,000 years has been generally agreed on as a likely limit, though a few believe that considerably greater antiquity will be revealed.[2]

When set against a history of such depth the European era in Australia shrinks in significance, representing a mere one half of one per cent of the time of human occupation – only eight generations out of 1600.

But it is not the great antiquity of Aboriginal society alone that has impressed contemporary scholars but also the evidence of creative adaption to a vast and varied continent over periods of dramatic environmental change. D.J. Mulvaney's book *The Prehistory of Australia* was probably the first work to draw this to the attention of a wider audience. Australia, he wrote in the introduction:

stretches from about 43° south latitude to within 11 degrees of the equator, while a third of the continent lies within the Tropics; in recent times an equal area has received an average rainfall of less than ten inches; it is further from Perth to Melbourne than the distance separating London and Moscow. The dispersal of the Aborigines throughout this vast land, their responses and adjustments to the challenges of its harsh environment, and their economical utilization of its niggardly resources, are stimulating testimony to the achievements of the human spirit.[3]

In the opening sentence of the book Mulvaney directly challenged traditional historiography with its emphasis on the achievements of the European explorer and pioneer. 'The discoverers, explorers and colonists of the three million square miles which are Australia', he wrote, 'were its Aborigines'.[4]

The dramatic discovery of a vast pre-history was important enough in itself. Its significance was increased because it co-incided with an international re-assessment of the nature of hunter-gatherer societies summed up in the phrase 'the original affluent society' coined by the celebrated, American anthropologist Marshall Sahlins. In Australia this radical re-evaluation was popularized by historian Geoffrey Blainey in a book celebrating the 'Triumph of the Nomads'.[5] At the same time there has been a wide-ranging re-assessment of Aboriginal land use spanning many disciplines. The Aborigines now appear not the aimless wanderers of traditional accounts but as people who systematically exploited their environment by means of a profound knowledge of its resources. In open grasslands the local clans harvested vast fields of self-sown yams and indigenous cereals. On sea coasts and permanent rivers sophisticated fish traps were constructed; in the Western District of Victoria archaeologists have discovered a massive system of canals and drains which allowed exploitation of eels passing from fresh water lagoons to the sea. We have also come to appreciate the importance of the controlled and systematic use of fire over many generations in shaping the Australian environment. The lightly timbered eucalypt woodlands which first attracted the sheep farmers were not an untouched wilderness but a human artifact shaped by centuries of deliberate 'fire-stick farming'. The implications for traditional historiography are clear. European settlers did not tame a pristine continent but turned a usurped land to new uses. While exploring its surface and testing its potential they followed Aboriginal paths, drank at their wells, slept in their gunyahs and were highly dependent on the sophisticated bushcraft of black guides. Writing of the south-west corner of the continent, the pre-historian Sylvia Hallam emphasized that local blacks had 'opened up' the landscape in which the settlers were able to 'move around, to pasture their flocks, to find good soils . . . and water sources'. The Europeans, she argued, 'inherited the possibilities of settlement and land use' from the people they dispossessed.[6]

Other certainties are currently under siege. Even such a basic fact as the size of the pre–1788 population is in dispute. Radcliffe-Browne's estimate of 300,000 has been widely accepted as the most likely figure since published in the *Australian Year Book* of 1930. But now one of Australia's leading economic historians has argued that the population was probably much larger. Concentrating on south-east Australia, N.G. Butlin asserts that all previous assessments have paid too little attention to the devastating impact of the two smallpox epidemics of the 1790s and 1829–31, and that we need to multiply previously accepted figures by four or five, that ancient Australia may have had a population as high as one and half million.[7] Prominent pre-historians, taking account of the most recent work on Aboriginal land use, concede that Butlin may be closer to the mark than the 1930 estimate he has so vigorously challenged.

In the last 20 years Australian scholars have broken the Great Australian Silence and in so doing have transformed our knowledge of the Aboriginal past – multiplying the time of human settlement by four or five, challenging accepted notions of population density, reassessing alike our view of the quality of life of individual hunters and gatherers and the creative achievements of Aboriginal society as a whole.

But what of more recent history – of the relations between the Aborigines and the European interlopers?

While archeologists have employed a wide range of new techniques to unlock the ancient past, historians, uncovering new source material and asking fresh questions of old, are examining the Aboriginal response to European invasion and settlement, are exploring the other side of the frontier. At the same time there is a tremendous upsurge of interest in the past among Aboriginal communities seeking to preserve their history both for its own sake and to buttress claims to traditional land.

Much research awaits to be done but it is now possible to piece together a generalized picture of the impact of the European settlement. There are numerous stories of the awe and alarm felt by coastal people at the arrival of the first sailing ships. Swan River Aborigines told confidantes among the early settlers:

with great vividness their impressions when they saw the first ship approach the land. They imagined it some huge winged monster of the deep, and there was a universal consternation. One man fled inland for fourteen miles without stopping and spread the terrifying news amongst his friends.[8]

Europeans have left many accounts of first meetings with Aborigines in which the actors on both sides display that uneasy amalgam of anxiety and curiosity, the sudden unpredictable shifts from amity to aggression and back again, the mutual discovery of commonality and novelty. 'We were so novel to one another', wrote the French scientist Péron of his meeting with the Tasmanians in 1802.[9] As in other parts of Australia the island Aborigines were fascinated by the Europeans' white skins, their clothes and shoes and strange possessions. The gender of the fully-clothed, clean shaven Frenchmen was a matter of earnest debate and insistent exploration. As Péron explained:

the natives wanted to examine the calves of our legs and our chests, and so far as these were concerned we allowed them to do everything they wished, oft repeated cries expressing the surprise which the whiteness of our skin seemed to arouse in them. But soon they wished to carry their researches further. Perhaps they had doubts whether we were the same sort of beings as themselves, perhaps they suspected we were of a different sex. However it may be, they showed an extreme desire to examine our genital organs, but as this examination was equally displeasing to us all, they insisted only in the case of Citizen Michel, one of our sailors, who by his slight build and lack of beard seemed he must be more likely to set their minds at rest. But Citizen Michel, who I begged to submit to their entreaties, suddenly exhibited such striking proof of his virility that they all uttered loud cries of surprise mingled with loud roars of laughter which were repeated again and again.[10]

But the experience of coastal clans was not typical. For most Aborigines the Europeans did not arrive unannounced. News of them

travelled inland well in advance of the wave of settlement while straying
domestic animals and assorted European commodities long preceded
the bullock drays into the interior. We know that iron, glass and cloth,
axes and tobacco were received by Aborigines far in the interior as long
as thirty years before the appearance of the first permanent settlers,
having passed along the traditional trade routes which criss-crossed the
continent. Iron and glass were quickly and successfully incorporated
into traditional tool kits. Skilfully crafted glass spear heads were fitted
to traditional shafts, sharpened scraps of iron were hafted with wooden
handles. European animals escaped from settlements all around the
continent and strayed into the interior. There are many stories which
relate the Aborigines' amazement and fear when they came face to face
with the exotic animals. A North Queensland story tells of a meeting
with a stray horse sometime during the middle of last century:

Somebody lost a horse – first time they ever saw a horse . . . and they got their
spears and boomerangs and nulla-nullas and they chased this horse and they
speared the horse and they put so many spears in the horse that the old horse
fell down. And they walked up and had a look at him and they lift his head up
and said 'What sort of creature is this?' They never seen an animal so big. They
said 'I wonder where this animal has come from it's so big.'[11]

Information about the white men also travelled quickly back from the
fringes of European settlement. News of the danger and mysterious
power of guns passed on to tribes all over the continent before they came
into physical contact with Europeans. Explorers found that blacks were
highly apprehensive of guns even before they had been fired. The artist
and writer Dick Roughsey recalled that on Mornington Island in the
Gulf of Carpentaria his father was told of guns before he had seen white
men. Mainland blacks had related 'how white people could kill a man
with thunder that sent down invisible spears to tear a hole in his body
and spill his blood in the sand'.[12]

The origin and nature of the white men provoked an intense debate
in Aboriginal society. Initially it was commonly thought that Europeans
were spirits returned from the dead, although eventually it was concluded that they were 'nothing but men'. All over the continent in areas
of early settlement the Aborigines applied to Europeans traditional
terms meaning 'ghost', 'spirit', 'departed', 'the dead'. In many cases
whites were thought to be not merely re-incarnated blacks but actually
returned relatives, a fact which often saved the lives of convict escapees
and wrecked sailors, as well as shielding fragile infant settlement from
black hostility. Settlers so designated were given the names of recently-
deceased relatives and the vacant place in the kinship network. George
Grey, explorer and later colonial Governor, related his experience in
Western Australia when claimed as the son of an old Aboriginal woman:

A sort of procession came up, headed by two women, down whose cheeks tears were streaming. The eldest of these came up to me, and looking for a moment at me said . . . 'Yes, yes, in truth it is him', and then throwing her arms around me, cried bitterly, her head resting on my breast . . . she then cried a little more, and at length relieving me, assured me that I was the ghost of her son, who had some time before been killed by a spear wound in his breast. . . . My new mother expressed almost as much delight at my return to my family, as my real mother would have done, had I been unexpectedly restored to her.[13]

Recent studies from all parts of Australia have emphasized the ubiquity of frontier conflict. The traditional picture of peaceful pioneering by unarmed frontiersmen has been shattered. Frontier settlements bristled with guns and almost every district settled during the nineteenth century had a history of conflict between local clans and encroaching settlers. A small town pioneer explained in 1869 that his community 'had its foundations cemented in blood'.[14] Another looked back ruefully on a decade of frontier conflict during which 'our cowardly fears led us to believe that our safety lay in reckless appeals to powder and lead'.[15] Black resistance in its many forms was an inescapable feature of life on the fringes of European settlement from the first months at Sydney Cove until the early decades of the twentieth century. Edward Curr, pioneer, squatter and amateur ethnographer, provided an overview of Australian frontier warfare. Writing in 1883 he explained:

In the first place the meeting of the Aboriginal tribes of Australia and the white pioneer, results as a rule in war, which lasts from six months to ten years, according to the nature of the country the amount of settlement which takes place in a neighbourhood, and the proclivities of the individuals concerned. When several squatters settle in proximity, and the country they settle is easy of access and without fastnesses to which the Blacks can retreat, the period of warfare is usually short and the bloodshed not excessive. On the other hand, in districts which are not easily traversed on horseback, in which the Whites are few in numbers and food in procurable by the Blacks in fastnesses, the term is usually prolonged and the slaughter more considerable.[16]

In the early stages of contact conflict often resulted from mutual fear, anxiety and misunderstanding. Once settlement had been established deaths occurred in the course of conflict about property. Innumerable small skirmishes involving European possessions, which on the surface appear to be little more than unseemly brawls, were manifestations of a fundamental conflict between the Aboriginal concept of reciprocity and sharing and the European one of private property. Many whites were put to death in revenge for specific injuries or for serious transgression of traditional law frequently relating to sexual relations between Aboriginal girls and womanless white frontiersmen. Such action was aimed at particular individuals or groups of offenders with the intention of inducing them to behave in morally acceptable ways. Initially, then, the blacks attempted to deal with the Europeans as though they were Aborigines. Their actions were judicial rather than martial. But as violence escalated and European competition for land and water intensified many Aboriginal groups moved decisively from feud to warfare, engaging in concerted guerilla attacks on the settlers, their crops and flocks, huts and herds.

Considering the advantages possessed by the Europeans, Aboriginal resistance was surprisingly prolonged, and effective, exacting a high price from many pioneer communities in tension and insecurity as much as in property loss, injury or death. Aboriginal attacks on property had devastating effects on the fortunes of individual settlers and at times appeared to threaten the economic viability of such pioneer industries as squatting, farming, mining and pearling. There were occasions – as in Tasmania in the late 1820s, New South Wales in the late 1830s and early 1840s and Queensland in the early 1860s – when Aboriginal resistance emerged as one of the major problems of colonial society. An editorial in Queensland's leading newspaper in 1879 assessed the impact of Aboriginal resistance in the colony:

During the last four or five years the human life and property destroyed by the Aboriginals in the North totals up to a serious amount. . . . Settlement on the land, and the development of the mineral and other resources of the country, have been in a great degree prohibited by the hostility of the blacks, which still continues with undiminished spirit.[17]

Yet Europeans were only rarely willing to recognize the intelligence and courage which informed the resistance. When they did their comments were particularly interesting. In 1830 a writer in the Hobart paper *The Colonial Times* referred to 'a cunning and superiority of tactics which would not disgrace some of the greatest military characters'.[18] Another island settler remarked that the blacks had 'oftentimes evinced superior tact and clearness of head'.[19] The official Tasmanian Aborigines Committee thought the blacks a 'subtle and daring enemy', a 'sagacious and wily race of people'.[20] A report of 1831 observed that the island blacks:

now conduct their attacks with a surprising organization, and with unexampled cunning, such indeed is their local information and quickness of perception, that all endeavours on the part of the whites to cope with them are unavailing.[21]

In 1834 Governor Stirling informed his superiors in England that West Australian settlers had found the blacks 'very formidable enemies, and if they could avail themselves of the advantages of combination it would be useless to attempt a settlement in this quarter with our present numbers'.[22] A pioneer colonist concurred, remarking in 1833 that if in addition to their knowledge of the country the local Aborigines had 'firearms and a little discipline' they would 'put an end to the settlement in less than a month'.[23]

But perhaps the most generous tribute was paid by Edward Eyre who wrote:

It has been said, and is generally believed, that the natives are not courageous. There could not be a greater mistake . . . nor do I hold it to be any proof that they are cowards, because they dread or give way before Europeans and their firearms. So unequal a match is no criterion of bravery, and yet even thus, among natives, who were labouring under the feelings, naturally produced by seeing a race they were unacquainted with, and weapons that dealt death as if by magic, I have seen many instances of an open manly intrepidity of manner and bearing, and a proud unquailing glance of eye, which instinctively stamped upon my mind the conviction that the individuals before me were very brave men.[24]

The cost of frontier conflict was high. It seems probable that about 2,000 Europeans and more than 20,000 Aborigines died violently in the course of Australian settlement and many others carried scars of shot and spear with them into a more peaceful era. Such a degree of violence may surprise outsiders less than it has Australians raised on historical works which stressed peacefulness of national development. Australia was the 'quiet continent', which has been colonized, not conquered; settled not invaded. The numbers killed greatly overshadowed those involved in all other forms of internal conflict and can only be compared with the death rate in Australia's overseas wars. Many white Australians are acutely embarrassed by the findings of the new history of the frontier. They would prefer that past bloodshed be forgotten. But in black communities memories are fresh and the wounds have not healed. Oral history has already tapped some of these sagas of bitter skirmish and sudden death. As an example I turn to a story of the 1870s or 1880s related a few years ago by an old man who had probably heard it as a boy from eye-witnesses to the events. It tells of an attack by the Queensland Native Police on a group of Aborigines who had taken bullocks from nearby settlers and were caught while cooking them. Such 'dispersals' happened many times in colonial Queensland. Despite the lapse of time, despite the broken English, the story has a powerful impact:

All the Native Police come up All got the rifle, all got handcuffs
Shoot im altogether, Shoot im altogether Chuck im in the fire
All the revolvers going on Talk about smell Nobody gonna be alive Chuck im in the fire, half alive Sing out
Native police shoot im all Widow come back cryin She lose im husband All finished, they shot em live All cryin come home To this valley here[25]

But conflict and resistance are not the only notable feature of the Other Side of the Frontier. There is much else besides. Enough work has been done in the last ten years for us to see that the Aboriginal response to invasion was far more positive, creative and complex than generations of white Australians have been taught to believe. W.K. Hancock's judgement of 1930 that Aboriginal society was 'pathetically helpless'[26] when assailed by Europeans can now be seen to have been a travesty. Indeed the story which is now emerging is one which has many parallels with the chosen themes of nationalist historiography.

The courage of European explorers pushing out into the interior was matched by that of the Aborigines who met them on the way and by those who travelled in towards the settlements to observe and evaluate the interlopers. Voyages of discovery were never the preserve of white frontiersmen. The explorers' fear of savages was echoed in Aboriginal alarm about evil spirits and malignant alien magic. The improvisation and adaption of Europeans settling the land was paralleled by tribesmen who grappled with a new world of experience on the fringes of white settlement. The stoical endurance of pioneer women was matched by that of their black sisters who bore children and battled to keep them alive in conditions of stark adversity. All over the continent Aborigines bled as profusely and died as bravely as white soldiers in Australia's twentieth-century wars. How Australians will relate frontier conflict to cherished military traditions, to the ANZAC legend itself, has yet to be determined. Will white Australians come to accept fallen tribesmen as national heroes who died defending their way of life against powerful invaders? Will their actions ultimately seem more relevant than those Australians who died overseas pursuing the tactical ends and strategic objectives of a distant motherland? That such questions now confront us is the clearest indication that the Great Australian Silence has been shattered, the cult of forgetfulness abandoned. Slowly, unevenly, often with difficulty, white Australians are incorporating the black experience into their image of the national past.

Meanwhile the achievements of the new historiography must be sought in the public as well as the private sphere, in the street as much as in the seminar room. Current political activity provides apt illustration. The Land Rights Movement seeks to reverse, in part, the annexation of 1788 and gain compensation for generations of deprivation and oppression. A committee of prominent white Australians has called for a treaty, or Makarata, to be signed with Aboriginal leaders in time for the Bicentenary in January 1988. The manifesto of the committee contains this observation:

We believe there is a deep and wide concern among Australians of European descent that our ownership of this land, as defined in the imported European law, should still be based solely upon force. . . . It is time to strike away the past and make a just settlement together.[27]

More recent, and even more relevant, was the speech delivered by the Federal Minister for Aboriginal Affairs Clyde Holding in 1983 entitled *Aboriginal Past: Australia's Future*. 'We have to admit and accept the past', Holding argued, noting that 'we have, only recently, begun to admit to ourselves that the widely accepted version of our beginnings, of the white man bringing the benefits of civilization to benighted heathens, is rather less than the whole truth'. He believed that the approaching bicentenary provided Australians with the opportunity 'not merely to contemplate our achievements as a nation, but also to come to terms with our history'.[28]

During the last twenty years many scholars in numerous disciplines have transformed our knowledge and understanding of Aboriginal Australia in the past and in the present. It has been one of the major achievements of Australian intellectual and cultural life since the Second World War. White Australians now accept a less flattering image of their past, but a much more realistic one. In coming face to face with black Australians they have at last come face to face with themselves.

NOTES

1. F.K. Crowley (ed.), *A New History of Australia*, Heinemann, Melbourne 1974, p. 1.
2. T. Murray and J.P. White, 'Cambridge in the bush? Archaeology in Australia and New Guinea', *World Archaeology* vol. XIII, no.2, October 1981, p. 257.
3. D.J. Mulvaney, *The Pre-history of Australia*, Thames & Hudson, London 1969, p. 12.
4. Ibid.
5. *Triumph of the Nomads. A History of Ancient Australia*, Sun Books, Melbourne 1975.
6. S. Hallam, *Fire and Hearth*, Aust. Institute of Aboriginal Studies, Canberra, p. 65.
7. N.G. Butlin, *Our Original Aggression*, Allen & Unwin, Sydney 1983.
8. G.F. Moore, *A Descriptive Bibliography of the Language in Common Usage Among the Aborigines of Western Australia*, London 1842, p. 108.
9. N.J.B. Plomley (ed.), *The Bundin Expedition & the Tasmanian Aborigines 1802*, Blubber Head Press, Hobart 1983, p. 84.
10. Ibid.
11. H. Reynolds, *The Other Side of the Frontier*, Penguin Books, Ringwood Victoria, 1982, p. 10.
12. D. Roughsey, *Moon and Rainbow*, Rigby, Sydney 1971, p. 13.
13. G. Grey, *Journal of Two Expeditions of Discovery*, 2 vols, London 1841. Vol I, pp. 301–302.
14. *Port Denison Times*, 1 May 1869.
15. Ibid., 21 May 1870.
16. E. Curr, *The Australian Race: Its Origin, Languages, Customs* 4 vols, Melbourne 1886–87, I, p. 100.
17. *Queenslander*, 15 February 1879.
18. *The Colonial Times*, 16 July 1830.
19. Ibid., 1 June 1831.
20. Papers of the Aborigines Committee, Tasmanian Colonial Secretary Papers, Tasmanian State Archives, CSO/1/319.

21. Papers Relative to the Aboriginal Tribes in British Possessions, British Parliamentary Papers, 1834, p. 158.
22. Dispatches to Colonial Office, 14 September 1834; 6 December 1838; Battye Library, Perth.
23. *Perth Gazette*, 30 March 1833.
24. E.J. Eyre, *Journals of Expeditions of Discovery*, 2 vols, London 1845, II pp. 216–217.
25. H. Reynolds, *The Other Side* op.cit., p. 127.
26. W.K. Hancock, *Australia*, Jacaranda Press, Brisbane 1960, p. 20.
27. S. Harris, *It's Coming Yet*, Aboriginal Treaty Committee, Canberra 1979, p. 12.
28. Speech to House of Representatives, 8 December 1983.

4 Constructing Australian Subjects: Critics, Writers, Multicultural Writers

Sneja Gunew

(i) From within...

Speaking from the position of a literary critic practising in Australia one may well, these days, pose the question, of what relevance is multiculturalism to the concept of Australian culture and/or Australian literature? In brief, as far as the first is concerned, it becomes a question of cultural franchise instead of cultural colonialism. As far as the second goes, it draws attention to the fact that all definitions of the literary and all readings of texts involve the political or the exercise of power relations. To name or define is to exercise forms of control. The one pervasive and enduring effect that Marxist and feminist theory has had is that of making it impossible to speak any longer of an aesthetics which transcends the political. Here, for example, is Terry Eagleton:

> The difference between a conventional critic who speaks of the 'chaos of experience' in Conrad or Woolf, and the feminist who examines those writers' images of gender, is not a distinction between non-political and political criticism. It is a distinction between different forms of politics – between those who subscribe to the doctrine that history, society and human reality as a whole are fragmentary, arbitrary and directionless, and those who have other interests which imply alternative views about the way the world is. There is no way of settling the question of which politics is preferable in literary critical terms. You simply have to argue about politics.[1]

A definition of Australian culture which does not take into account the cultural production of all its citizens is not extending a full cultural franchise and needs to justify this practice. A concept of a national literature which silences some of its citizens on the grounds of race, gender, or class, needs to be interrogated. Let us consider a for moment how a national culture is created in the first place. Usually we prefer to take terms like 'Australian literature' or 'Australian culture' for granted as being manifestations of an 'Australian way of life', which is also a given. The so-called explanation becomes circular. 'We' all know what 'we' mean and those who don't had better remain silent: cultural

51

totalitarianism. It might, therefore, be more useful to speak of culture in the terms of another British Marxist critic, Raymond Williams, as 'the signifying system through which . . . a social order is communicated, reproduced, experienced and explored.'[2] How is this signification produced, how is meaning created? Once again, a useful approach might be to think of meanings as being created through difference. Words gain meaning through their relation to other words so, for example, male is what female is not; Australian is what migrant is not.

Now, as regards culture, the previous difference against which (on the whole) Australian had been measured and defined had been that of Britain or, sometimes, on occasions of greater specificity, the Anglo-Celtic. Behind the need to structure this meaning had been the desire for a unified identity, to discover a cultural territory after the geographical land mass had been sighted. This impulse to establish meaning had been, perhaps, the most difficult part of the colonizing process. From this eighteenth- and nineteenth-century legacy of differences which construct meanings, Australia acquires meaning by differing itself from Britain. At the same time, in this particular binary equation, Britain is the dominant term. British culture is the standard, the model, against which Australian culture is measured and defined. The suppressed or unconscious difference against which Australian culture was measured and defined was of course the gaping absence of Aboriginal culture so that against that difference, Australia is *not* what it has been; Australia *is* the negative shadow of Aboriginal culture. But, as we know from Freud, the repressed always returns. Witness, for example, the current ways in which Aboriginal culture is being reconstructed with a vengeance. Those are two kinds of multiculturalism which have been operating without being visible in quite those terms. The influx of European migrants after World War II created other sets of differences which threw into relief the previous sets of differences that had operated to make Australian culture a meaningful term. The recent arrival of new Asian settlers has foregrounded once again the criteria of selection which operate to establish meaning. That notions of culture are based on difference and exclusion is usually suppressed. When new and obvious differences arise we are forced to confront the suppressed.

In a paper delivered at Stirling University, Scotland, in 1983, Professor Colm Kiernan situated Australian culture in relation to British culture as being one of 'the outcasts and rejected'. Certainly that equation makes sense in a previous context in relation to British culture when the early settlers were primarily from England and when what was really being defined here was a difference *within* British culture itself i.e. the Celtic as measured against the Anglo. But even if one accepts for the moment Professor Kiernan's construction of Australian culture, what happens to this culture of outsiders and outcasts when it in turn must accommodate a new group of outcasts and outsiders? What happens then to this new definition of Australian culture? The former outcasts (the Celtic ones?) have eventually become the solid verandah posts of the community. In a sudden vision of infinite regression the verandah posts are joined by the solidity of imported Italian balustrades and Greek terra-cotta as new waves of Indo-Chinese outcasts and outsiders re-position who is now 'in' and who 'out'. We extract ourselves from this abyss of specificity and cultural vertigo by re-posing the first question. How have the differences posed by multiculturalism contributed to Australian culture? An easy answer (with far from easy implications) is that multi-cultural voices have contributed their personal histories to Australia, but only recently. Together with Aborigines, the working class, and women, the significant difference of migrant voices may eventually shift our received notions of Australian history.

Another further answer is that multiculturalism is forcing Australians to read their own culture, their own differences, in self-conscious ways. I am of course speaking of reading not in terms of any simple literacy but in relation to reading sign systems, Williams's signifying systems, which form languages of food, of dress, of faith, of custom. In coming to Australia migrants rescued it from its own marginality *vis à vis* British and European cultures by creating a protective margin of multiplicity or *multi*culturalism. Like other cultures Australia, too, now had its marginal protection/protectorate. Australia was framed now, set off to advantage by a baroque frame of endless decorative details. But framing what? A still life? (We are heading towards vertigo again.) Frames draw attention to what they enclose, to the centre, or to centres of interest. For those who position themselves on those margins, or frames, they draw attention to what is left out. Of what relevance is multiculturalism to Australian culture? It has framed Australia culture and, yes, of course, in some ways indicted it. It has drawn attention to what Australia is by speaking of what it is not, what it excludes. (Frames and margins offer ambiguous protection).

These migrant voices read Australia from the outside, culturally speaking, because this is where they have been positioned by dominant cultural discourses. It is as though these dominant discourses were saying to the marginal, 'We will only listen to you when you speak what we already know, when you become the same, when you silence difference.' Where these marginal voices themselves speak from is massively complicated. Their framing of the dominant culture is not always a negative one. There are many degrees of collusion, of sympathy. These voices draw attention to heterogeneity rather than homogeneity as do their personal histories, which I mentioned earlier. Much of what is generally called migrant writing is in fact first-person reminiscence or oral history. But how do these migrant histories differ

from other marginal voices who have been, until recently, not autho-
rized to speak? What migrant voices do in general (and here I am not
saying that these voices *are* necessarily the same as migrant writers, i.e.
those born outside Australia or outside the English language) is to alert
us to the intersection of culture and nationalism. Consider some other
marginal voices insofar as they adopt the mode of personal histories:
women's voices alert us to the construction of gender differences within
culture, working class voices to class and culture, black voices to race
and culture. With migrants the focus is on nationalism and culture,
culture as it relates to nationalism. Migrant voices raise questions about
what constitutes national consciousness or national cultures. To read
them with this in mind is not, as I have argued, a matter of con-
taminating aesthetics with politics. All interpretations or readings *are*
political and there are good reasons why they should be political and
why we should affirm this instead of denying it. The more we identify
and deconstruct the absences in our discourses the less we are controlled
by them. Multiculturalism is, therefore, a strategy of writing and
reading which focuses on discursive heterogeneity in relation to culture
and nationalism. Migrant voices are those who interrogate hegemonic
notions of the intersection of the national and the cultural. Finally,
multiculturalism may teach us to speak not English but Australian.

(ii) From without . . .

We have to write because they've been telling stories about us. Word
has gone out but not our words. The following purports to be the voice
of the migrant writer:

> There are far too many New Australians in this country who are still mentally
> living in their homelands, who mix with people of their own nationality, and
> try to retain their own language and customs. Who even try to persuade
> Australians to adopt their customs and manners. Cut it out. There is no better
> way of life in the world than that of the Australian. I firmly believe this. The
> grumbling, growling, cursing, profane, laughing, beer drinking, abusive, loyal-
> to-his-mates Australian is one of the few free men left on this earth. He fears
> no one, crawls to no one, bludges on no one, and acknowledges no master. Learn
> his way. Learn his language. Get yourself accepted as one of him; and you will
> enter a world that you never dreamed existed. And once you have entered it,
> you will never leave it.[3]

Where *we* migrants are writing from is this territory, stories such as the
one from which I have been quoting, stories which comprise both
history and literature, two ends of the same narrative spectrum. As
Donald Horne puts it:

> . . . one of the great battles for multiculturalism must be fought in the schools,
> but far more important than the teaching of community languages is the
> teaching of history, and of literature.[4]

Whether we choose to regard it as history or literature depends on a strategic emphasis but the two modes are always intertwined. Currently, we are preoccupied with histories. One could appeal to a rough rule of thumb here and argue that history generally demands the voice of the witness, the authenticity of the eye-witness account, the raw materials of fragmented experiences which are then processed into a unified narrative. In those circumstances one must examine the motives of the court historian who produces this homogenised narrative. Here is a very early description, from the twelfth century, of that process from eye-witness to what purports to be history:

Finding himself left all alone in this far-distant land on Egypt's confines, Bors put on all his armour and, leaving Sarras, went down to the sea where he boarded a ship. Circumstances favoured him, and after a short voyage he arrived in the kingdom of Logres. After landing there he journeyed on horseback as far as Camelot where he found king and court. Never was there such exultation as greeted his arrival, for they thought to have lost him for ever, since he had been so long abroad.

When they had dined King Arthur summoned his clerks who were keeping a record of all the adventures undergone by the knights of his household. When Bors had related to them the adventures of the Holy Grail as witnessed by himself, they were written down and the record kept in the library in Salisbury, whence Master Walter Map extracted them in order to make his book of the Holy Grail for love of his lord King Henry, who had the story translated from Latin into French. And with that the tale falls silent and has no more to say about the Adventures of the Holy Grail.[5]

The result of that particular first-person account was to bestow upon the kingdom of Logres a secular messiah and a sacred history which has in turn been an invaluable resource mined, at strategic intervals, by the subsequent rulers of Logres/Great Britain. One could argue that the Australian equivalent of Walter Map was C.W. Bean and that the sacred history we have here begins with Anzac and Gallipoli rather than Camelot.

We migrants have also contributed many first-person accounts to Australian historians. In fact what is labelled 'migrant writing' is commonly perceived as encompassing only that mode – the precarious authority of the first-person account. By definition almost, this mode needs another, purportedly more objective one, in order to give it the status of received truth. In the unified narrative of official history the first-person account has been returned to us as the collective migrant success story. Our sufferings either took place beyond these shores, before our rebirth here, or, even when they did occur here, they functioned, eventually, as a healing process. Like the Grail knights, 'we' have redeemed the wasteland. We, too, in our eye-witness accounts have testified to Logres and Camelot, to Australia as the Promised Land instead of the Penal Colony. Today this process of mythmaking, to which the migrant writer was relegated, is healthily satirised in a different kind of migrant writing. For example, Walter Adamson's *Australia of all places*. In this extract his two protagonists, both of migrant extraction, are revisiting rural Germany:

... we two Australians had become well-known characters, conspicuous by our extremely casual, not to say sloppy, clothes on weekends and holidays, in contrast to the natives. In every shop we entered, they downed tools and talked to us. What was it like 'down under'? What was the weather like, the money, beer, water? Their faces became transfigured when we talked of 'down under'. The most difficult thing was to convince them that we also had strikes and inflation, demonstrations and discontent. That Australia is no land of milk and honey. That it is only marginally smaller than Europe, and yet has only fifteen million inhabitants. That in the 800 or so kilometres between Melbourne and Sydney there are hardly any cities worth mentioning. That Christmas is celebrated in summer. Ho hum. Not many believed us, and when we eventually left, they were all convinced that we had returned to Paradise.[6]

That Australia is finally the Promised Land is no doubt comforting news to the official historians who are labouring, like Master Walter Map, in the wilderness of contradictory events on the eve of various questionable celebrations of white settlement.

From history to literature and I have already, of course, indicated how blurred these boundaries really are. But, for the purpose of argument, let us say that literature is the way in which human subjects transmute their own physical implausibility into metaphysical terms. The mere fact of physical presence carries little substance until it has been recreated in storytelling: 'In the beginning was the word...'.

But, as I've been trying to point out, the kind of story told is crucially determined by who tells it, to whom, and for what reasons. A national literature is the way in which, collectively, we re-build this continent inside our own heads. It does not have a recognizable reality until it has been named and, having done this we are then able to recreate it for others. Australia was discovered through the five senses only when it was physically encountered. Its immediate reproduction occurred in one kind of language, the semiotics of cartography, maps as sign systems which comprise, amongst other things, a language of imperialism. Then it was named according to the terms of other sign systems and stories organized it. Australia began circulating as discursive currency in ways which differed from its previous issue as the imaginary Great South Land.

Now, on the eve of bicentennial inflations, there are renewed and concerted attempts to revalue this currency, to tell Australia again. There is a sense that the continent is still eluding our re-creation. Why, otherwise (as a recent visitor reminded me), do we continue to reproduce its outline (usually minus Tasmania) as a fetish in every aspect of our lives? Have you ever noticed how often we are bombarded with the metonymic outline of Australia? Theoretically, there is nothing more real than this familiar shape so why do need to keep on reproducing it? Of what are we reminding ourselves? Richard White's recent book, *Inventing Australia*, bears our what I have been saying: 'There is no "real" Australia waiting to be uncovered. A national identity is an invention'.[7] We are obsessed by the drive to rediscover Australia discursively. In White's book we find a succinct summary of that group, putative *bona fide* Australian subjects, who have been telling stories about us, New Australian subjects.

And here, finally, the second part of this topic: who are we writing for? Ourselves; or, rather, we are writing ourselves into being as subjects within the multicultural history of Australia. For the moment we will keep this 'we' in suspension because it is, of course, bristling with interrogations. And what about this fraught term *'multi*-culturalism'? According to nineteenth-century co-ordinates (Matthew Arnold & Co.) and their legacies of unity and consensus, *multi*-culturalism is a contradiction in terms. Here is a definition of culture by Edward Said, a Palestinian academic incongruously dissident in New York:

...culture is a system of discriminations and evaluations...for a particular class in the State able to identify with it; and it also means that culture is a system of exclusions legislated from above but enacted throughout its policy, by which such things as anarchy, disorder, irrationality, inferiority, bad taste, and immorality are identified, then deposited outside the culture and kept there by the power of the State and its institutions. For if it is true that culture is, on the one hand, a positive doctrine of the best that is thought and known, it is also on the other a differentially negative doctrine of all that is not best.[8]

To label oneself *multi*-cultural may be at best an attempt at an alibi which rescues one from such an accusation. Said labels culture as the means whereby the rulers control the ruled. Multiculturalism may represent an attempt to camouflage vested orthodoxies. Donald Horne echoes this fear:

I would now say that in the sense that they should seek Australian, not British, definitions of Australia, all multiculturalists in Australia should be as it were 'anti-British'. Failing this, *there is a danger that multiculturalism becomes a way of keeping 'the ethnics quiet while the 'anglos' can go on running things*, as destiny demanded they should. If the aim is to define Australia as a multicultural society and to set multiculturalism as a national goal, how, at the same time, can Australia be declaredly monocultural, as, not only symbolically, but constitutionally, it still is?[9]

In a recent compilation which yokes history and literature together, *The Oxford History of Australian Literature*, Professor Leonie Kramer's introduction[10] speaks of the disjunctive ways in which colonial writers tried to discover a language to fit their new experiences. Perhaps we recall more easily to the mind's eye the beginnings of Australian painting where for quite a while the flora and fauna, as well as the Aborigines, resembled pictorial transplants from other prior and more familiar cultures. Did these early painters really see gum trees in terms of such European outlines? Perhaps not, but to communicate with others they had to employ an iconography of the already known. The folks back home saw as they had been taught to see until there was a consensus that reality was otherwise, after which they were ready to see differently. Professor Kramer goes on to say that the need for public utterance, the drive to have the alien experience confirmed (we are *not* dreaming this place in mad solitude) drove those early writers to favour the conventions of public utterance derived from the more formal discourses of the eighteenth century. This was in contrast to what were, at that time, the actual contemporaneous conventions of nineteenth-century romanticism which, with their emphasis on private intro-spective meditations, were not deemed appropriate. It was far too risky to meditate in private on those early experiences which would, in their namelessness, surely confirm one's lunacy.

This sense of discrepancy, the feeling that experience is not being matched by language, recurs. Surveying Australian literature as it has been disseminated by various State institutions (the review pages of newspapers and journals, school and university curricula) we become aware of several ghosts and gaps. In recent literary history there has been the belated discovery of women writers. And now the question is being posed: where are migrant writers from non English-speaking backgrounds? Where is *their* experience told in a way that we do not know already?

To reiterate: where are we writing from? Australian Literature has produced us and our positions already as surely as Australian paintings produced those early European gum trees. We have had a place mapped out for us already: the migrant as object. This ranges from the unsubtlety of O'Grady's sterotypes, to the complexities of Patrick White's Greeks, or Tom Shapcott's Old Hungarians confronting Inno-cent Australia with Jamesian subtlety and paradox:

> ... On those damp logs
> innocence glows phosphorous as fungus. I write
> from a place of stilts. There are many growths:
> I no longer differentiate corruption. Innocence
> can look with monstrous padlocks.[11]

Other discourses besides the literary ones have produced and con-tinue to produce us: the official forms which reduce the migrant subject to essentials, beloved by sociologists and historians. Welfare agencies:

the migrant problems; the migrant *as* problem. And further signifying systems: Channel 0/28 (*The migrant experience* in six parts) and, before that, those films made by the Department of Immigration. This is why 'we' need to write because we are already constructed as objects by Australian history and Australian literature. We are not, strictly speaking, an absence at all but we do need to re-invent ourselves.

And now, at last, who are 'we'? Above all, there is no unified 'we'. Insofar as 'we' exist it is as a group cemented by the kinship of having in common the experience of migration, both em- and im- (leaving and arriving) and sometimes this experience has been exacerbated by the knowledge of a language and culture other than the official white English one.

In some respects every person who migrated here, including the British, have had to contend with the psychic schizophrenia of a prior culture. Such an experience is beautifully described, for example, by the Glaswegian writer Mary Rose Liverani in *The winter sparrows: growing up in Scotland and Australia*:

> I am waiting for Australia to enchant me.
> To distract me from the past. To become
> the hypnotic present.[12]

All migrants have to contend with a profoundly felt renegotiation of cultural certainties. It is as wrong for us to construct a spuriously unified Anglo culture as it is for 'them' to homogenise all migrants or multiculturalists as 'ethnics'. Anyone who has encountered the kingdom of Logres/Great Britain recently becomes aware of the many multicultural cracks in the erstwhile monolithic British Empire. Similarly, in retrospect, we become aware that even within Australia there has always been a consciousness of the split between the Anglo and the Celtic. Indeed, as I have argued elsewhere,[13] the Celtic or Irish dissidence was one upon which Australia initially reinvented its own difference from the cultural paternalism of Britain. So the 'we' may sometimes include all migrants. What it does not include, as far as I'm concerned, are those who wield cultural unity and cultural dominance as their 'natural' prerogative. Here I must pause because the effort to be heard in the face of exposure to Anglo-Australian complacencies has produced some so-called ethnic writers who do resort to their own brand of cultural totalitarianism. Richard Bosworth and Janis Wilton[14] have produced a useful summary of some of the reactionary elements they have found reproduced in some ethnic writing. One can understand that the culturally disenfranchised might have sought comfort in a nostalgia about Old Europe (or even Old Asia) with its exclusive patina of ancient cultures.

At its best this nostalgia can provide a vantage point for satire as, for example, in Pino Bosi's short story, 'That ... thing in "Via della Topaia"' in which a sensitive Australian visitor to Italy, Professor Samuel Pipps, cannot bring himself to desecrate a urinal built by the Emperor Vespasian.[15] But where finally does it lead us? On the positive side, to an awareness that cultural history comprises more than British culture. Texts other than British ones are still rarely studied as part of literary curricula. But at its worst this nostalgia for old cultures produces both an inappropriate Eurocentrism (witness the recent Blainey debate) and functions as an atrophying force, the weight of the dead hand of the past. In this respect the critics of multiculturalism (both conservatives like Lachlan Chipman[16] and those from the migrant community like George Michelakakis[17]) are right in identifying a certain limited concept of multiculturalism as being derivative and custodial. Energy goes into preservation instead of innovation. Ethnic cultures reek of formaldehyde and all the energy is expanded in preserving, anachronistically, the 'old ways'. Not surprisingly this has often had a paralysing effect on the young.[18]

In the new wave of migrant writers the 'we' is not simply located in a past preserved elsewhere nor is it simply constructed in or by opposition. It is suspicious of such naive polarities. One encounters such a sceptical 'we' in Antigone Kefala's recent novella, *The Island*, on the face of it about New Zealand, but with wider relevance. The narrator in this text certainly at times recognises the reality of being constructed in opposition. Here is an encounter betweeen a New Zealander and the foreign narrator:

I spoke. I could see from his face that he had not the faintest idea what I was saying, the meaning stopped somewhere mid-air between us, he incredulous that he will ever understand me, I incredulous that he will ever understand me. He was busy swallowing thin mouthfuls of vinegar, watching me with preoccupied eyes, rubbing his hands as if drying them of sand, trying to get rid of it. I could see in his whole attitude the immense surprise at being confronted, here in his own room, at the University, by something as foreign as myself. The implied extravagance of my voice, the rapid nervousness of my movements, my eyes that looked too directly at him. He made social concessions outwardly, but inwardly he kept repeating to himself – why the hell do I have to put up with this in my everyday life, one is not safe anywhere these days.[19]

At the same time the narrator has a sardonic awareness of taking refuge in the easy glamour of the exotic:

Now, in the lighted room, Aunt Niki filling the air with puffs of smoke, trying to find the right card for her patience, I launched enthusiastically, for I loved to talk, and Aunt Niki liked me, admired me as something out of the ordinary, as if she recognized in me things that she considered of value, giving me scope to do things and say things that she would not give to others. I felt at home with her, yet sometimes with a slight, but very slight foreignness towards myself, so that as I talked I watched myself from the corner of my eye to see if the finishing touches were aesthetic enough. For Aunt Niki loved decorum, the living decorum of one's life that must be kept always cultivated, polished, so that one could move gracefully among centuries of stylized gestures.[20]

Who, finally, are we writing? What kinds of subjects are we re-inventing? We are not blank pages, our experiences of migration are inscribed on the already written: a palimpsest. We cannot speak unmediated experience innocently. When we tell *our* stories we are addressing, in part, all those other stories already told about us and must take issue with them. It is not a question of being original for we must bear the responsibility of refusing originality. Entering literature and history means recognizing those discourses which have already produced us. It means doing our homework. Like women, migrants are already enmeshed within many sign-systems. We are all constructed as subjects the moment we enter any of those sign-systems. As migrants we must contend with a whole history of representations: two images which stand out immediately are that of the child and that of the women. The former, the migrant as child, is illustrated by Ania Walwicz's poem 'helpless':

before they were big i was small they could do things more than me they were something now they are nothing he was a doctor of animals now he was learning to speak properly he talked funny they made mistakes she was clumsy she works in a factory he cleans the floors of the serum laboratory now life can be everybody clean and nice and we are all wrong here i was the translator i was the mother of my mother they were more helpless they were useless nervous didn't know what to do i was too serious for me it was too early to be like this we walked lost on the street we were looking for john street i was bigger than them my parents were again small old children they were heavy for me they couldn't do much you are helpless useless[21]

The migrant as woman is celebrated, for example, in the film *Silver City* (dir. S. Turkiewicz, 1984). I am not condemning either text but only saying that we cannot afford to be ignorant of these familiar metaphors if we are trying to produce new stories about ourselves within history and literature. To speak merely from the first person is no immediate guarantee of a new authenticity. Oral history can, as we have seen, also be used in such a way that it supports the already-known. The new subjects we produce must question cultural certainties and, above all, must not allow the new banner of multiculturalism to become synonymous either with Eurocentrism or with a-politicism. It should not function against Asians or Aborigines as a consolidatory European charter myth of origins. If we allow ourselves to be co-opted as Old Europe to support a new White Australia then, like Sir Bors, we are being co-opted by Master Walter Map for Logres and will be helping to write merely a new chapter in the sacred history of imperialism. Instead, like the Chinese–Australian protagonist of Brian Castro's *Birds of passage*, we need to carry the multiple manuscripts of our ancestral multi-cultures 'as talismans for other points of departure'.[20] To reinvent, what else, New Australians.

NOTES

1. T. Eagleton, *Literary theory: an introduction*, Basil Blackwell, Oxford, 1983, p. 209.
2. R. Williams, *Culture*, Fontana, 1983, p. 13.
3. Nino Culotta, *They're a weird mob*, Ure Smith, Sydney, 1957–60, p. 204.
4. Donald Horne, 'The perils of multiculturalism as a national ideal', Third Annual Address to the Australian Institute of Multicultural Affairs, AIMA, Melbourne, 1983, p. 4.
5. *The quest of the holy grail*, trans. P.M. Matarasso, Penguin, Harmondsworth, 1969, p. 284. My emphasis.
6. Walter Adamson, *Australia of all places*, Hodja, Richmond, 1984, pp. 68–69. See also, for another example, a chapter title, 'The promising land', in Brian Castro, *Birds of passage*, Allen & Unwin, Sydney, 1984.
7. Richard White, *Inventing Australia: images and identity 1688–1980*, Allen & Unwin, Sydney, 1982, p. viii.
8. Edward Said, 'Secular criticism', in *The world, the text, and the critic*, Faber, London, 1984, pp. 11–12.
9. D. Horne, op. cit., p. 3. My emphasis.
10. Leonie Kramer, 'Introduction', *The Oxford history of Australian literature*, Oxford University Press, Melbourne, 1981, pp. 1–23.
11. Thomas Shapcott, *White stag of exile*, Allen Lane, Ringwood, 1984, p. 165.
12. Mary Rose Liverani, *The winter sparrows*, Sphere, Melbourne, 1978, p. 195.
13. S. Gunew, 'Migrants in Silver City', BASA (British Australian Studies Association Journal), No.1, 1, Spring 1984, pp. 21–26.
14. R. Bosworth and J. Wilton, 'Novels, poems and the study of Europeans in Australia', in *Teaching history*, July 1981, pp. 43–65.
15. Pino Bosi, *The checkmate and other short stories*, Kurunda, Sydney, 1973, pp. 145–151.
16. L. Chipman, 'Multiculturalism and Australian Writing', talk on ABC's *Books and writing*, 13/6/84.
17. G. Michelakalis, 'The cultural structure of the Greek minority in Australia', *Aspect*, no. 29/30, Autumn 1984, pp. 54–66.
18. For a discussion of the pros and cons of 'multiculturalism' as it circulates currently within Australia see S. Gunew, 'Australia 1984: a moment in the archaeology of multiculturalism', forthcoming in the Proceedings of the conference held at the University of Essex, July, 1984, 'Europe and its others'.
19. A. Kefala, *The Island*, Hale & Iremonger, Sydney, 1984, pp. 22–23.
20. Ibid., p. 40.
21. A. Walwicz, 'helpless', in S. Gunew (ed.) *Displacements: migrant storytellers*, Deakin University Press, Victoria, 1982, p. 2.
22. B. Castro, op. cit., p. 4.

5 Setting up an Australian literature course: some conceptual and practical reflections

Werner Senn

What incentive, beyond that of getting additional credit points, can there be for students of English literature struggling with overloaded reading lists, harassed by exams and worried by bleak professional prospects, to take up yet another field? We might begin by pointing out the exciting and invigorating experience of reading in an area so patently unfamiliar to the continental European. Today, indeed, as Anna Wulf in Doris Lessing's *The Golden Notebook* complains, 'We read *to find out what is going on*,' and we think of novels, in particular, as original 'in the sense that they report the existence of an area of society, a type of person, not yet admitted to the general literate consciousness'. (Bantam Books, 1981, pp. 60–61).

Legitimate as this may be, it still does not exhaust the interest which Australian literature holds for the student of English literature who seeks to understand not only how the past took shape in the canonical works but also how it affects and shapes our vision of the present. It can be extraordinarily instructive to see ideas and concepts familiar from traditional 'Eng. Lit.' courses transplanted into a colonial context, to trace, for example, the impact of European intellectual and political forces on the colonization of the Australian continent. Equally fascinating and informative for Europeans is Australia's own more recent encounter, as an industrialized 'western' country, with its Asian neighbours. It is clear that these areas of interest are interrelated and mutually illuminating: confrontation with Europe, with Asia (and America!) necessarily leads to a rethinking of the past and to new self-definitions.[1] The insights that may be gained from this process, the way the past and present forces shape the images which Australian writers project of themselves and of their experience of Australia, would seem to make this a very worthwhile approach to the study of Australian literature.

Australia's short literary history (if we exclude 'oral' literature) makes it possible to look at a couple of issues in an introductory course, which should ideally be followed up by more specific courses on more

63

narrowly defined topics. What is offered here is a number of reflections on how such a basic course might most usefully be conceived and realized; these will be followed by an illustration of some teaching possibilities in one area, the Australian short story. The readers I have in mind are 'pioneers' rather than experts.

Given the still undisputed predominance of English literature in our curricula (and the indisputable claims of the other 'new' literatures in English), the Australian course may be limited in scope and time, so that the selection of texts becomes a crucial question. The temptation is great to offer 'the best', but is this necessarily also the most representative or the most suitable for our purpose? Leaving aside the often vexing problem of obtaining books from Australia, the criteria for selection are obviously determined by various factors. There is, especially for a course of this kind, a need to present a spectrum as wide as possible in style, form and content. There is, on the other hand, the need to give information to students for whom Botany Bay or Gallipoli are mere names, to whom Burke and Wills or Ned Kelly mean nothing at all, and whose image of Australia may well derive from recent films such as *The Thornbirds* and *My Brilliant Career* (both shown on German television).

There is nothing wrong with reading (also), in Lessing's sense, 'for information', provided that the term is inclusive enough and the information conveyed selected carefully enough and processed properly. Thus to argue, for example, that in order to learn about the 'real' Australia of the early twentieth century, students should read *Such Is Life* (1903), *Capricornia* (1938) and *The Tree of Man* (1955) would be inadequate simply because of the very real difficulties presented by the sheer bulk and local detail of the former two works, and the knotty style and often stubborn complexity of the latter. If the course is to be followed up later, both Herbert and White, as well as other major novelists like Christina Stead and H.H. Richardson would benefit from being discussed at a more advanced stage. On the other hand, works with a topical appeal, like Thomas Keneally's 1972 novel *The Chant of Jimmie Blacksmith* (racism and the Aboriginal question) or David Williamson's 1972 play *The Removalists* (sexual politics and the abuse of power) will go down well, without necessarily giving a typical – let alone balanced – view of modern Australia. For this kind of course the question of whether to read *in* the texts or *through* the texts (Todorov's 'commentary' and 'projection') – or whether to engage simply in what he calls 'reading' – seems to remain unanswerable and to make compromise mandatory.

This is not the place to join in the debate on what constitutes the Australianness of Australian writing.[2] The poet Les Murray made the valid point that Australian literature today does not have to be about Australia at all (*The Peasant Mandarin*, 1978, p. 224). Yet for a didactic purpose, books with Australian settings and themes are clearly an advantage at this stage. At the same time, of course, a work based on a purely local incident, such as Patrick White's *A Fringe of Leaves* (1976), is just as much 'about' modern Australia as it is about Europe, while, conversely, a novel dealing with Ovid's exile on the Black Sea – David Malouf's *An Imaginary Life* (1978) – is patently relevant for Australia and its European heritage as well. In full awareness of their inescapable subjectivity, therefore, I would propose the following criteria of selection: the texts studied and discussed should be (*a*) representative (*b*) manageable in size and degree of difficulty, (*c*) of intrinsic interest, (*d*) recognizably 'Australian' in a wide sense. These criteria – to stress the point – might not be valid for a more advanced course. In practice, a satisfactory compromise can be reached by choosing texts of some thematic or generic coherence, which allow an exploration of topics both synchronically and diachronically. Such topics might include: the colonial history of early settlers and convicts; the encounter with, and attitudes toward, the Aborigines; images of Australia in poetry; the short story; city and bush; women in Australia; contemporary drama.[3] A certain amount of overlapping can do no harm: Henry Lawson, say, would figure in both 'The Short Story' and 'City and Bush'. Moreover, many of the themes can be approached through texts which reflect them as well as those which reflect *on* them. 'City and Bush,' for example, could include both Lawson's 'The Never-Never Land' and Les Murray's 'Sydney and the Bush'; 'Aborigines' could deal with writings both about and *by* Aboriginals (of which there is an increasing amount).[4]

Australia's early colonial history, which is of course basic to an understanding of Australian culture, can be introduced by studying some of the popular ballads collected in Douglas Stewart and Nancy Keesing's *Favourite Bush Ballads* (Angus & Robertson, Sydney, 1967). These afford an opportunity of looking at some of the images created and projected by early colonizers, convicts and bush-workers alike. By and large they evince 'an irreverent or hostile attitude towards authority and social pretension, a solidarity in the face of natural difficulty or social wrong, a capacity for initiative and improvization.'[5] But more than that: they allow us to see radically opposed views of, and attitudes towards, the new continent, which has to do with differences not only in social status but also in origin, notably with the large number of Irish convicts, whose background 'produced an identifiably different behavioural pattern' (*Intruders in the Bush*, p. 85). Ballads like 'The Wild Colonial Boy' and 'Jim Jones at Botany Bay' on the one hand, and 'Van Diemen's Land' on the other, neatly illustrate this basic contrast between violently egalitarian desires and the prudent moralizing of a cautionary tale. The latter reflects not only a temperament made servile by centuries of oppression but also the prevailing policies of dissuasion adopted by the authorities in Britain, for whom Botany Bay was the epitome of the penal settlement and functioned 'as a weapon in the control of working-class crime in Britain'.[6] A fruitful discussion of the complex problems of the early settlement can be initiated by contrasting the ballads with two superb modern novels that cover the same historical ground, Thomas Keneally's *Bring Larks and Heroes* (1967) and White's *A Fringe of Leaves*.[7] Contrasting attitudes towards Australia as edenic Utopia or infernal prison may be traced through the later literary ballads (Lawson, Barcroft Boake, 'Banjo' Paterson) to such 'classics' as Dorothea Mackellar's 'My Country' and Mary Gilmore's 'Old Botany Bay'. The juxtaposition of Judith Wright's early 'Bullocky' with her later 'Australia 1970' provides some fascinating insights into recent revisions of concepts (and also an opportunity of looking at women's contribution to Australian writing).

Let us now explore some of the rich possibilities which the short story holds for a coherent and rewarding approch to our subject. The short story is perhaps the most firmly established genre in Australian literature – which does not mean the most uniform – and it is possible to base an entire course on it. Recent anthologies by Kerryn Goldsworthy, Bill Scott and the well-established volumes edited by Harry Heseltine and Brian Kiernan offer a wide and representative selection which includes some of the major authors such as Herbert, Richardson and Stead, whose longer works, for the reason given above, do not figure on my initial syllabus.[8] I can do no more than highlight a few selected items here, in the hope that they will be useful to teachers and stimulate further discussion. Henry Lawson is my obvious (in fact inevitable) first choice, to be followed by Hal Porter and two contemporaries, Murray Bail and Peter Carey.

For readers brought up on the laconic restraint of Hemingway, the symbolic sophistication of Joyce and the curiously dispassionate intensity of Kafka, it might be well to recall the social and ideological impulses behind the stories of Henry Lawson, whose strident pathos and homely humour our students may find hard to appreciate at first. Lawson's own remarks, in a *Bulletin* piece of 1897 entitled ' "Pursuing Literature" in Australia', might be helpful here:

In the first fifteen years of my life I saw the last of the Roaring Days of Gulgong goldfield, N.S.W. . . . saw selectors slaving their lives away in dusty holes amongst the barren ridges . . . saw how the gaunt selectors' wives lived and toiled. Saw older sons stoop-shouldered old men at thirty. Noted . . . the pile of chimney-stones, a blue-gum slab or two, and the remains of the fence – the ultimate result of ten years', fifteen years', and twenty years' hard, hopeless graft by strong men who died like broken-down bullocks further out. And all the years miles and miles of rich black soil flats and chocolate slopes lay idle, because of old-time grants, or because the country carried sheep – for the sake of an extra bale of wool and an unknown absentee. I watched old fossickers and farmers reading *Progress and Poverty* earnestly and arguing over it Sunday afternoons. And I wished that I could write.[9]

The point to be made is that the famous 'realism' in Lawson's writing is a direct result of his desire to write a kind of 'littérature engagée': again (if we may trust the artist rather than the tale) he makes this clear in the conclusion to 'Some Popular Australian Mistakes':

We wish to Heaven that Australian writers would leave off trying to make a paradise out of the Out Back Hell; if only out of consideration for the poor, hopeless, half-starved wretches who carry swags through it and look in vain for work – and ask in vain for tucker very often. What's the good of making a heaven of a hell when by describing it as it really is, we might do some good for the lost souls there? (p. 130)

The knotty problem of literary realism – which students of German literature are well aware of – can be illustrated by reference to one of the classic Australian short stories, Lawson's 'The Drover's Wife'.

It has been argued recently that the notion of realism which dominated much Australian writing well into the twentieth century (the 'Lawson tradition') meant an objective and impersonal method of writing from which the author's personality as well as any awareness of an audience was completely removed, but that Lawson himself broke away from these *Bulletin* conventions, and that 'even in one of his most objective stories, 'The Drover's Wife', one finds direct addresses to the reader and personal asides'.[10] It is not my intention to go into, or add to, the ongoing critical debate about the precise nature and the implications of Lawson's narrative technique, of which the 'prominent authorial role' has been declared to form 'an essential part'.[11] But – unfamiliarity of setting and subject matter apart – the contemporary (European) reader's difficulty may lie precisely in those personal asides, which seem to be not only a matter of technique but of feeling, affecting the emotional impact of the story. The undercurrent of strong emotion which is given oblique expression only in the boy's final assertion, 'Mother, I won't never go drovin', blast me if I do!' would seem to suggest a powerful, if unacknowledged, condemnation of the drover himself (elsewhere one of the heroic figures) for the sort of life (or non-life) he is inflicting on his wife, albeit through force of circumstances.

Although there is nothing inherently comic in it, incipient sentiment is time and again defused or deflated by attempts at humour which seem half-hearted to us but may in fact be quintessentially Australian. One example must suffice: Tommy's question, when he cannot go to sleep, 'Do you think they'll ever extricate the (adjective) kangaroo?' is meant to be funny both through its malapropism and its coy use of the generic term for the specific Australian 'bloody', i.e. we have two comic effects on two totally distinct levels. The first is on the level of story, in the 'dramatic method' (Jarvis, p. 59); the second, syntactically contiguous, is on the level of discourse, drawing attention to the authorial presence in the act of narration. If this feature, which occurs repeatedly, superficially links Lawson up with the postmodern experimenters (as E. Webby claims, p. 154), its purpose is nevertheless diametrically opposed to theirs: Lawson seeks to achieve identification of reader with events and characters, stresses the referential nature of his fiction, while they stress its fictionality; to jolt the reader into an awareness of this is their whole point. The many jolts the reader of Lawson's early stories receives both through the attempts at comic deflation of sentiment and through the brazenly sentimental authorial intrusions (e.g. at the end of both 'The Drover's Wife' and 'The Bush Undertaker') work – at least for many – against the sought-for identification or empathy and tend to obscure at first Lawson's splendid achievement.

The postmodern variation which Murray Bail's 1975 story 'The Drover's Wife' (reprinted in Kiernan, *The Most Beautiful Lies*) plays on Lawson's theme can make us fully aware of the difference, but its very cleverness and playfulness enables us to recognize the intensity of Lawson's commitment and acknowledge the impact of his starkly pessimistic realism, and makes us more easily accept his story as 'an archetypal image of maternal isolation and loneliness – intolerably deprived',[12] and appreciate its powerfully evoked atmosphere and character. Against the backdrop of Lawson's story, Murray Bail's contemporary one is not just a clever skit but takes on multiple resonances and, through its postmodern emphasis on its own fictionality, invites reading on different levels. The identity of titles plainly refers to Lawson's story, yet this is nowhere made explicit. Instead, the narrator refers to Russell Drysdale's well-known painting 'The Drover's Wife' (1945) – itself a reading, in a different medium, of Lawson's story – as a portrait of his wife Hazel shortly after she ran away from him, some thirty years previously. In other words, he treats the work of art as a more or less faithful mirror of reality, draws inferences from it about Hazel's relationship with the man just barely visible in the background (presumably the drover she ran away with) whose facial expression he tries to scan with the help of a magnifying glass, finding him, predictably, 'nothing but brush strokes. A real mystery man'. Yet he continues to mistake art for life, criticizes the painter for failing to paint the flies, 'a serious omission: ... It is altering the truth for the sake of a pretty picture', a comment that exposes his realistic-mimetic view of art as patently absurd.

His criticism of the painting can be seen as part of his strategy of refuting accusations (from his daughter, from the painter, from the reader even) that it had all been his fault. On this level, the story offers a psychological study of the break-up of a marriage, focusing not only *on* the husband but *through* him, and properly so, since the man turns out to be a bully if not a male chauvinist. He blames it all on his wife's 'silly streak', her childish delight in outdoor activities and heavy practical work, such as chopping wood or killing a snake (the most obvious allusion to Lawson's story). The narrator is not aware of how totally his arrogant stance undermines his case.

Authorial irony extends to a larger issue, which the story tackles only obliquely: the much discussed theme of City vs Bush.[13] The narrator, a dentist from Adelaide, recalls how during a camping holiday in the outback he felt completely lost in the bush and merely found it 'stinking hot', while Hazel was 'in her element . . . she acted as if she were part of it. I felt ourselves moving apart, as if I didn't belong there, especially with her. I felt left out'. The marital conflict is thus embedded in this larger cultural conflict between city (male?) and wilderness (female?), which has affected Australian society from its nationalist days to the present and which could be discussed within the binary opposition civilization/nature.

Virtually left out of Lawson's story (where the narrator pretends not even to know whether the drover, like his wife, has got used to their long separations), the husband puts himself into Bail's story with a vengeance, displacing the wife, who has no more voice here than *he* has in Lawson's story. But he cannot and will not put himself in touch with the bush, and so he also commits the ultimate social offence by declining a drover's invitation to share tea with him, preferring to wait in the car until Hazel has finished, preferring to remain clean, cultivated, suburban.

The last and largest irony of the story, I think, takes us back to Lawson. The narrator, looking at the tiny silhouette of the drover in the painting, recalls the real drover they met, 'a thin head in a khaki hat, not talkative, with dusty boots. He is indistinct. Is it him? I don't know. Hazel – it is Hazel and the rotten landscape that dominate everything'. Given the complex 'anxiety of influence' that this sophisticated story betrays, is it too far-fetched to read this ending as a dismissal of the Lawson tradition as epitomized in 'The Drover's Wife'? For Michael Wilding, another contemporary author of short stories, this tradition has been 'dominant as a central, monolithic tradition for too long' (*Australian Literary Studies*, 8, 1977, 123). Murray Bail himself has declared his 'dissatisfaction with the barren, anecdotal realism of the local literature' (*ALS*, 10, 1981, 187), while another prestigious short story writer, Frank Moorhouse, has characterized the Lawson tradition as 'sympathetic to the working class and kind to kangaroos' (*ALS*, 8,

1977, 190) – a witty parody of Furphy's famous description of his *Such Is Life*: 'temper democratic, bias offensively Australian'.

Hal Porter, perhaps the most brilliant of Australian short story writers, reacts to this 'monolithic' tradition not by turning, like his younger contemporaries, to the models of Kafka, Borges and Barthelme, but by developing a regionalism of his own. He displays himself rather self-consciously as 'regional', 'parish-bound', 'almost pastoral', preoccupied with his native South Victoria:

I don't loathe the bush, the outback, the never-never, call it what you will, as a city-slicker like Henry Lawson did, and have skipped happily enough over most of these pretty deadly areas, as well as into and out of all the capital cities and a lot of the provincial ones.[14]

In 'Everleigh's Accent' (1962) Porter takes us into just such a provincial town, brilliantly evoked by the narrator in sharply observed, realistic detail, and in a richly figurative language which satirically highlights the social and cultural pretensions, the synthetic nature, of the town's sham values:

From the last hill-top the over-lit town declared itself an ante-room to coruscating gaiety. I knew better; perspectives of municipal moons showed streets naked except for three Italians dressed as New Australians but gesticulating like Italians in front of a display of Volkswagen and cyclamen; the Prince Regent Theatre lassoed out hectoring talkie voices towards the gibbous moon; from the rotunda in the strip of lawns, palms and claret ashes that divided Main Street the Shire Band was despairing its way through *Mélodie d'Amour*. (p. 179)

Very self-consciously, the narrator introduces himself as a commercial traveller and as a man who 'can well enough simulate the Intelligent Good Mixer. You understand?' This is both a prerequisite for the functioning of the story and, it would seem, for the functioning of Australian social life. Himself a part of the society he ridicules, the narrator dazzles by his display of artfully casual references to painting, classical myth, English literature and a whole range of popular and semi-popular culture. His stupendous linguistic competence convinces us that, despite his disclaimer, he *is* a Professor Higgins who can place any Australian by his accent and loves doing so.

All these faculties of discernment are trained on the elusive Everleigh, centre of attention at an after-hours drinking party in the private lounge of the Railway Hotel. A pale young man who has his audience in hysterics by his superbly performed music-hall acts, Everleigh mixes 'songs of blazing sentimentality' with *risqué* stories and impeccable imitations of accents. Yet even in private conversation with the inquisitive narrator – who, intrigued by the 'enigma of his accent . . . lust(s) to find out more' – Everleigh shifts from Welsh to Black American, French and Aboriginal accents, even imitating the narrator's own, 'so that each mimicked personality lay over its own, making him a mystery, a symbol behind fog'. The reader is by now fully enlisted in this compulsive but ultimately futile search for Everleigh's identity. Illumination comes unexpectedly, in a flash, after the party when the narrator comes across Everleigh sitting on the stairs, in the 'archaic light' of the moon, drunkenly stretching out his hand:

... I was forced not to ignore his outstretched hand in the hell of whose stained palm lay not only the ghastly town with its shattered verandas and the fly-besequined eye-sockets of his part-blood parents but the Main Street garden debauchees, the reeking ones, the outskirt-walkers skinny as their mongrels, the soft-eyed beggars whose lilting and smoky accent Everleigh was using at the foot of the moonlit stairs, for it was his by custom, practice, and heredity: 'Drink, man ... Drink gimme ... Gimme little cigarette, boss'. (p. 188)

It was these words that Everleigh had used in his 'imitation' of the part-blood Aboriginal, and with superb craftsmanship Porter has turned this into a powerful and illuminating punch line.

Porter's mastery of form and effervescence of style need not blind us to the remarkable thematic substance of his story. His analysis of 'good mixing' as the supreme social virtue entails a devastating indictment of the average Australian as a synthetic being with no identity of his or her own. Acting a part becomes a social necessity, demonstrated at the outset of the story in the behaviour of the three Italians. The town itself presents a surface of glitter and glamour that the seasoned commercial traveller recognizes as sham, as a composite of borrowings from other cultures and of cheap imitations put together in the crudest of tastes yet advertised as the real thing. The narrator himself, despite his awareness, accepts himself as a representative (a 'rep', as some of his mates call him) of this sham culture, simulating his part in it, although grudgingly. His smattering of an education which embraces Hogarth and Tiepolo, Landseer and Kate Greenaway, Fagin and Father Brown, is a perfect equivalent to the synthetic flashiness of the hotel's private lounge, this 'multicoloured box', which in turn is perfectly in tune with Everleigh's way of dressing:

... his fancy dress, as it seemed to me, had the same qualities of indirectness that the room had – the nickel-plated supports of the fluorescents; the walls each a different colour – Reckitt's Blue, magenta, stewed-quince, card-table green; the brandy-advertising ashtrays; the wire-and-paper irises stuck in troughs of sand; the white-framed reproductions of magnolias. (p. 183–4)

When Everleigh tries to describe his father's (non-existent) pub, he can only do so by gesturing towards the interior of this lounge, this 'harlequin box in which we all thus exercised towards death'. Even without the rather obvious straining after meaning in this instance, it should have become clear that Porter's story implies a severe critique of the pretentiousness of Australian social and cultural values, but there is a further, more radical implication: if to act the Intelligent Good Mixer is an Australian virtue, Everleigh becomes the arch-Australian – which, of course, in a sense he is – except that he is a pitiable example of a part-blood Aboriginal who, deprived of his cultural and racial identity, is left to ape white pseudo-civilization.

The stories of Peter Carey are mostly surrealist fabulations about modern life with a wide appeal beyond the immediate, Australian context, although this is still important.[15] 'Crabs' and 'American Dreams' (both reprinted in Kiernan, *The Most Beautiful Lies*) belong to his most original creations and are representative of the best in post-modern Australian writing. 'Crabs' presents a chilling vision of a bleak and violent future in a world reminiscent of *1984* and *A Clockwork Orange* but still faintly recognizable as Australian, heavily industrialized but in an economic slump, dominated by a network of mass media and terrorized by savage gangs of car thieves, the Karboys. The youngster Crabs, his heart set on becoming a truck driver, stealthily borrows his friend's hotted-up 1956 Dodge to take his girlfriend Carmen to a drive-in cinema, fully aware of the dangers this adventure involves. While they are making love in the car, two of its wheels are taken off. This means that the pair, like most of the other people at the drive-in, are stuck because there is no transport back to the city and it is forbidden (and too dangerous) to walk on or near the road. Thus the drive-in, surrounded by wire fence, virtually turns into a prison camp, although the government distributes meal tickets and blankets. More wrecked cars arrive on huge trucks, prefabricated huts are set up to house the growing number of people (mostly Italians and Indians, to Crab's horror) who arrive and have their cars wrecked or parts stolen. The wire fence is electrified, searchlights are installed, the gate is mostly kept locked.

Crabs starts saving up meal coupons and pinching petrol caps and hub caps, which he hopes to trade in to a Karboy for a wheel. Although in his job he had hated the Mini in which he used to deliver his goods, he now misses it, or rather: 'He misses that hate. He misses driving it, knocking shit out of its piddling little engine, revving it hard enough to burst'. While most of the 'inmates' of the camp set about improving their living conditions, even setting up a temporary cricket pitch, Crabs, by dint of hard thinking, succeeds in formulating for himself a crucial insight: 'to be free, you must be a motor car or vehicle in good health'. Accordingly, he wills himself to become, through a Kafkaesque trans-formation, a complete, well-functioning truck and thus manages to leave the drive-in which by now extends over many square miles. It is here that the story, in Carey's own words, 'fades' into surrealism. (*ALS*, 8, 1977, 185)

To move is everything; aim and direction do not matter, nor does the wasteland into which Australian suburbia has here been turned:

He has gone for an hour when he realizes that the road is empty. . . . He drives through empty suburbs. There are no neon signs. No lights in the houses. A strong headwind is blowing. He begins to take sideroads. To turn at every turn he sees. He feels sharp pains as his tyres grate, squeal and battle for grip on the cold hard roads. He has no sense of direction. (*The Most Beautiful Lies*, 63–64)

Crabs is relieved when he sees lights in the distance. They seem to him 'the only lights in the world', and when he approaches them, he finds himself outside the heavily barred gate of the drive-in cinema, behind which he can see people talking, laughing, dancing.

It becomes quite clear here that Carey shares the postmodern writer's preoccupation with the nature of reality and its perception, and that his surrealist invention is motivated 'not by gratuitous or merely subjective fantasy, but by an original and disturbing perception of the way the "ordinary reality" upon which we all depend can deceive us' (Clunies Ross, *ALS*, 10, 1981, 179). It is only logical that in a society dominated by the car, and in which mobility is the supreme god, the way to achieve freedom is to become a car. By the same logic, of course, you exclude yourself from the fellowship of men and find yourself, like Crabs, 'outside the fence'.

For Carey, 'Crabs' is a comparatively early story, with a 'cold hard surface' unlike the more recent 'American Dreams', in which his imagination takes a more humorous, though nonetheless critical turn. The story is set in a pretty dull country town not unlike that in 'Everleigh's Accent', where people, influenced by the postwar boom of American films, dream their dreams of affluence, glamour and adventure. Life drags on with little excitement except for that temporarily provided by shy and withdrawn Mr Gleason, who one day hires a group of Chinese workmen to build, for no apparent reason at all, a high brick wall on top of a hill, behind which he spends most of his free time. After a while, Gleason is shrugged off as a crank, until at his sudden death his widow has the wall knocked down to reveal to the astonished citizens a miniature model of their own town, faithful to the last details not only of building but also of posture and physiognomy of its inhabitants. Unalloyed, 'simple joy' is the general reaction to this 'most incredibly beautiful thing I had ever seen in my life', as the young narrator puts it. And his father thinks that it had been Gleason's aim 'to let (them) see the beauty of (their) own town' to cure them of their American dreams. But joy and pride give way to shock, fear and anger when they discover that Gleason has given more than just a faithful, realistic reproduction of the surface. The roofs of the houses can be lifted off to expose people's private affairs to the public. The immediate destruction of the model by the angry citizens is prevented only by the interference of the local press and then by the minister for tourism, who calls it a work of art and promises to market it to the American tourists. Soon these come in droves, their wallets full of dollar bills. American Dreams of a sort are realized, but with the Americans' money comes the obligation for the inhabitants of posing endlessly before their cameras in exactly the poses in which Gleason has fixed them in his model.

Like Crabs, these citizens spend their time trying to escape from something they find unsatisfactory, only to realize they are caught in an impasse. On one level, the story comments on a problem which causes many Australians increasing concern: the growing influence of the United States, especially since the Vietnam War, on numerous spheres of life in Australia. On another level, Carey's postmodernist concern with the perception and nature of reality is manifest in the prominent role the mass media are given in both his stories. The press, TV and film all create and popularize powerful stereotype images that may eventually be mistaken for reality, or which at least powerfully determine our view of what is real. So instead of driving into the outback, as Murray Bail's dentist at least tried to, Crabs goes to the drive-in theatre to make love in the locked car and watch a film possibly starring Rock Hudson and Kim Novak – the young narrator's idols in 'American Dreams'. In this story, the 'reality' of the small town is only apprehended through its faithfully mimetic reproduction in the 'work of art', which for a time dispels the vague yearnings induced by the Hollywood clichés.

With the self-consciousness typical of postmodern writing, the story also implies a reflection on its own status as fiction. It would seem that the absolutely mimetic representation of 'reality' of Gleason's model imposes on life a rigidity of vision that is fatal, forcing people to go forever through the motions of a fiction by which they cannot live and which separates them from real life; the result is that the tourists feel disappointed and the inhabitants feel guilty, as they both realize that life refuses to live up to the fiction. For both, ultimately, the unequivocal 'realistic' model (of the fiction) blurs the view of the living reality – Carey's own oblique comment on the Lawson tradition?

The few stories discussed here have been chosen for their inherent literary qualities and their variety of style and subject matter as well as for their common preoccupation with matters Australian. It should have become clear that through exploring ways of seeing Australia, they can open up for us many of the areas outlined at the beginning. In studying them, we may also find fresh ways of seeing ourselves; in analyzing these writers' endeavour to clarify and transmit their views of Australia and Australians, we may adapt our own perception, perhaps even discover our Everleighs and our American dreams, so that in reading about others we may be learning about ourselves.

NOTES

1. At the international conference held in Berne, Switzerland, in October 1984 on 'War: Australia's Literary Response', the search for a 'usable past' was seen as a major concern of contemporary Australian writers.
2. Cf. Brian Kiernan, 'Bibliographical Spectrum: What Is Australian Literature?', *Review of National Literatures*, 11 (special number on Australia), ed. L.A.C. Dobrez, New York, 1982, 211–234.
3. The growing literary output of non-English immigrants is a subject in itself. Its scope is well illustrated – in English – in the short story anthology *The Strength of Tradition*, ed. R.F. Holt, St Lucia, 1983.
4. For a useful bibliography see Adam Shoemaker, 'A Checklist of Black Australian Literature', *Australian Literary Studies*, 11 (1983), 255–63. A challenging recent study of the Aboriginal presence in Australia is Henry Reynolds, *The Other Side of the Frontier*, Penguin Australia, 1982. The literary image of the Aborigine is studied in J.J. Healy, *Literature and the Aborigine in Australia, 1770–1975*, St Lucia, 1978.
5. Ian Turner, 'Sydney and the Bush: Notes on Popular Culture', in *Readings in Australian Arts*, ed. P. Quartermaine, Exeter, 1978, p. 17. See also *Intruders in the Bush: The Australian Quest for Identity*, ed. J. Carroll, Melbourne, 1982.
6. Richard White, *Inventing Australia: Images and Identity 1688–1980*, Sydney, 1981.
7. On the convict theme in Australian fiction see Laurie Hergenhan, *Unnatural Lives*, St Lucia, 1983.
8. *Australian Short Stories*, sel. Kerryn Goldsworthy. Everyman's Library, Melbourne, London, 1983; *Impressions of a Continent: A Collection of Australian Short Stories*, comp. Bill Scott, Richmond, Vic., 1983; *The Most Beautiful Lies: A Collection of Stories by . . . Michael Wilding, Morris Lurie, Frank Moorhouse, Peter Carey, Murray Bail*, ed. Brian Kiernan, Sydney, 1977; *The Australian Short Story: An Anthology from the 1890s to the 1980s*, ed. Laurie Hergenhan. Portable Australian Authors, St Lucia, 1986. Useful bibliographical and documentary material is contained in two special issues of *Australian Literary Studies*, No. 8: 2, October 1977, and No. 10: 2, October 1981, and in Bernard Hickey's critical study *Lines of Implication: Australian Short Fiction from Lawson to Palmer*, Venice, 1984.
9. *Henry Lawson*, ed. Brian Kiernan, Portable Australian Authors, St Lucia, 1976, p. 202.
10. Elizabeth Webby, 'Australian Short Fiction from *While the Billy Boils* to *The Everlasting Secret Family*', *Australian Literary Studies*, 10 (1981), 154.
11. Doug Jarvis, 'Lawson, the *Bulletin* and the Short Story', *Australian Literary Studies*, 11 (1983), 62.
12. Ken Stewart, ' "The Loaded Dog": A Celebration', *Australian Literary Studies*, 11 (1983), 153.
13. See Turner, op. cit., and also Graeme Davison, 'Sydney and the Bush: An Urban Context for the Australian Legend', *Intruders in the Bush*, 109–30.
14. *Hal Porter*, ed. Mary Lord, Portable Australian Authors, St Lucia, 1980, p. 386–7.
15. This point is well made in Bruce Clunies Ross, 'Some Developments in Short Fiction', *Australian Literary Studies*, 10 (1981), 179; see also Teresa Dovey, 'An Infinite Onion: Narrative Structure in Peter Carey's Fiction', *Australian Literary Studies*, 11 (1983), 195–204.

6 Australian studies and Australian identity

Don Grant

In a 1978 article,[1] intended 'to stimulate lively debate on the problems of cultural analysis', John Colmer noted the large amount of small-scale investigation into various aspects of Australian culture that was then taking place and pointed to the need for 'fresh attempts at a larger synthesis'. He referred also to the lack of opportunities for inter-disciplinary exchange and co-operation:

Historians and literary scholars in Australia tend to operate quite separately and to be unaware of the implications of each other's research. We have nothing to compare with the Birmingham Centre for Contemporary Cultural Studies, a Centre that has attracted historians, sociologists, and literary scholars and has fostered research on the theory and practice of cultural analysis. In Australia the reaction away from Departmental structures in the new universities has not led to the founding of Schools of Australian Studies to anything like the extent one might have expected. No association exists to bring all scholars interested in Australian studies together. There is no journal that serves to publish important interdisciplinary research.

It is not the purpose of this essay to attempt the larger synthesis of Australian culture which Colmer believed was needed. Its aims are much more modest: to point to some developments in interdisciplinary and Australian studies since 1978; to speculate why these have occurred; and to suggest that these developments may both reflect and further contribute to reappraisals of cultural myths, especially those concerned with Australian national identity.

Let us take Colmer's points in reverse order. The *Journal of Australian Studies* has been produced twice annually since 1977 and has published articles on Australian history, politics, economics, sociology, pre-history, the arts, education, geography and literature. Most of the articles published to date have been single-disciplinary and a strong emphasis has been on history. In 1984 the *Journal* sought to broaden its concerns:

At a period in our history when there is an increasing awareness of the Australian identity we believe the *Journal* has an important role in publicizing

77

and initiating ideas and research on Australian problems. A recent feature has been forums on controversies of an inter-disciplinary nature. We hope to encourage this in future issues.[2]

Also published twice annually is the *Australian Journal of Cultural Studies*, which first appeared in 1983. This journal aims to provide a platform for research and debate in cultural studies:

The journal's interests embrace the full range of the production of the culture – accepting the value of analysis of such produced texts as television and film, of 'lived' texts such as sport and recreational activities, and cultural motifs such as the beach and the barbecue. The *AJCS* will encourage articles dealing with the theory and practice of culture, the reception and creation of texts, and the particular ways in which the Australian culture endows its members with a cultural identity, Australian ideologies and myths.[3]

The *Journal of Australian Studies* is based at Melbourne's La Trobe University; the *Australian Journal of Cultural Studies* comes jointly from Perth's Murdoch University and the Western Australian Institute of Technology. All three are 'new' tertiary educational institutions, and each has experimented with variations from traditional departmental structures.

The inaugural conference of the Association for the Study of Australian Literature, held in May, 1978, agreed that the 'Study of Australian Literature' should be interpreted in a sense 'which encompasses the pursuits of sociologists, historians and students of culture, so far as these pursuits relate in any way to Australian literature'.[4] At successive conferences of ASAL, papers have been read on a variety of topics including film, drama, the visual arts, comparative literary and cultural studies, social and historical writing and journalism as well as Australian literature. Although its primary emphasis is on 'Australian literature and study and research in Australian literary culture',[5] ASAL has successfully encouraged pluralist approaches to literary cultural studies. Its journal, *Notes and Furphies*, which has been produced twice yearly since 1978, is one of the liveliest of its kind in Australia.

The formation of the Australian Studies Association (AUSTA) was announced in September 1983. During 1984 one *Newsletter* and two *Bulletins* (joint productions from Deakin University and the Western Australian Institute of Technology) were distributed to more than 300 people in Australia and overseas who had indicated their interest in the Association. An editorial in the first *Bulletin*[6] stated that the Association's role would be both to foster Australian studies and to encourage an approach which would be broad-ranging rather than conventionally defined. The first meeting of AUSTA's interim executive in May 1984 endorsed the specific aims of the Association as being to:

• Promote Australian studies in educational institutions and in the community.

- Consider the Australian experience in its international, social, cultural and economic context.

- Facilitate communication between persons working in Australian studies (e.g., performers, teachers, writers, archivists, etc.).

- Encourage research and writing in Australian studies.

- Encourage the collection and preservation of Australian materials.

- Support Australian studies overseas.

Athough the majority of its foundation financial members were academics, AUSTA has attracted substantial numbers of people whose work or primary interest is in schools, libraries, archives, galleries, museums, publishing and writing. Among the academic members there is a wide spread of disciplines; many members are already actively engaged in the teaching of Australian studies or Australian culture.

The two *Australian Studies Bulletins* have drawn attention to the recent proliferation of Australian studies programmes and courses in Australian and overseas tertiary institutions. The first course in Australia was probably that offered by General Studies at the new University of New South Wales in the early 1960s. The first major in Australian studies was probably that introduced by the Schools of English and Social Sciences at the Western Australian Institute of Technology in 1974. Most activity is occurring in the newer universities and colleges of advanced education, for example, at Ballarat, Deakin, Flinders, Footscray, Griffith, James Cook, Magill, Murdoch, New South Wales, WAIT, Warrnambool and Wollongong. Some of the older universities have also entered the field including ANU, Queensland and Sydney.

An Australian Studies Centre was established at the University of Queensland in 1979 and another at WAIT in 1983. Overseas there are Australian Studies Centres at the University of London, at Pennsylvania State University and at the Beijing Foreign Languages Institute. Chairs of Australian Studies have been established at Harvard and Dublin universities. Other centres are being planned both in Australia and abroad.

During 1984 new school curriculum guidelines were issued in Victoria, and in Western Australia the Government adopted the recommendations of a committee of inquiry into education. Among other recommendations, there was in both reports emphasis on promoting interdisciplinary teaching by breaking traditional subject boundaries and by increasing the attention given to Australian studies.

In August 1984 the Australian Minister for Education and Youth Affairs, Senator Susan Ryan, announced the establishment of an Australian Studies Project. Senator Ryan said that the Government had agreed to allocate $1.3 million to the Project over a two year period commencing in 1984–85. 'The Government is keen', she said, 'to encourage all Australians to develop an understanding of their history and culture and the Project will do much to assist in this process'. The Project, which will form part of a National Programme developed by the Australian Bicentennial Authority to mark the Bicentenary in 1988, was formulated in response to public concern that there be greater emphasis on Australian studies in educational institutions. The Project will comprise two main elements. First, the development of curriculum materials in Australian studies for primary and secondary schools. Second, a review which will cover Australian studies in tertiary institutions, concentrating on needs in teacher education, on the place of Australian studies as an academic discipline, and on ways of promoting a greater understanding of Australian culture in the community at large.

The evidence is clear that interest in Australian culture has increased considerably since Colmer wrote in 1978. Not so clear are the reasons why this has occurred. A useful starting point is to look at initiatives taken by Government, of which the Australian Studies Project is the latest example. The Project was first referred to by the Prime Minister, Malcolm Fraser, in his Australia Day address on 26 January 1983. In an outline of the programme of national and international events which would commemorate Australia's Bicentenary, Fraser referred to educational and information activities which would include 'an inquiry into Australian studies programmes in schools which lead to a deeper appreciation among young Australians of their heritage and Australia's path in the future'. A Bicentennial Authority publication released early in 1983 indicated that the Inquiry might be broader than Fraser had intimated:

The proposed inquiry would study and report on the status of teaching and research in Australian studies throughout the education system. The report of the Inquiry would provide a basis for future action.[7]

Reaction was immediate, and both the Bicentennial Authority and the Government were urged to consider a more comprehensive inquiry than the modest one proposed. Teachers in tertiary institutions especially, many of whom were aware of the ramifications in Canada of the investigations and reports of the Commission on Canadian Studies established in 1972, pressed for the extension of the inquiry into tertiary education. The response from Government was quick and positive: substantial funds were allocated for the Project which, although still seen as making an important contribution to the education and information activities of the Bicentennial programme, was transferred administratively to the Department of Education and Youth Affairs; the Project itself was divided into two parts, one concerned with the schools, and the other with tertiary education and the wider community.

Although negative examples could be cited as well, Government stimulus for Australian cultural studies has also been provided in other areas. Obvious examples are the encouragement of a variety of cultural activities through the Australia Council and State Arts Councils, the enforcement by regulation of a minimum amount of Australian content on television, and more recently the activities of State Film Commissions and the provision of taxation concessions for film producers.

Government financed the rapid growth of tertiary educational institutions in the 1960s and 1970s. Many of the Australian academic staff members recruited during this period of rapid expansion came from educational backgrounds somewhat different from those of traditional university academics. They also found themselves in institutions which were willing to encourage experimentation. In addition, the shortage of qualified staff in Australia led to the employment in these new institutions of considerable members of staff from overseas. This also was a contributing factor to the challenges mounted in some of them to traditional English-derived university orthodoxies of subject organization and course structure. New staff, from North America especially, were familiar with interdisciplinary programmes, in American and Canadian studies for example, and saw nothing particularly threatening or remarkable in the development in their new institutions of Australian studies programmes.

Most of the activities mentioned above had been conceived well before John Colmer made his comments in 1978. Gestation apparently was fairly slow until the recent surge of interest in Australian studies. The role of Government in this matter is difficult to define. The positive contributions sketchily outlined above are obvious, but, as is frequently the case, they may reflect not Government initiative so much as Government reaction to community pressures and needs. However, attention should be drawn to the influence of Government leaders on the resurgence of interest in Australian culture. Although poles apart in politics and personalities, Prime Ministers Gorton, Whitlam, Fraser and Hawke have all contributed personally to what might be called the new nationalism of which interest in Australian cultural studies is a part. Whitlam and Fraser, especially, enjoyed casting themselves in Australian roles on a world stage. Under their leadership, for example, the Australia Council and the Department of Foreign Affairs were encouraged to sell Australia abroad, not only for the usual economic reasons, but also for the purpose of fostering in overseas countries a greater understanding and a closer study of Australia. The Chair of Australian Studies at Harvard University was a pet project of Whitlam; Fraser was personally involved in the establishment of the Australian Studies Centre at the University of London.

In scores of universities around the world students are now able to take courses in Australian history, literature, geography or more broadly in Australian studies. In seeking the answers to why this situation has come about in the last decade or so, we might ask several questions. To what extent does this reflect an increased interest in Australia generally by people overseas? How important has been the enthusiasm of particular individuals like Bernard Hickey in Italy, Peter Quartermaine in Britain, Anna Rutherford in Denmark, Horst Priessnitz in Germany, Henry Albinski in the United States, Hu Wenzhong in China, and many more? Is the interest perhaps not so much in Australia itself as in the availability of a new area for scholarly studies, comparable, say, with Canadian studies which is also enjoying a boom abroad? How important is the support given by Australia through Foreign Affairs, the Australia Council, tertiary institutions, which provides financial assistance for conferences, study visits to Australia, library acquisitions, and so on?

The answers to these questions are perhaps less important than the situation which gives rise to them. The essential point is that not only has there been a quickening of interest in Australian studies at home, but also Australians have felt it appropriate to foster a similar interest in foreign countries. Both activities are reflections of the new nationalism. Within Australia this new nationalism goes back at least as far as the Vietnam War and the polarities it created in regard to Australia's relationship with the United States. The triumph of Whitlam in 1972 was an expression of the desire of Australians for an independent identity which served as a catalyst for a brief period of nationalistic euphoria. The excesses may have been trimmed during the period of the Fraser government, but there could be no returning to the pre-Whitlam days.

Although attention to Australian studies in the tertiary institutions is a comparatively recent phenomenon, general studies of Australian life and culture have proliferated during the last couple of decades.[8] In recent years a broadening of the field has become apparent in works on Australian popular culture.[9] Writing in *Overland*, Stephen Alomes reflected 'on the short history of the study of popular culture in Australia and overseas':

The first hesitant moves towards the study of popular culture during the 1960s came more out of academic or 'high culture' traditions. The early work of Ian Turner on children's books, graffiti, jazz and football . . . came out of such a tradition. Turner's pioneering work was complemented by the writings of a later generation who were, in a sense, his contemporaries in the celebration of popular culture. A university generation from lower middle-class and sometimes working-class backgrounds, which was more influenced by teenage culture than by the official culture of the school and university, looked sympathetically at popular culture. Their empathy differed greatly from the downward glance and frowning condemnations of their often Leavisite middle-class predecessors.[10]

Outside academe, Alomes noted various critiques-cum-celebrations of popular culture, including recent confessional novels and in drama and popular song. He might also have noted the enormous success and popularity of performers such as Barry Humphries and Paul Hogan. One satirises the cultural aspirations of 'ordinary' Australians; the other celebrates them. But they present different sides of the same coin. Intellectuals and British people may deplore the ocker ascendancy which Humphries sees, perhaps correctly, as reflecting the cultural aspirations of most Australians. They may sneer at the boxing kangaroo emblem which floated above Australia II, the yacht which won the America's Cup in what was for many Australians probably the outstanding world event of 1983. They may cringe at wares offered in the new kitsch Australiana shops, at I-Luv-Australia bumper-stickers and T-shirts, and at the friendly Qantas koala. To many Australians, however, these things are as valid and as precious manifestations of the new nationalism as are the serious academic explorations of Australian studies.

Even the serious endeavours have not passed unchallenged, as Eugene Kamenka showed in a recent edition of *Australian Cultural History*:

There is a legitimate and important intellectual (here slightly different from cultural) interest in exploring the social history of Australia, in the development of attitudes and lifestyles in Australia, and in the life of the mind in Australia. In these areas interest is stronger than it has ever been. The results form an important part of the intellectual background to culture in Australia, and in principle they could be both culturally enriching and conducive to the production of great work. But they do not guarantee it. In practice, indeed, because so many of those immersed in this activity, especially the young, see it as a substitute for a universal culture, it can and does pedestrianize thinking in Australia.[11]

In the same edition of *Australian Cultural History*, Jim Davidson convincingly argued against Kamenka's position. 'For many writers', he averred, 'the changed climate Kamenka rails against merely means a firmer, geocentric grip on the world. The point is not so much to decry Australianization as to consider whether our historical predicament allows us much choice'.[12]

Davidson's last point is an important one, for it enables the rules of the debate to be broadened. Australia is not alone in its historical predicament. Nor is Australia uniquely experiencing the new nationalism and its concomitant cultural explorations. The example of Canada has already been cited, and others could be, which might indicate that a certain stage has been reached in post-colonialism, or in economic and political maturity, which finds its expression in increased self-confidence and awareness, and in seeking both to establish and to proclaim a unique national identity, mythical though it might be.

The new nationalism in Australia has nowhere been more apparent than in the film industry. Prominent among the most successful Australian films have been those (*The Man From Snowy River*, *Breaker Morant*, *Gallipoli*, *Phar Lap*, for example) which have drawn upon that most pervasive of Australian myths – the myth of the bushman, later transposed to the digger. The myth embraces the Aussie battler: democratic, egalitarian, independent, laconic, resourceful, tough, nationalistic, whose natural home is the bush rather than the city. The popularity of the films indicates that the myth still has strong general appeal. The myth itself remains central to any examination of Australian cultural identity as evidenced by many of the recent literary and critical, as well as filmic, forays into Australian studies. The final section of this essay will look at some aspects of the myth, especially at recent explorations of it, and also at how these may be relevant to the first point made by John Colmer, that 'Historians and literary scholars in Australia tend to operate quite separately and to be unaware of the implications of each other's research'.

John Docker's recent book, *In a Critical Condition*,[13] is subtitled 'Australian Literary Criticism'. It is primarily concerned with the deficiencies Docker sees in the orthodox academic establishments which, he argues, control university English departments and determine the content and structure of courses. The first thing to be said about Docker's arguments is that they are too narrowly based. He seems unaware that the broader contextual as well as textual analysis of Australian literature, for which he pleads so vigorously has, in fact, been an important principle in the development of Australian studies courses in the newer colleges and universities. That aside, however, Docker's book is useful in drawing attention to the restricted nature of Australian literary studies in universities since they were first hesitantly introduced in the 1950s.[14] Although one may dispute the conspiracy theory which Docker seems to espouse – that senior academics in English departments have colluded in establishing the canon of Australian literature which may be taught – indeed which is worthy of critical discussion – the evidence is clear that until recently certain orthodoxies dominated Australian literature courses in the universities, and Docker argues that they still do.

Docker refers to this phenomenon as the 'Metaphysical Ascendancy', its proponents as belonging to the 'new right'. It is characterized by 'text-centric formalism' and an emphasis on moral and metaphysical values. Although not peculiar to Australia, it has produced in this country, Docker argues, an important variant or sub-genre of the metaphysical orthodoxy: the gloom thesis:

The contributors to the gloom thesis not only assert the centrality of certain metaphysical themes in Australian literature, but attempt to produce a new

Australian literary and cultural history. In particular, they wish to contest what they see as the radical nationalist version of Australian cultural history as a story of egalitarianism, group loyalties, and social optimism – a spirit supposedly established in the vigorous days of the 1890s (Australia's adolescence) and built on ever since (our maturity as a nation in the 20th century).[15]

The views of the 'Metaphysical Ascendancy' have been widely published since the 1950s. Representative books have been *Australian Literary Criticism, The Stockyard and the Croquet Lawn* and *The Oxford History of Australian Literature*.[16] Docker is certainly correct in drawing attention to the disparagement by many of the academic critics whose work is contained in these volumes of the critical position of those whom Docker calls the 'radical nationalists', and also of the literary worth of much of the writing by Australian authors who are identified as belonging to the radical nationalist tradition.[17] His attack on these critics is directed as much at their ideological position (the 'new right') as it is at their critical approach to literature (formalist, metaphysical, moral). Thus he casts doubts on their rejection, allegedly solely on the grounds of literary merit, of left-wing, social realist writers such as Palmer, Davison, Mann, Tennant, Cusack, Prichard, Marshall, Morrison, etc.

One Australian writer whose works did not appear on the set text lists for university literature courses in the 1960s, when the metaphysicals were certainly in the ascendant, was George Johnston. In a 1978 article, historian Russell Ward claimed that 'the most influential Australian novel published in the 1960s was George Johnston's *My Brother Jack* (1964) which was made into a film and shown to mass TV audiences':

Its immense appeal to Australian readers and viewers sprang from the contrast between the successful, bourgeois, 'Moonee Ponds' life-style of the narrator and the legendary, egalitarian, rolling-stone, 'good mate' character of his admired brother Jack. Quite obviously readers, viewers and author alike identified strongly with Jack, though most of them lived lives which were in fact much more like his brother's.[18]

In this passage Ward updates the thesis he developed in his 1958 book *The Australian Legend*. Jack has become the mid-twentieth-century version of Ward's nineteenth-century 'typical frontiersman [who] was the romanticized, ideal, stereotype of the bush-worker'.[19]

Today, *My Brother Jack* (and works by many of the other social realist writers mentioned by Docker) is set for study in some of the newer tertiary institutions. The domination of Australian literature courses by what Docker calls the 'metaphysical orthodoxy' is certainly under challenge. Intriguing, though, is the orthodoxy's apparent belief that it has been the challenger through its assessments of Australian literature by the application of correct 'literary' judgements in contrast to the postition of the so-called radical nationalists, who are alleged to be overly concerned with the place of literature in Australian social history. Perhaps the first extensive statement of this position was that made by G.A. Wilkes in a 1958 article entitled 'The Eighteen Nineties'.[20] In 1984 Michael Wilding showed that the attack on the nationalists was still continuing when he argued that the 'weight put on the nationalist nineties by the new nationalist critics of the 1930s, 40s and 50s has produced its particular and predominant version of Australian literary history':

... there is the nationalistic cult of the short story, with Henry Lawson as the particular native genius.... A single, narrow tradition took its increasingly barren way on; it became established, enshrined, protected, and the literary magazines gave it a home ... [there was a] single, utilitarian, insular, aggressively anti-experimental, philistinely parochial 'write Australian' line: something caused not so much by the nationalistic nineties writers, but by the new nationalistic theorists, critics, and publishers and magazine editors from the 1930s through the 1950s.[21]

Wilding believed that 'the new nationalist critics immensely damaged Australian literature'. By 'new' he seemed to imply a continuing influence since the 1950s of such critics. John Docker is certainly not one of these, despite his attacks on the 'metaphysical orthodoxy'. In fact, Docker pointed to serious limitations in the radical nationalists' contextual approach to cultural history and literary criticism. He was especially critical of a contextual approach which is usually at the expense of detailed analyses of texts; he saw limitations in 'the historicist premise that a literary or cultural period can possess a single unified essential spirit'; and he found crippling the evolutionist view that literature could be seen 'as evolving towards a goal, that of the mature, confident expression of distinctive Australian values'.[22]

Docker's consistent use of the term 'radical nationalists' is intriguing. Goeffrey Serle, in his 1973 book, *From Deserts the Prophets Come* did refer to the bushmen of the nineteenth century as a class who had 'developed a range of radical nationalist assumptions',[23] but Docker is innovative in his application of the expression to a wide range of twentieth-century literary critics, social historians and creative writers. This is somewhat remarkable since the notion of a general congruence in Australia of radicalism and nationalism repeatedly has been seriously challenged,[24] and Docker's text and references show that he is familiar with the relevant works. They also show that Docker is one literary scholar at least who is aware of, if not always in agreement with, the implications of the research of historians and sociologists. Scholars in these areas are also increasingly using the research of their literary colleagues, a situation which would, no doubt, be welcomed by John Colmer. In 1978, the year in which Colmer voiced his concern about their lack of awareness of each other's work, historian Michael Roe, in an article 'Challenges to Australian Identity',[25] drew upon the research of literary scholars as well as that of historians and sociologists. The publication, in the same year, of sociologist Tim Rowse's wide-ranging *Australian Liberalism and National Character*[26] inextricably brought the two groups together (assuming that they had ever been as far apart as Colmer suggested), and was itself a powerful stimulus for future Australian cultural studies.

Throughout this essay I have been suggesting that today the situation in regard to Australian cultural studies is rather different from the one sketched by Colmer in 1978. Certainly there have been significant developments in the intervening six years. I see these as being evolutionary rather than revolutionary. In 1978 Tim Rowse detected 'a greater concern with and confidence in popular attitudes and national character' since 1945, and he observed that this was also part of an evolutionary process:

With the passing of time since federation, there has been a gradual sedimentation of national preoccupations among the intelligentsia. This does not necessarily imply 'patriotism', it may mean as little (or as much) as more university courses, books, radio and T.V. programmes, and general knowledge, about Australia – an unbending of the cultural cringe.[27]

Sedimentation following the froth and ferment of the last decade or so of the nineteenth century? Scholars keep returning to those years, the most recent being Donald Denoon in an article in *Australian Society*, January 1985:

White Australia had its biological origins in 1788, but a century passed before many Australians became self-conscious, and it was mainly from the 1890s that ordinary Australians imagined that they had a separate destiny, and began to plan for it.[28]

Vance Palmer, Russell Ward, Arthur Phillips,[29] and others have written about the 1890s as the decade which above all others shaped an 'Australian Legend'. John Docker emphasized its importance in the construction of the radical nationalist version of Australian cultural history. Film-makers continue to exploit the attractiveness for their mainly city audiences of the bushman myth. The authenticity of the conditions or processes which form the basis of the legend/myth has been widely challenged, but with little apparent effect on its continuing widespread acceptance as an essential ingredient in the collective Australian self-image.

In 1978 Graeme Davison argued that the genesis of the myth in the 1890s 'was not the transmission to the city of values nurtured on the bush frontier, so much as the projection onto the outback of values revered by an alienated urban intelligentsia'.[30] If Davison is correct, and his argument, with its essentially pastoral connotations, is a convincing one, then it may be as applicable to Australians living in the 1980s as to those who lived in the 1890s. The importance of personality and individual experience in the shaping of interpretations of Australian life and history has been examined by several historians and sociologists including Michael Roe[31] and R.W. Connell. In 1968 Connell claimed that the research of political scientists and psychologists 'suggests that images of country tell us more about their individual owners than they do about the country concerned . . . how much descriptions of Australia describe their authors and what they have read'.[32] The next few years hold the promise of broader and deeper explorations of Australian images. We can watch with interest any reinterpretations of Australian myths of identity which may emerge from the new interdisciplinary Australian studies courses, the journals of Australian studies, the Australian Studies Association, and the national inquiries into Australian studies.

Colmer raised important issues in 1978, at the beginning of some quite significant developments in Australian cultural studies, several of which, as has been noted, were replications of developments which had reached more advanced stages overseas. I hope I have addressed some aspects of those issues and that the people cited in my notes have addressed still others. Six years after Colmer's article, and in light of the subsequent developments, other questions should now be asked. They fall under the category of 'Whither Australian Studies in This Country?' and they really take the form of caveats.

If we are moving from multidisciplinary studies to interdisciplinary studies, then there must be some coherent philosophy which informs the interdisciplinary approach, a fact which has been observed by several critics.[33] This may itself present another problem if ideology comes to be used as a justification for exclusivity. The conundrum of values in culture, and therefore culture studies, must be much more clearly articulated if not entirely resolved. It has been argued that cultures merely *are*, that they are neither 'good' nor 'bad'. Yet some culture studies courses set themselves up as better than more traditional studies which they oppose; and others (for example, some Marxist-informed versions) often prefer certain forms of cultural expression to certain other ones, even to the point of a counter-productive dismissiveness of the other positions (for example, the low-brow versus the high-brow opposition). The problem of jargon must also be dealt with. Previously in the traditional Australian universities there may well have been a conspiracy of silence against some specific literary texts, and even more so against the new 'definition' of texts which encompasses virtually all expression in any medium. Now there is the very real possibility that the tower of silence will become a tower of Babel. Convoluted critical terminology, often in obtuse translations of foreign language terms, may serve to distance the community at large from the very culture which the terminology purports to explain.

It seems clear that Australian cultural studies will continue to develop in Australia and elsewhere through the rest of this century. What is problematic is the manner in which it will do so, a worthy and probably essential question for the discipline of cultural studies itself. Another question arises from this. In what ways will Australian cultural studies relate to the quality of life of the nation?

NOTES

1. John Colmer, 'Australian Cultural Analysis: Some Principles and Problems'. *Southerly*, No. 3, 1978, p. 244.
2. *Journal of Australian Studies*, No. 14, 1984. The quotation is from a publicity brochure included in the *Journal*.
3. *Australian Journal of Cultural Studies*, Vol. 1, No. 1, May 1983, p. 1.
4. *Notes and Furphies*, No. 1, April 1978, p. 2.
5. *Notes and Furphies*, No. 7, October 1981, p. 6.
6. *Australian Studies Bulletin*, No. 1, April 1984, p. 2.
7. *National Projects and Events*, Australian Bicentennial Authority, 1983, p. 12.
8. See, for example, J.D. Pringle, *Australian Accent*, London, 1958; P. Coleman (ed.), *Australian Civilization*, Melbourne, 1962; Donald Horne, *The Lucky Country*, Melbourne, 1964; Craig McGregor, *Profile of Australia*, London, 1966; Ian Turner (ed.), *The Australian Dream*, Melbourne, 1968; Ronald Conway, *The Great Australian Stupor*, Melbourne, 1971; John Docker, *Australian Cultural Elites*, Sydney, 1974; W.F. Mandle, *Going It Alone*, Melbourne, 1978.
9. See, for example, Craig McGregor, *People, Politics and Pop*, Sydney, 1968, and *Sound Tracks for the Eighties*, Sydney, 1983; P. Spearritt and D. Walker, *Australian Popular Culture*, Sydney, 1979.
10. Stephen Alomes, 'Australian Popular Culture Revisited', *Overland*, No. 5, 1981, p. 12.
11. Eugene Kamenka, 'Culture and Australian Culture', *Australian Cultural History*, No. 3, 1984, p. 17.
12. Jim Davidson, 'So-Called Culture', *Australian Cultural History*, No. 3, 1984, pp. 20–21.
13. John Docker, *In A Critical Condition*, Melbourne, 1984.
14. In fact, Docker published many of the essays in this book well before 1984. Others who have contributed to the debate are noted in Footnote 1 to Greg Manning's review of *In A Critical Condition* in *Meanjin*, No. 3, 1984, p. 422.
15. Docker, op. cit., p. 110.
16. Grahame Johnston (ed.), *Australian Literary Criticism*, Melbourne, 1962; G.A. Wilkes, *The Stockyard and the Croquet Lawn*, Melbourne, 1981; Leonie Kramer (ed.), *The Oxford History of Australian Literature*, Melbourne, 1981.
17. See Docker, op. cit., p. 83, for Docker's list of radical nationalist critics and metaphysical critics. See p. 95 for his list of radical nationalist writers who are rejected by the metaphysical critics.
18. Russell Ward, 'The Australian Legend Re-Visited', *Historical Studies*, Vol. 18, No. 71, 1978, p. 176.
19. Ibid, p. 181.
20. G.A. Wilkes, 'The Eighteen Nineties', *Arts* 1, 1958, pp. 17–26.

21. Michael Wilding, Introduction to Marcus Clarke, *Stories*, Sydney, 1984, pp.xii–xiii.
22. Docker, op. cit., pp. 37–38.
23. Geoffrey Serle, *From Deserts the Prophets Come*, Melbourne, 1973, p. 61.
24. See, for example, Terry Irving and Baiba Berzins, 'History and the New Left', in R. Gordon (ed.), *The Australian New Left*, Melbourne, 1970; Humphrey McQueen, *A New Britannia*, Melbourne, 1970; David Walker, *Dream and Disillusion*, Canberra, 1976; J.B. Hirst, 'The Pioneer Legend', *Historical Studies*, Vol. 18, No. 71, 1978.
25. Michael Roe, 'Challenges to Australian Identity', *Quadrant*, Vol. 22, No. 4, 1978.
26. Tim Rowse, *Australian Liberalism and National Character*, Melbourne, 1978.
27. Ibid, p. 253.
28. Donald Denoon, 'Australians and Race', *Australian Society*, Vol. 4, No. 1, January 1985, p. 5.
29. Vance Palmer, The Legend of the Nineties, Melbourne, 1954; Russell Ward, *The Australian Legend*, Melbourne, 1958; A.A. Phillips, *The Australian Tradition*, Melbourne, 1958.
30. Graeme Davison, 'Sydney and the Bush', *Historical Studies*, Vol. 15, No. 71, 1978, p. 208.
31. Roe, op. cit.
32. R.W. Connell, 'Images of Australia', *Quadrant*, Vol. 12, No. 1, 1968, p. 9.
33. See, for example, Brian Head, 'Australian Studies: Establishing a New Discourse', in Carole Ferrier (ed.), *Australian Studies: Theory and Practice*, Australian Studies Centre, University of Queensland, Brisbane, 1983, and Delys Bird and Graeme Turner, 'Australian Studies: Practice Without Theory', *Westerly*, No. 3, 1982, pp. 51–56.

Writing Women/Reading Women: The Double-Voiced Discourse of Australian Women's Fiction

7

Delys Bird

But it is obvious that the values of women differ very often from the values which have been made by the other sex; naturally, this is so. . . . And these values are inevitably transferred from life to fiction. This is an important book, the critic assumes, because it deals with war. This is an insignificant book because it deals with the feelings of women in a drawing-room. A scene in a battle-field is more important than a scene in a shop – everywhere and much more subtly the difference of value persists. The whole structure, therefore, of the early nineteenth-century was raised, if one was a woman, by a mind which was slightly pulled from the straight, and made to alter its clear vision in deference to external authority.

Virginia Woolf, *A Room of One's Own*, London, Panther, 1977, pp. 70–71.

in dealing with women as writers, as much elasticity as possible is desirable; it is necessary to leave oneself room to deal with other things beside their work, so much has that work been influenced by conditions that have nothing to do with art.

Virginia Woolf, 'Women and Fiction' in *Women and Writing*, Michele Barrett (ed), London, The Women's Press, 1979, p. 43.

In a series of speculative essays concerning women and writing, Virginia Woolf initiated many of the ideas that have been taken up by feminist literary criticism since its inception in the late 1960s. Two of these ideas, one to do with the connection between values and sexual difference, the other with the connection between writing and its enabling conditions, both concerned with the connection between literature and life, provide an introduction for my own speculations on the subject of Australian women's fiction. When Woolf spoke of women as writers, separating them from male writers and their work, she recognized a specific body of literature, writing by women, which was defined and differentiated by the sex of the author. Her reason for doing this is made clear in *A Room of One's Own*; it is unquestionable, she argues, that 'the values of women differ very often from the values which have been made by the other sex; naturally this is so'. This difference of value affects the writing and the criticism of prose fiction, and since prose fiction is of all literary genres dominated and characterized by its connection with and concern to reproduce a reality, the status of that fictional reality will be judged ideologically as well as aesthetically.

Social as well as literary conventions require that 'A scene in a battlefield is more important than a scene in a shop'. And not only the content, the story, but the discourse of fiction written by women will be affected by those masculine values: 'The whole structure, therefore, of the early nineteenth century novel was raised, if one was a woman, by a mind which was slightly pulled from the straight, and made to alter its clear vision in deference to an external authority'. When a writer has altered her values in deference to the opinions of others this alteration will be evident in her writing. Hence Woolf's second contention (for my purposes) that women's writing 'has been influenced by conditions that have nothing to do with art'. These conditions may be private and psychological or social and political (categories which are, of course, inextricably related), but they are presumed by Woolf to be uniquely female. Hence, too, her plea for critical flexibility when 'dealing with women as writers'.

Woolf perceived a difference in writing and a difference of value, and argued implicitly for a difference in criticism when 'dealing with women as writers', one that recognizes the nature and cultural experience of those women. Since she wrote, and especially over the last two decades, feminist critics have been preoccupied with the problem of locating and specifying a difference in women's writing and with the search for a method to read this difference. Theories regarding the imposed or inherent differences that separate men's and women's lives and influence their writing are now organized not around the sex of the writer, but through the notion of gender. Unlike sexual difference, gender difference is culturally assigned and inscribed; it is the 'cultural meaning attached to sexual identity'.[1] This differentiation has meant that the stereotyping of qualities and characteristics as specifically male or female, so difficult to undermine or destabilize while these attributes were credited by essentialist theories of human nature and language, can now be related to ideology not biology. Thus the question of difference, in life, in values, and in writing, can be recognized and analysed in a range of social practices.

What follows depends on two related notions. Firstly, as Woolf says, connections exist between a woman's life and her writing, and knowledge of the social and literary situation of a woman writer enables us in part to specify what makes a woman's text different from a man's. Further, at any particular historical moment ideology enters literary discourse in indirect, subtle ways, but necessarily (in the instance I want to argue) by way of the writer's historical and cultural situation. This is not to say that the writer consciously or knowingly transfers lived experience, saturated in ideology, to the literary text; rather that since the social is the ideological, then any literary text must encode and transform elements of ideology which will be reproduced in its various textual aspects and which are available to the reader of that text. My reading of Australian women's fiction depends on difference, and since that (sexual and textual) difference is in part located in the relationship women have to their culture's history and ideology, the concept of ideology I rely on needs explanation.

Here, ideology will be used not in the sense of 'false consciousness', in which the contradictions inherent in any social structure appear not to exist, or are smoothed over through the illusory function of ideology activated by those in power to serve class or self interests. The concept of ideology I will use depends on that articulated by Althusser. It can be understood as a 'complex system of representations by which people are inserted as individual subjects into the social formation'.[2] Ideology functions to 'naturalize' real social contradictions by offering false resolutions to those contradictions; false, that is, because the resolutions are understood to be natural or obvious. Ideology, then, structures and encodes social relations of power, those of male dominance for instance, while it can also accommodate the idea of conflicting ideologies, that of feminism for instance.

Woolf's assumption that the difference of values which exists between women and 'the other sex' is 'natural' is itself ideological. Unable to question the basis of this difference of values, Woolf did feminize her object of study, the work of the woman writer, and gave female values primacy by making men's values and opinions 'other'. While she could not theorize the difference she perceived, she did recognize that values (part of ideology) move between life and fiction, affecting the writing and the criticism of fiction. Moreover, Woolf understood that the writing of the woman dominated by a masculine value system who is therefore forced to 'think of something other than the thing itself' will be distorted in some way as the writer's mind is 'pulled from the straight' by her cultural experience. And when Woolf urges the need for a more expansive perspective from which to read women's writing, taking into account things other than the aesthetics of the writing, she textualizes while contextualizing women's writing, pointing to the possibility of a political criticism.

Thus Woolf defined a series of related issues which have become central to contemporary feminist theories. She particularized the practical and aesthetic problems that a middle-class woman writer in her period and in other historical moments faced, and she intimated a special reading stance to 'deal' with women as writers. Although this smacks of the be-kind-to-women brand of feminist criticism in which women's writing is to be read as a true reflection or expression of female experience, while men's writing is subjected to savage, aggressively suspicious criticism, a 'different' reading stance is the theoretical basis of feminist criticism. And Woolf proposed strategies to adopt in that dealing. We may, however, ask what are those 'conditions' that have nothing to do with art? Are they, as Althusser would argue, the conditions of the way people experience their relation to the social relations of production and the social formation? And how or in what ways may these 'conditions affect women's writing? Is it, indeed, 'natural' that women's values are different from those of the other sex? And is 'elasticity' sufficient to deal with women's writing? If the site from which we read that writing is a gendered one, we need also to define what it is we are seeking and the means we will use to seek it. That is, if it is asserted that writing by women and writing by men are different categories, a strategy to locate that difference, a method by which to read it, and a theory to explain it, are all needed.

For my purposes, those 'conditions' that so affect women's writing, far from having nothing to do with art, are the conditions within which a woman lives and which prescribe and explain the way she lives, as well as the potential and parameters of her life. These conditions are, of course, material and ideological, and I will argue that the material conditions of a woman's life and the ideologies that encode that lived experience provide the context from which women's writing emerges and in relation to which it may be read. That these conditions influence the kinds of literature a woman writes, the topics and themes of that writing and the way it is written, will become clear through an examination of the complex relationship between women's writing and its historical, social and ideological context. These things are un-avoidable, inherent pressures necessarily affecting the writer, and her writing will be 'marked' by them in more or less discernible ways. Under these circumstances, 'woman' as an idea is constructed by the society and its ideologies as a gendered subject in ways that relate to, and are explained by, her biological nature. And the literary text may be read in relation to these things. This 'woman' is abstracted from the power structures that organize Australian society as she is domesticated and rendered a moral being. She is also a sexual being, objectified through a classic polarization as virgin or whore, desirable bitch goddess or despised suburban incubator. In all of these ways the female sphere is made the personal. Woman has been written out of history in part as a consequence of the ascription to her of emotional not intellectual life, a nurturing, passive role, and either a purely moral or solely sexual selfhood. This reading of Australian woman as a gendered being, a cultural construct, avoids the stereotyping of the term with a collection of qualities and characteristics which are seen as 'naturally' female-specific, although the construction of woman follows the same lines. What changes is the understanding of how woman is so specified. Female qualities and charactistics can no longer be understood as given; they are created by and reside within those social and discursive formations that constitute a culture.

By specifying woman as Other, not born but made so, Simone de Beauvoir named woman's cultural condition and its ideological causes. An androcentric culture legitimizes and validates the male by opposition: what is masculine is positive and superior, what is feminine is negative and inferior. Australian ideologies, too, naturalize this dichotomy with its associated values. In *The Australian People* (1972), Donald Horne, Australian social critic and perpetrator of the lucky country image, deplores a movement that occurred during the inter-war period in Australia. He defines it as a shift from the nationalist impulse which was open, communal and progressive, to the surburban which was private, domestic and repressive. Noticing this, Tim Rowse annotates what he calls Horne's ambivalent attitude to suburbia, uncovering a sexist bias. Although Rowse is 'not concerned with sexism as a feature of Australian social criticism' he has

noticed more than once that the negative image of surburbia is equally a negative image of woman. A rough equation that seems to be employed is: women, domesticity = spiritual starvation. (Men, wide open spaces, achievement = heroism of the Australian Spirit). The female influence in the 'culture' is often taken to amount to a destructive obsession with status and difference. It seems that Lady Macbeth has been written into the myth of mateship.[3]

In Australia, this oppositional labelling based on a gender distinction operates as class distinctions do, creating a hierarchical structure that denies value to that which it designates feminine. By implication, the strength and worth of the masculine is continually reinforced. If 'woman' is the other, negative, then man must be it, positive.

Australian society and its dominant ideologies project insistently and debilitatingly crude attitudes towards women, repressing what is repressible and displacing what is not. Those qualities encoded as feminine (instinct, emotion, the unconscious and the irrational, aptitude with language, lack of physical strength, and so on) are displaced in a culture that approves and establishes a national identity by way of their opposites (laconic speech, physical strength, unemotional endurance, rational life, and so on). Women's traditional childbearing, nurturing role is similarly repressed, as it is culturally inscribed as natural. This displacement and devaluation of woman and repression of the feminine in Australian life is both literal and symbolic, and can be briefly accounted for historically and ideologically.

Australia's founding by white settlers, the majority of whom were convicts, was historically unusual, and promoted the growth of ideologies based on an exaggerated dominant/dominated structure. These first white settlers came to this land not from choice nor with the idealistic impetus that marked American colonial settlement. Although an Arcadian ideology informed settlement during the early decades of the nineteenth century, Australian colonial culture was marked by its initial enforced displacement from its parent culture; symbolically Australia was a prison and imprisoning. Further, those first settlers discovered a natural antipathy to their new world; its 'weird melancholy' was strange to them and in turn the land itself seemed resistant to these unwilling immigrants. A fallacious but persuasive myth links the inability to live in harmony with the natural world and a society unable to accept or integrate female life.[4] A more persuasive, if equally fallacious, myth equates nature with the feminine and culture with the masculine in this way: nature is to culture as woman is to man.[5] Myths organize and explain reality; if nature is unsympathetic to an emergent culture, perhaps in turn that culture will develop ideologies that marginalize the feminine.

The process of national and individual self-definition in an embryonic culture whose internal relations were at best uncertain was problematical; to achieve it by defining woman as other, thus elevating the male traits that made survival possible in this world, was perhaps the only recourse of an impoverished society. Statistically, an overwhelming proportion of Australia's early settlers were male: in colonial Australia, a low-status male population, already accustomed to accord woman a lower rung on the caste ladder than their own, labelled the female minority damned whores and treated them as such. Vulnerable in a male world, women either accepted this sexual role or escaped it by way of the moral stereotype established in the alternative tradition of the good woman, most familiarly situated in a surburban domestic space as wife and mother. This good woman was introduced to Australia through Caroline Chisholm's notion that what she saw as a degenerate Australian society could be regenerated by them in their role as 'God's Police'. These alternative but equally undesirable and limiting roles for women in Australia have been incorporated into Australian ideologies and identified in Anne Summers' socio-cultural history of Australian women, *Damned Whores and God's Police* (1975). Women in Australia were either abused as purveyors of immorality or lauded as purveyors of morality; in either role they were discriminated against by the dominant national masculine ideology.

Defined as other, and therefore deviant in relation to the values of the patriarchal order, colonial Australian women were further distanced from participating fully in their culture by emergent masculine ideologies such as mateship and myths like the bush, which operated – and still do – as excluding practices and discourses to position and construct woman as a silent or invisible cultural entity. This exclusion of woman or the feminine by the androcentric Australian culture also extends to other cultural concepts that lie outside those inscribed by convention as masculine. Notably, these include intellectual as well as creative and emotional life. Thus the now familiar signification of the sign woman as the other widens in Australia to incorporate all those things defined by their difference from the ideological meanings attached to and inscribed in the masculine pursuits and interests that relate to the male ethos of the culture. These things are categorized as feminine, therefore worthless and subject to derision. Expatriate Australian writer Shirley Hazzard links rejection of women and 'the arts' as an attribute of Australia's masculine culture:

It may be that gender has to do with this – the arts, though forceful enough in their way, being (or being seen as) part of the 'feminine' aspect of humanity, and for this reason lying under particular proscription in a country whose 'maleness' was a matter for strident and even panic-stricken assertion, and whose derision of all artistic expression was not unconnected with derision of women as a sex.[6]

This excluding activity privileges the masculine and denies all that is signified feminine, which is placed outside the cultural space described by and constituted in the dominant ideologies.

These generalizations presume a monodimensional, ahistorical social structure and apparently ignore the numerous class and race positions within Australian culture. They also appear to endorse an understanding of the situation and ideology of women (as well as the contempt in which activities like writing or painting and areas such as emotional life are held) as always present and unchanging. This is, of course, a gross simplification of a complex matter. Nevertheless, it is true that the strength of the dominant masculine ideologies that organize and explicate Australian life are such that despite social and political change, attitudes and dogmas continue to repress (sometimes subtly, sometimes overtly) the feminine, marginalizing all that is considered female by representing it as located outside the central masculine beliefs and concerns of the culture. These notions lead to an articulation of the nexus between history, ideology and literature. If the condition of being a woman in Australian society is socially, politically and psychologically definitive, woman being inserted as a gendered subject into a particular position in the social formation, then as a writer her work will in its turn record in some way that situation, which is ideological. Analysis and criticism of women's writing will both derive from an ideological position, a feminist one, and acknowledge that those 'other things beside their work' influence that work, and that knowledge of them helps illuminate it. However, Woolf's proposition that these influences have 'nothing to do with art' becomes not just redundant, but contrary to the idea that an intricate interrelationship exists between women's writing, the place of woman, and the nature of female experience in a culture, for all these things are encoded by ideologies that produce masculine superiority.

The feminine, then, is effectively devalued and silenced within Australian history and culture, and the consequences of that devaluation and silencing can be discerned in different ways in Australian women's writing. Curiously, a remarkable proportion of women write and publish fiction in Australia. Indeed, in the 1930s, according to Drusilla Modjeska's recent socio-historical, literary survey of the women writers of the period 1925–45, *Exiles at Home* (1981): 'Women were producing the best fiction of the period and they were, for the first and indeed the only time, a dominant influence in Australian literature'.[7] Oppressive cultural determinants may produce a positive reaction in this way, and a counter ideology of female life in Australia is perceptible. Crude devaluation and dismissal by dominant masculine ideologies allow a struggle against these power structures, which, according to Michel Foucault, are dynamic and productive rather than merely or predominantly repressive and negative. In this case the imposition of power to dominate and control parts of society and areas of its life will result in *relations* of domination rather than a simple opposition, dominator/ dominated. A strategy of this power relation, one of its modes of struggle, may occur in writing. In their texts women may speak their experience of their culture, including its literary manifestations; through a reading of those texts which is attentive to that culture and its ideologies the specificity of both women's writing and women's lives may be explored. In an Introduction to her 1982 edition of poems by four Australian women poets, *Journeys*, Fay Zwicky, West Australian poet and short story writer, points to the difference and the potential aesthetic freedom of these writers: 'Perhaps . . . women have been more free to express their awareness in our culture, more able to synthesize in the teeth of fragmentation around them'.[8] A more simplistic evaluation of the reason for the number of Australian women writers in a culture antagonistic to women's achievement is analogous to Henry James's remark that Jane Austen's writing is like a woman absent-mindedly picking up stitches in her knitting. In a *Bulletin* article 'Women and the Novel' published in 1926, Vance Palmer presents all the gendered assumptions that link the feminine with the novel, concluding that 'writing a novel seems as easy to almost any literate woman as making a dress',[9] neatly abstracting effort and intellect from women's activities and implicitly valorizing the concomitant work of a male writer.

Women in fiction by women, like those women who write, are significantly less sanguine about the costs involved in attempting to speak out of their imposed and culturally determined silence. In Christina Stead's early Australian novel *Seven Poor Men of Sydney* (1934) her central female character, Catherine, speaks of her hopeless struggle against the masculine hegemony: 'I've fought all my life for male objectives in a male world.... I fight so hard and suffer so much and get nowhere'.[10] Dorothy Hewett, dramatist and poet, specifies the dual contradiction inherent in the position of a woman who is also a writer in Australia in noting that 'the role of the woman writer is always doubly subversive in a predominantly male ethos. She *thinks* subversively by nature and experience, and she writes from that other country of spirit and physicality, which still remains, for us, largely uncharted'.[11] Women writers, thinking against the masculine literary tradition and its prescriptions, and writing from a place unrecognized (and therefore unnamed by that tradition), find themselves in a curious cultural situation in Australia. Since Australian society is organized according to a patriarchal order and by way of masculine ideologies, it denies female life any central value, abstracting it from the concerns and practices of the androcentric culture. Women are confined by domestication and defined by an ideology of the female which is limiting and negative in all its aspects. Further, Australian society disparages the value of intellectual or creative life. It mocks its artists and thinkers by feminizing their activity, labelling it non-masculine and thereby denying it value. Because Australian ideologies reject intellectual and creative life as they reject female life, women are given access to these things.

But to be female and creative in Australia is to invite a dual alienation; in Dorothy Hewett's words it means to place oneself in a position of double subversion. And despite the artistic freedom allowed her by an ideology that equates creativity with gender, stereotypically conflating 'female', 'creative', 'emotional', 'feeling' and so on, the Australian woman who writes doubles the number of roles she must play which lack social and ideological sanction. Although this series of premises seems to reduce complex conditions to simple equations, it does allow the possibility of a reading position for the question 'How do women write?' in Australia. With no sustaining or mediating ideology, Australian woman's fiction will reproduce (in its voice, perhaps, or its formal structures, or by way of thematic irresolution or textual dislocation) those contradictions that derive from an aggressive ideological repression, or exclusion, of women and the arts.

An Australian woman will write, then, from one of two positions, each of which is a product of the situation I've described. She may suppress her 'nature and experience' and 'that other country of spirit and physicality' of which Dorothy Hewett speaks, and become a token male. In this case, she will adopt what are culturally valued as the characteristics of the Australian literary tradition. Despite numerous re-writings of this tradition, it is still valorized as the mode of radical nationalism. Like Virginia Woolf's nineteenth-century writer with her mind 'pulled from the straight', like Catherine in *Seven Poor Men of Sydney*, this women writer will fight for 'male objectives in a male world', and the experience will be debilitating. Compromised aesthetically in this position as she negotiates a relationship with the masculine values of the national ideology in order to be heard, the writer and her writing will suffer. Miles Franklin's novel *My Brilliant Career* (1901) is a clear example of this kind of writing. Alternatively, she may accept her cultural position as other, exacerbated as it is by her creativity. Since both her gender and her writing are made insignificant and inconsequential she will write from a position of dual alienation, one that is difficult but paradoxically free. In this case, too, her work will be different, and such a female writer runs the risk of its being misunderstood, subjected to critical ridicule, or simply ignored. Christina Stead's fiction demonstrates the problems of writing from this position. These two broad patterns of choice suggest a dialetic between whose two poles women's writing will be situated (moving from one to the other extreme to varying degrees), and offer both a reading position and a methodology to deal with that writing.

Rereading Australian women's fiction from this position, which sees each text as part of a larger context (one in which women's experience is radically different from men's) allows for new perspectives as well as new interpretative strategies to illuminate this writing. It also creates problems in practice, since the claim of 'difference' in life, and therefore in art, implies something against which this difference is measured – women's writing is different from men's and that difference, according to my argument, stems from woman being constructed by Australian ideologies as different, as other – yet how or in what ways is that difference to be specified in women's writing? A great deal of evidence is now being documented in Australian literary studies that women writers have been excluded, ignored or patronized in a national literary context. This work parallels that recuperative feminist criticism undertaken in England and America. Although the number of women writers in Australia is proportionately large – and, as I have said, this may be so because of the disrepute an excessively or aggressively male-centred Australian society has accorded to the life of the intellect or the creative arts – they are poorly represented in anthologies, and have until recently been given less critical attention (or critical attention of a different kind) than male writers. Women writers have not been well represented on courses in Australian literature or Australian studies. Some adopted the by now familiar tactic of writing under a male pseudonym so as to be considered *not* as women writers – Henry Handel Richardson and Miles Franklin are the two most obvious examples. Women, moreover, have had no public tradition from which to write, and the networks between women writers have been private ones – one such is well documented by Modjeska in *Exiles at Home*. Their writing was given no status and usually had to be fitted in with other demands, most often domestic ones. Literary circles were, and are, dominated by men. All these familiar signs of discrimination, well-documented by female literary critics in England and America, exist in crude forms in Australian literary and cultural history.

Obvious and more subtle forms of oppression and suppression have operated against the Australian woman writer, and there is much work still to be done both in documenting this women's literary history, in assessing the effect on these women and their writing of those forms of oppression and suppression, in recovering lost or forgotten writing by women, and in re-writing the history of Australian writing (rather than creating a new or parallel tradition) in this more inclusive sense. As Modjeska says in her introductory remarks to *Exiles at Home*:

> Women had . . . been writers of fiction for the better part of a century. And they had been so against unequal odds. They had written in spite of poor financial returns, the demands of family responsibilities, a frequently depressed publishing industry, their own low self-esteem and a view of Australian literature that was predominantly masculine.

These writers of the thirties, she points out, were much more emancipated than those earlier ones, but their situation remained difficult, as it still does.

This immediate context for the work of the writing woman, then, can be seen as an extension of a socio-historical context and of the place of women within that context. But the woman writer's situation is a peculiarly ambiguous one, since in aspiring to be a writer, she will either be seen as stepping out of her allotted role or doing something that comes naturally to women. Both attitudes neatly deny her activity status by seeing it as either unnatural or 'natural'. Analogously, for the woman writer the choice remains to write like a man or acknowledge her doubly disadvantaged position and write freely from it. In the work of one Australian writer, each of these tendencies is discernible. Barbara Baynton's slim volume of short stories, *Bush Studies* was first published in London in 1902. It provides a useful starting point for a reading that theorizes those differences of experience and values in relation to writing. Baynton wrote *Bush Studies* during the 1890s, that decade when the colonies were moving towards Federation and Australian literature is said to have come of age. The dominant characteristics of this Australian literature were established in this period; a sense of nationalism, a focus on the bush and bush life that included a sense of affinity between the bush and its inhabitants, mateship as a central value, and a formal preoccupation with realism conveyed through the structures of the text and the language and speech patterns of the common man. Henry Lawson is of course its illustrative representative, conveying its myths and values in his short stories, the preferred form of the 1890s. Baynton's work, like that of Lawson and many other writers, was first published in the *Bulletin* (in its Christmas edition, 1896). Thus Baynton shares many qualities with male writers of this definitive period in Australian history and literature.

It is true that the legend of the nineties has been reconstructed in the literary criticism of the last decade or so. Furphy has been rediscovered, as has the complex irony that lies behind Tom Collins as narrator of *Such is Life*, complicating the apparent geniality (even banality) of the tales of an Australian drover's life. Lawson is now recognized as rejecting the harshness of bush life and deploring its sentimentalization in the work of many of his contemporaries. But although Lawson writes of the emptiness, loneliness, even the threatening quality of the bush (the opening sentences of 'The Drover's Wife' provide a clear example of that narrator's negative attitude toward the bush setting of the story) those who people it are united in a common human bond – they're mates. And although the quality and meaning, the very ideology, of that mateship is now being critically examined, it is the central value in Lawson's literary world. However, Baynton's *Bush Studies* fulfil few of the thematic or even formal expectations produced by the legend of the nineties. In her stories the bush world is malignant, and its inhabitants exist within it in a situation of almost permanent hostility, fear and non-communication. A savage natural world, it contains equally brutal human beings, and it is striking that in the six stories the only relationships that convey feeling, compassion and understanding are between human beings and their dogs, or centred in the concept of motherhood.

Like Lawson's, Baynton's bush is largely peopled by men. Far from being laconically good-humoured, considerate of each other, honestly living according to a code of bush ethics, Baynton's characters (men and women alike, and almost without exception) are lazy, shiftless, amoral, thieving, murderous, sly, foulmouthed, greedy, inhospitable, and so on. The exceptions are all women, and all are outsiders. They range from the classic female victim of 'The Chosen Vessel', protecting her baby even in death, to the ageing half-caste of 'Billy Skywonkie', rejected as a housekeeper by the absolute inhumanity of those at the isolated station she travels to, to the daughter who risks her life to see her mother again in 'The Dreamer', and (most interestingly) to Squeaker's mate in the story of that name. This woman has all the male characteristics of the myth of the mate; stoicism, endurance, loyalty to the indescribably awful Squeaker, and an understanding of the bush and its ways, yet in the story she is literally immobilized. Her back is broken when the tree she is felling snaps, rotten at its core, and a branch falls on her, making her a victim of the unpredictable bush. Squeaker deserts her, introducing a new, younger 'mate' into the hut and relegating her to a lean-to. A victim of her sexuality, she is also clearly a victim of the age and its ideologies. The men who have regarded her as a mate desert her when she is paralyzed, reacting to her now as a woman – a loss of strong physicality seems to equate with a loss of token masculinity – and their wives come once and then no more, still reviling the mate for her lack of femininity, her 'uncompromising independence'.

It is significant that in all Baynton's stories women are vulnerable and subject to varying degrees of torment, ranging from rape and murder to wife-beating, at the hands of brutish men or the malignant environment. It is also significant that the strongest virtue in these women (and the only admirable human feeling portrayed in the stories) is the mothering instinct. Even barren Squeaker's mate is his surrogate mother – this is the secret of the 'mystery' of the strong woman's devotion to the despicable little man. In *Bush Studies*, 'woman' is a term of derision. The other men in 'Squeaker's Mate' disparage Squeaker as 'a nole woman', a remark, the narrator comments, 'after man's fashion to eliminate all virtue'. It is not surprising, then, that what we may see as a stereotyping of womanly virtue in the valorization of the mothering instinct and the potential to nurture, is made a positive value. What is surprising is that in the two stories most directly concerned with mothering, 'The Dreamer' and 'The Chosen Vessel', the subject is treated with often embarrassing overstatement, melodrama and cliché. This is not unlike the inept, stereotyping sentimentality Lawson uses when he depicts 'good women'. Yet in 'Squeaker's Mate' Baynton has avoided any such loss of narrative power although the situation is potentially open to bathos. Is this because the mate is more of a man than the men are, so that her never-uttered pain, physical and emotional, is realized with shocking impact precisely through a lack of emotional language or any straining for effect? In other words, is it only by writing 'like a man' that Baynton creates her finest story?

Bush Studies are more stories of incident than of character, and their situations are fully and often horrifyingly revealed through the devices and techniques of realism. And realism – which Patrick White decried in his often-quoted remark as 'dreary and dun coloured'[12] – is the traditional mode in the male-dominated Australian literary culture. Baynton's stories, then, seem to be written in the style and form necessary to be successful in the 1890s. Yet these stories, realistically told, often use melodramatic language and the situations of melodrama – they have a Gothic flavour. The melodramatic and the Gothic are modes of writing which have become identified with women writers. Minor genres, they are accessible to women who feel (or are) excluded from writing in what are regarded by phallocentric critics as the major genres. Moreover, they arise, according to David Punter in *The Literature of Terror*, 'from a need to fantasise an unsatisfactory reality'[13] and the reality of being a woman and a writer in Australia at the turn of the century posits a pretty unsatisfactory reality. Good and evil are polarized in Baynton's stories, which are suffused with an atmosphere of lurking terror and imminent destruction. Even the comic-grotesque device in 'Bush Church', when the illiterate bush people converse and move around while the town parson ineffectually conducts a service which they neither comprehend nor value, is disturbing, conveying social chaos as the bush intrudes into the polite middle class environment of the grazier's house where the service is held. Again, it is argued that melodrama or Gothic have allowed female (and male) writers to convey aspects of existence that threaten the social order or are conventionally unspeakable. Sexuality has been one of these areas. For all its imported religiosity (the Peter Hennessey episode was written into the story after its first publication) 'The Chosen Vessel' is pure horror story in its classic Gothic situation, in which an unknown, active male relentlessly seeks a confined, passive female. The threat to the woman in 'A Dreamer' is nightmarishly contained in the darkness of a terrible story, and the lashing willow branches that produce the hostility of the whole natural world are not-very-latently suffused with male sexuality. And through the powerless female at the centre of the meaningless, sexually-charged activity in 'Billy Skywonkie' the narrator conveys a sense of the surreal: 'A giddy unreality took the sting from everything, . . . she felt she had lost her mental balance. Little matters became distorted, and the greater shrivelled'. Women are imprisoned and rendered powerless by some phallic force which is equated with the male and the unresponsive, malicious natural world. The polarization of acquiescent slave woman and aggressively-sexual master male is a Gothic trait. Squeaker's mate is given both traditional, male qualities and a nurturing, female role, yet she too is ultimately powerless against those outside forces.

A surreal atmosphere that induces a kind of madness is most clearly linked with the appalling heat of Baynton's bush. Heat becomes another enemy in the melodrama of the stories, draining energy from nature and human beings or producing bursts of manic activity. The brutish listlessness induced by this heat adds to the anti-realism of Baynton's fiction. This woman writer, then, writes within an accepted masculine tradition of short fiction, realistic in its form and content, deriving meaning through themes which are an acceptable part of this tradition, of the hardship of life in the bush, of saintly women, of human endurance. Yet the stories actually parody, or invert these qualities. Realism becomes surreal as it is juxtaposed with Gothic or melodramatic elements, and these modes of writing are used to speak an experience which realism cannot deal with. Realism reaches out to a social context, while Gothicism and melodrama produce fantasy, and in this mixture the writer textualizes women who, whether they are saints or whores, are exploited, victimized and sometimes destroyed by a malevolent power identified with male sexuality. Baynton, as a recent analysis of her work concludes, writes out of anger and in a spirit of revenge against the bush and all its representatives.[14] It seems that once these emotions were expiated, or perhaps when the more comfortable and secure circumstances of her later life influenced her, Baynton lacked the impetus for her writing. Although Woolf claims that writing in anger – almost inevitable for a woman but a practice she must overcome – distorts women's writing, such distortion is a productive one for Baynton. Her curious, compelling stories in *Bush Studies* explore, and obliquely explain, the despair of being a woman in a rejecting, alienating environment. Little known for many decades, it is significant that Baynton's work and life have recently become important in the history of Australian literature.

I have spent some time exploring the specificities of Baynton's writing in the light of my previous remarks in part because her work is accessible and demonstrates clearly, sometimes even crudely, that she writes out of a debilitating social and personal experience. An alternative ideology, of the female, of the bush, and of Australia, to the dominant masculine one is produced by her writing. Baynton is also significant because she wrote in the 1890s, a time of great importance in national and literary history, so that her work has an immediate literary context and measure of its difference in Henry Lawson's short stories. In this sense, Baynton's work invites a reading against Lawson's narratives, making *Bush Studies* an alternative female text.

Baynton has obviously adopted the masculine values of a national and literary ideology, yet, with more or less damage to her work, has circumvented the central tenets of those ideologies, using at times different generic modes, unrealistic language and symbols to indict savagely the very bases of that masculine national ideology. Her use of Gothicism and melodrama, fantastic generic elements that allow her freedom of expression denied by realism, is strong in a number of later writers, for example in Elizabeth Harrower's novel *The Watchtower* (1966) which has recently attracted a number of feminist critiques. This novel concerns two orphaned sisters, Laura and Clare. They are taken up by Felix who marries Laura. Felix, a surrogate father, is a kind of

Bluebeard; Laura is kept in sexual, economic and political bondage to him. The tower of the title is Clare's bedroom from whose window she watches and waits. It is imprisoning, signifying the self divided from other hostile selves, or the phallic oppression that is Felix's power. The novel gradually acquires sinister meanings as Laura and Clare are insidiously rendered powerless, subject to Felix who represents the dominant culture that defines women negatively and often forces them into the same self-definition. Gothic images and situations convey those meanings. Barbara Hanrahan's novels, always fantastic, often use Gothic elements. Perhaps most effectively in *Dove* (1982), innocence and evil are the only possibilities for characters' lives; the settings are grotesque, and the female protagonists are conscious of a constant feelings of threat, not least from their own bodies. Helen Hodgman, a contemporary Tasmanian writer (*Blue Skies*, 1976 and *Jack and Jill*, 1978) also makes strange the banal domestic life of which she writes, in which her women characters are trapped and by which they are maddened. Suburban life itself is threatening, and made to seem bizarre by the Gothic perception of the author and the shifted perspective of the central female characters.

In these readings, language and literature produce constructions of reality that run counter to the ideology of the dominant culture, rather than reflect or mirror that masculine reality. Katharine Susannah Prichard's writing, too, conveys obvious textual and thematic tensions that can be explained by a clash between the Australian national ideology that the texts reject, and their presentation of alternative ideologies, Marxist and feminist. In *Intimate Strangers* (1937), the female protagonist Elodie is offered that social and sexual freedom which is denied her by her society. Yet an unintentionally ironic compromise finally portrays Elodie as a castrating female who apparently makes the ideological choice for motherhood her society demands, but at the expense both of the text's socialist and feminist commitment. And a recently published novel by Georgia Savage, *Slate & Me and Blanche McBride* (1984) shows the persistence and power of the national ideology, exclusively masculine. Slate and Wyn are brothers, united against middle-class Australian society and its values. They carry all the codes of the national ideology; they're mates, they defy authority and espouse individual freedom, the rights of ordinary men, the power of the underdog, and the ability of this kind of individual to survive in a hostile social and natural environment. But when they take a girl hostage after their bank robbery fails and they become fugitives, the female disrupts this bonding and their downfall becomes certain. Thus the novel textualizes the threat female life holds for those masculine ideologies. As Wyn watches his brother Slate cut the girl's hair in what is written as a symbolic killing/rape of femininity, he has 'the feeling that he was attacking her for being female and that if he'd had a bayonet he'd have sliced her chest as flat as his own'.[15] So this novel by an Australian woman reproduces the gendered power relations that structure Australian culture; woman destroys the potential wholeness of a male world while the masculine ideologies that make her a despised victim continue to naturalize that victimization. Female life signifies aberrance as it threatens the dissolution of those masculine values. *Slate & Me and Blanche McBride* re-writes in an astonishingly pure form those historical and cultural practices that encode difference in Australian society, and the ambivalent narrative triangle of the book reproduces the ambivalent relationship of the Australian woman writer to her society.

NOTES

1. Sally McConnell-Ginet, 'Linguistics and the Feminist Challenge' in *Women and Language in Literature and Society*, (ed.) Sally McConnell-Ginet et al., Praegar, New York, 1980, p. 16.
2. This concise explanation of a dense theory of ideology is given by Penny Boumelha in the Introduction to her study, *Thomas Hardy and Women*, Harvester Press, Brighton, 1982, p. 5.
3. Tim Rowse, *Australian Liberialism and National Character*, Kibble Books, Melbourne, 1978, p. 208.
4. In the first chapter of her exploratory work of social history, *The Real Matilda*, Penguin, Harmondsworth, 1976, Miriam Dixson introduces this concept: 'In long historical perspective Lewis Mumford sees man's relation with nature and with the earth as crucial to his feeling about woman and thus to her social standing' (p. 23) and relates it to the position of women in Australia.
5. This binary opposition derives, of course, from the notion of woman as essence. The structuralist equation was constructed in the form of a question by Sherry B. Ortner in her article, 'Is female to male as nature is to culture?' in *Women, Culture and Society*, (ed.) Michelle Zimbalist Rosaldo and Louise Lamphere, Stanford University Press, Stanford, 1974, pp. 67–87. The answer was no.
6. Shirley Hazzard, 'Australian Authors', *Australian Literary Studies*, Vol. 10, October 1981, p. 207.
7. Drusilla Modjeska, *Exiles at Home*, Sirius Books, London & Sydney, 1981, p. 1.
8. Fay Zwicky (ed.), *Journeys*, Sisters Publishing Ltd, Melbourne, 1982.
9. Modjeska, *Exiles at Home*, p. 8.
10. Christina Stead, *Seven Poor Men of Sydney*, Angus & Robertson, Sydney, 1971, p. 214.
11. Dorothy Hewett, 'The Garden and the City', in *Westerly*, No. 4, December 1982, p. 102.
12. Patrick White, 'The Prodigal Son', in *Australian Letters*, Vol. 1, No. 3, April, 1985, p. 37.
13. David Punter, *The Literature of Terror*, Longmans, London, 1980, p. 409.
14. Lucy Frost, 'Barbara Baynton: An Affinity with Pain', in *Who is She?* (ed.) Shirley Walker, University of Queensland University Press, St Lucia, 1983, pp. 56–70.
15. Georgia Savage, *Slate & Me and Blanche McBride*, Penguin, Melbourne, 1984, p. 111.

8 Film and Fiction: Dealing with Australian Narrative

Graeme Turner

Although there has been an increasing amount of cross reference between film and literary fiction in Australian literary and cultural studies over the last few years, most of it has been informal and incidental. This discussion is aimed at repairing that deficiency by exploring the theoretical connections between the two forms.

'The Union Buries Its Dead' is one of Lawson's most subtle stories, where the interplay between the narrator, the implied author, and the values of the community being observed is complex and delicately balanced. It is possible to argue long into the night about how convincingly Lawson dismisses a sentimental view of that community, or whether his is an Australian variant of that tough, but self-regarding sentimentality Leslie Fiedler calls the Higher Masculine Sentimentality and locates in realist writers such as Hemingway. The key point in discussions tends to be the problem of the narrative voice, the duplicity of that voice, and the selection of the key locations of its tone. Whatever the reading, Lawson's story is a demonstration of the flexibility of prose and of the sensitivity of the narrative point of view in preferring and generating meaning in fiction.

The film version of this story makes up one of three parts in Cecil Holmes' film, *Three in One* (1957). Titled 'Joe Wilson's Mates' but based on 'The Union Buries its Dead', the film lacks the ambiguity of the story: its focus is firmly on the nature of the bush community, its nationalist virtues and values, its solidarity. Much of the film is taken up with renditions of bush songs, tall tales and cameo appearances from stock bush characters – the swagman, the spiv from the city. The level of identification with the community and its values is not qualified by any narratorial objectivity or ambivalence. The role of the dead man dwindles to the simple facts of the coffin and his union card – the latter slowly passed around the group in the pub with more reverence than the coffin is accorded. Introduced by a short series of remarks by actor John McCallum, the story is typed an 'amusing commentary' on mateship. 'Joe Wilson's Mates' is an uncomplicated narrative to read, only providing one position from which the viewer can make sense of it, that of a celebration of the national type and the exemplary community in which he finds his place.

These two texts are an example of, and are introduced to expose, the problems in talking about film and literary fiction together, and particularly film versions of fiction. There are usually two opposing responses to such an example as this. The first defends the film's apparent simplification of the point of view of the story by insisting that the difference between the two media is so great as to make comparison pointless; the film has its own story to tell and must be accepted on its own terms. The second response prefers the literary version to the film, citing the inevitable trivializing of the material drawn from Lawson's story as evidence of the inadequacy of film to deal with ambiguity, a variety of narrative points of view, or an ironic tone. This response depends on the intuition of an 'ideal' version of the story drawn from, but independent of, the literary source which it is film's task to materialize. Both views are crude in this description but they do provide a sense of the outer boundaries of the following discussion. In placing itself within these boundaries this discussion has a number of objectives: to look at the difficulties inherent in the application of the practice and standards of literary criticism to the analysis of film; to suggest ways in which film and fiction can be interrelated without overlooking their formal differences; and to place such a study within the framework of an enquiry into the formal and ideological determinants of Australian film and fiction as products of a specific national culture.

The obstacle before literary critics who want to respond to their interest in film is that film and fiction are two different forms; most tend to walk through this obstacle by the straightforward strategem of articulating film's structures and language in terms of those of fiction, as if the two media were entirely analogous to each other. The problem is frequently encountered, but rarely acknowledged; we have a recent example in Brian McFarlane's book, *Words and Images*,[1] which evades it by talking about the two forms separately but from the same critical point of view, while offering tentative value judgements on the comparative success of each book/film he discusses. In many ways one's training as a literary critic provides one with a set of assumptions and techniques that are exactly wrong for the study of film. Gerald Mast has talked about this in a useful and argumentative study where he develops a critique of the literary response as one intrinsically antipathetic to film studies.[2] First, he says, film is a new art form and one to which the more traditional modes of high art criticism are not always applicable. The nomination of a text as high art places it within particular cultural contexts, within particular audiences, and within particular conditions of production and reception – most of which are not those of the feature film. The problem of the popularity of the form, the subsequent expansion of the role and genre and convention, and the manner in which the success of a popular art is (or is not) measured, are all aspects of film criticism which Mast maintains are not easily addressed through a high art model. Further, the socio-economic placement of film is different to literary fiction; there is some truth in the proposition that those who spend their leisure time watching films occupy a different class position to those who spend their leisure time reading novels.

Mast, Chatman and others[3] have indicated that there are assumptions absorbed with a literary training that need to be recognized, both because they are there and because they often operate unconsciously – as prejudice rather than judgement. For instance, literary training creates a respect for the integrity of the text that motivates resistance to translations of a text from one medium to another. In their dealing with texts, literary critics also develop a preference for the reflective, contemplative and intellectual pleasures over the more passionate, sensual and stimulating ones. This can take the form of a somewhat puritanical distrust of the senses. Film takes words out of narrative and replaces them with sights and sounds, appealing directly to the senses; in Mast's words, film offers us a 'sensuous metaphor for the experience of an event',[4] rather than an ironic or reflective understanding of its significance. An important and debilitating consequence of this preference is the common disregard for films which are clearly conventional, operating comfortably within the boundaries of their genre, such as most of the entire output of Hollywood. This disregard for genre is implicated in the modernist preferences of early film criticism in the sixties, which was attracted to the films of Fellini, Antonioni, and Godard, while American films simply attracted audiences. The sense that a genre film (westerns, thrillers, horror films and so on) was inherently inconsiderable because it made so few claims for its own uniqueness, is implicated as part of a range of attitudes which accompany a respect for the literary and a discomfort with the popular. In many cases this is a theoretical blind spot; the distinction between the literary and the popular is assumed rather than understood, and there is little discussion of the different ways in which the various modes construct their meanings – to do with, for instance, a greater ambiguity and multiplicity of reading positions, a greater space for the idiosyncracies of the individual text, distinguishing a literary use of language from the popular.

There are, of course, *real* differences between the forms – they are not all invented by literary critics. Film does not use narrative point of view in the same way fiction does; irony is difficult to achieve, symbol is difficult to avoid, and the clearly asserted description of scene and setting we are accustomed to in the novel gives way to a more generalized depiction in the cinema: in film, the camera's proliferation of information creates a problem of focus, highlighting those aspects of setting which are crucial to the film's meaning. Character in film is radically different in its construction; while some may regret the star syndrome, film stars do have an important ontological function in film. As Richard Dyer points out, stars are semiotic systems – signs – and carry a detailed and precise range of meanings with them.[5] They present an important advantage to the film-maker in that they provide a reservoir of significance which can be drawn upon in the representation of particular types and values. Further, the film-maker has the advantage of presenting a concrete, physical presence which can then be overlaid with nuances, accretions of meaning. The novelist starts in the reverse position, building collections of traits, features, values in the hope of eventually establishing a concrete-like physical presence for the character. Even if this is achieved, there is not that physical particularity in our reception of character in fiction; hence the disagreements about the casting in translations of novels into films, where the choice of actor or actress fails to mesh with our mental image drawn from the prose. This disagreement is a legitimate one because the face of the star is *part* of the characterization and not separable from it; the Philip Marlowe played by Humphrey Bogart is not the same character as the Philip Marlowe played by James Garner or Robert Mitchum.[6]

The genuine problem of formal comparisons is often exacerbated by discussions of film which talk of it possessing a visual 'language' that is more or less precisely comparable to verbal language. Unfortunately, while this is a helpful metaphor in explaining the way film communicates in a *general* way, film language is not analogous in any *detailed* way to verbal language. Despite Eisenstein's assertion that the shot is equivalent to the word, it is not; there have been films compiled with as few as 12 shots, and some shots in conventional films can last for many minutes, suggesting they relate more accurately to the sentence or paragraph rather than the word. The most we can say with any certainty about the grammar of film language is that it is clear that two successive shots are held to be in some way related, and the understanding of this connection – which can take many forms – is more akin to understanding lines of poetry than a word or a sentence of prose.[7] Some attributes of verbal language – metaphor, irony – seem to be intrinsically verbal and are difficult to reproduce in film, certainly within the dominant mode of realism. Metaphor becomes symbol or convention, and irony tends to occur through dialogue or dramatic structure rather than in the manipulation of the camera's (the narrator's) point of view. The effects of verbal irony can be duplicated by visual means – through the manipulation of identification through close-ups and reaction shots, for instance – but the complexity of Lawson's narrative voice in our example would be almost impossible to achieve by other than verbal means in Holmes' film without departing from the realist mode altogether.

This brief glossing of some of the differences between film and fiction is partly to shoot down a few fallacies still airborne, but primarily to establish the inadequacy of innocently regarding film as fiction with pictures. The relation between literary fiction and film is an interesting but not an uncomplicated one, and we are not justified in feeling that we can move easily between the two forms without making some adjustments to our approach. If we do feel it useful and worthwhile to include film within our discussion of Australian fiction from time to time, or to enclose it within the larger field of Australian studies, we need to make the connection between them a theoretical as well as a practical one.

To start at the rudimentary level, what film and fiction have in common is that they both tell stories – they are narrative forms. The recent developments in the study of narrative provide us with a rich body of theory that can assist in our attempts to explore the interrelation between film and fiction as narrative. The work of the Russian Formalists, the various structuralists and structural anthropologists such as Lévi-Strauss provide us with ways of reading narrative that do not depend entirely upon a literary orientation. To simplify a very disparate group of theory, the basic procedure of all these schools is to approach narrative through its most primitive forms, and to see it as a particular use of language; simply, narrative is a culture's way of making sense of itself. Narrative is argued to serve the same functions in all cultures; the studies in folk tales, myths and legends in Propp and Lévi-Strauss lead towards the articulation of a universal grammar of narrative that structures all story. Lévi-Strauss underlines the universality of narrative structures in all cultures, but also insists on the cultural specificity of the particular formulation of this structure in each culture. While narrative may perform the same ideological function in all cultures, the specific manner in which any one narrative is articulated is also determined by its particular culture. Since the role of narrative in primitive cultures is to resolve contradictions within experience, to explain the apparently inexplicable, and to justify the inevitable, and since there are many different manifestations of contradiction, inexplicability and inevitability, there is always the need for the culture's narrative to deal explicitly with those specific aspects of experience which are meaningful to that culture.

In general, these are useful concepts, although in my opinion there is a limit to the applicability of theories about the function of myth, legend and folk tale in primitive societies to the function of mass-produced filmed and printed narrative in developed industrialized societies. The fairy tale and the film, for instance, enjoy a different status as texts. The fairy tale's plot is primary – the story itself is central and will survive a number of different storytellers. In film and prose fiction, the way in which the story is told (point of view, setting, characterization, lighting, form in general), its range of discourses, becomes more important. We do not think of the film or the novel as simply plot, and the inseparability of plot from other formal characteristics of the novel has become one of the most widely held *dicta* for those who deal with these more sophisticated narrative forms. Reducing the novel or the film to its most basic plot structure does establish the universality of that structure and does tell us something about the work accomplished by narrative. But it will not necessarily help in the work I'm outlining here. The analysis of a nation's film and fiction inevitably interests itself in the features of the discourse of the individual texts, as culturally specific transformations of universal structures. The cultural specificity, the Australian-ness of texts, lives in recurring principles of organization and selection, in the application of a particular language – drawing on the myths, connotations and symbols which have currency in the culture – and in such determinants as the activity of formal preferences – the encouragement of certain genres, conventions, and modes of production. In the patterning of such influences we can see which meanings are most easily articulated within, are preferred by, and are seen to be the most significant to, the culture.

One of the most useful propositions deriving from post-Saussurean linguistics is that we do not make our meanings by inventing fresh concepts as the need arises (by inventing names as new objects materilize) but by making new constructions out of material already provided for us by the culture. Lévi-Strauss's analogy of the *bricoleur*,[8] who makes the best he can out of the materials at hand, is one that still fits the role of the storyteller even in such potentially idiosyncratic forms as the novel. The materials for the story, its detailed and individualized representation of life, is drawn from the narrative *langue* of the culture. This *langue* is not only linguistic in the narrow sense but also ideological. The nation's narratives are defined not so much by factors such as the birthplace of the author or whether it was written in Sydney or London, but by the bank of ideologically framed myths, symbols, connotations and contextual associations upon which they draw. The Australian, for instance, 'sunbakes' while the English 'sunbathe'; this difference does not simply imply that you are more likely to be rained on at an English beach, but invokes a whole battery of ideological positions towards nature and the natural environment that is inscribed into the language of the two cultures. English nature is under control, orderly, and one may abandon oneself to it; Australian nature is harsh, hostile, and the enjoyment of it depends on proving one can survive its worst excesses: survival on these terms confirms one's Australian-ness as does a bronze tan during the summer. The language of narrative is 'bathed in ideology', in Althusser's phrase, and the formal and thematic structures of narrative seem to be too; the way a culture's narratives represent the type of the hero, for example, reveals much about the ideology of the individual and his or her place in the society. A comparison between Australian and American heroes would highlight important variants in the values and beliefs governing individual behaviour between the two countries as well as those governing their literary traditions.

I've referred to two broad ways of looking at narrative. The first depends on the argument that all narratives possess a deep structure which is independent of their medium and is ultimately universal. This approach stresses the similarities between narratives, the lack of individuation at this deep structural level. The second approach is the one I am most interested in here and the one in which I see the greatest possibilities for the study of film and fiction within Australian culture. This approach focusses on the Australian articulation of these universal structures, examining what is 'national' about the narratives, tracing the activity of the culture's own sets of values and beliefs, and the ways in which it reproduces these values and beliefs in the individual text. The texts examined are not then seen as natural, organic products of our emerging national character, but as cultural constructions, as 'national fictions'.

Put as baldly as this, the practical applications of this theory may seem obscure or undetermined. But before moving from theory to practice, there are a number of theoretical assumptions which this approach challenges and they need to be nominated. Certain definitions of literariness are clearly discounted. The importance of value judgements as part of the equipment of the critic who asks 'is it any good' before asking 'what is it' is minimized. Along with this goes the preference for individual perceptions as intrinsically more interesting and important than those cultural perceptions which transmit themselves through the novelist or film-maker. The balance of power between the text and context is reorganized in ways that reduce the valorizing of the individual text. (There are many strands of pure literary theory that do this, too.) The author suffers, therefore, and although this approach does not require the death of the author it does require that he regularly be given a sleeping pill. Further, the preference for the 'novel', the unconventional, discriminates against film by precluding the recognition of the possibility of narratives working within conventional boundaries while still retaining the possibility of seriousness. Finally, the assumption that literature is prior to and

therefore superior to film as an art form inevitably distorts comparisons
and is an obstacle to the analysis of film's contribution to the expansion
of the potential of narrative.

There are more positive ways than these of describing the opportunities provided by the study of narrative, however. Laurie Hergenhan, for instance, gently intimates in *Unnatural Lives* that the role of
value judgements in creating the insistence on articulating our literary
traditions around only those works which are seen to be the best has
excised the typical, the simply realist, the political and the conventional
as lacking any cultural or contextual importance in creating the conditions in which all our fiction – good, bad or indifferent – is written. This
creates an impression of Australian literary traditions as consisting of
a 'broken chain of waterholes', and is unnecessarily prescriptive.[9] John
Docker's familiar attacks on the colonizing of Australian literary traditions, the patrolling of the borders of what he calls the 'metaphysical
ascendancy', and the exclusion of a rich and important body of
Australian writing from consideration is relevant here, too.[10] The best
feature of *In a Critical Condition* is that it attacks the constant
hierarchizing of texts in literary criticism; the worst aspect of it is that
it suggests that Docker has his own hierarchy waiting to slouch out of
Sydney to be born. From what we know about the ways in which a
culture produces its stories, the intertextual links between fictions and
the conditions of production are not solely proscribed by distinctions of
quality any more than they are solely proscribed by the national culture
in isolation from any wider narrative traditions. Any comparative study
of Australian narrative must have the objective of widening the field of
enquiry, the extension of the purchase of literary studies onto the study
of culture. Unlike the parodical critic, Simon Lascerous, in his article
in *The Pooh Perplex* entitled 'Another Book to Cross off Your List', the
endeavour here is to enlarge the sense of context, to widen the scope of
the interrelations we trace between literature and society, between
national fictions and national culture.

This larger sense of context is immediately appreciable to all who
have applied themselves to reading Australian films, fiction and their
respective bodies of criticism. The multiplicity of connections this
activity reveals is especially illuminating for critics of Australian literature. The same arguments go on, the same perceptions circulate, in
Australian film studies as in Australian literary studies. At all levels of
critical discussion we find accounts of the film tradition which strike
very familiar notes. An example would be the orthodox account of the
plight of the individual in Australian film, articulated in our literary
tradition by way of the outline of the battler trying to survive, in one
formulation, or the post-romantic nihilist stranded between the opposing poles of nature and society, in another. Similarly, Tom Ryan,

from Scott Murray's *The New Australian Cinema*, comparing Australian and American cinema:

[Australian films] are far more modest, preferring to define the individual as a battler against overwhelming odds which cannot be defeated even if they are confronted head-on, but which will allow survival if he/she suffers the indignities without asserting resentment. This individual is a victim, a consumer of history, rather than a participant in its course.[11]

This is not an unfamiliar account. Further, the widespread use of the fact and metaphor of imprisonment has been noticed by Ian Reid, Laurie Hergenhan, Brian Kiernan and others, and it crops up again in Bob Ellis's description of the Australian star in the movies: 'while American stars look as if they are Superman on furlough, our actors look like crims on parole'.[12] The metaphor, with its suggestions of the precariousness of freedom, is one more familiar to students of the 'double aspect' of freedom and exile in Australian literature than to students of film. At times, the use of essentially literary generic terms, such as in Susan Dermody's discussion of the quest motif in Australian cinema,[13] reveals a need for an acquaintance with the history of the formal characteristics of this mode in media other than film. This indicates the usefulness of both areas of study visiting each other's bibliographies from time to time, but the more important point of the comparison is to emphasize the fact that many of the patterns we have found in fiction recur, or are seen to recur, in precisely analogous ways in our films. The fact that these patterns – thematic, formal and ideological – surface not only in literature but also in a more popular and conventional medium tells us much about their currency within the culture as a whole, while also indicating how direct a relationship even the most idiosyncratic of our novels have with the culture.

Tracing these connections brings us into contact with constructions of meaning that are not exclusively literary; they are rather literary articulations of the myths of the culture. The discussion of the bush legend, for instance, has largely been confined to a literary context, even by historians. Yet the bush legend dominates early Australian film in the same ways it did early Australian fiction, and this is made clear in John Tulloch's *Legends on The Screen*.[14] While there are separate studies of the phenomenon in each discipline, there is no chance of asking how they might be the same phenomenon; the answer could have important repercussions on our view of the fiction.

There are numerous theoretical connections available for analysis in the comparative study of Australian film and fiction. We can find similarities, say, in the representation of character in Lawson and Furphy – characters presented not as highly individualized 'essences' but as metonyms for certain aspects of Australian life – in a wide range of early and contemporary Australian films. The use of character as setting, too, is part of the Australian narrative tradition which derives from a common cultural source, not just the formal exigencies of the dominant modes of documentary realism in film or social realism in fiction. The role of the yarn, the saga, the objective social realist tale in fiction, and the function of documentary realism in film is ideologically comparable: all these forms place the individual within an historical frame which partly obscures its fictional character while minimizing the importance of individual actions through the translation of social change into the movement of history or nature rather than the actions of men and women. In Australian narratives the characters tend to be acted upon by events and circumstance, and the way this positions the individual within the society reveals a particular ideology. If such connections do exist, the role of the culture itself in producing them across such a breadth of textual formations seems to demand close attention.

To conclude, we can return to the two versions of the Lawson story armed with more appropriate analytical perspectives. Rather than arguing over the merits and demerits of the two versions, it is more productive to see the Holmes film as a revision and reformulation of the Lawson material that has particular objectives and problems. What I would see as the main burden of the Lawson story, the role of the individual and its subordination to the centrality of the community, survives the translation but the main difference between the two versions is the level of overt commitment to this ideological burden. Holmes' film is less ironic, but it is less 'narrated', too; it presents itself as more of a natural, unmediated creation of a world than the clearly mediated, observed, constructed view in Lawson's story. The film's apparent innocence in its naturalizing of its point of view tends to defuse analysis, encouraging acceptance in a straightforward way that is explicitly avoided by Lawson. Rather than seeing this as a mis-understanding of Lawson, it might be useful to see it as a formal strategy that is partly determined by the context in which it was made. Its naive celebration of the bush legend occurs not at a time of widespread nationalism at all; it occurs at a time when the appropriation of the national character is essentially in the hands of a radical populist left wing. Released in 1957, it is bracketed by such events as the publication of the *Legend of the Nineties*, (1954) the foundation of *Overland*, (1954) the publication of *The Australian Legend* (1958) and *The Australian Tradition* (1958), and the appearance of a number of definitively Australian productions on stage and screen in *The Summer of the Seventeenth Doll*, (1955) *Reedy River*, (1953) and *Smiley* (1956). Despite the success of *Reedy River* and *Smiley*, there was still little chance of Australian films attracting a large popular audience, and the radical nationalism of the trio of stories in *Three in One* should not be seen as reflective of, but rather renovatory of, the dominant ideology of the time. The populism of the form is not conditioned by the realistic expectation of a mass market but by the growing movement for an alternative, indigenous popular culture based on 'the Australian tradition', which can be seen in *Overland* and Ian Turner's early work.[15] While there seemed to be some ground for hope at the time, this enterprise looks romantic from the nineteen eighties. Nevertheless, and given this context, the formal differences between the story and the film can be seen as products of the film's essentially political attempt to re-invent an Australian identity, which is necessarily more reliant on an active mythologizing of the model community Holmes is celebrating than the Lawson story; the context for the Lawson story itself provided the mythology and his ironic tone partly derives from his attempt to distance himself from the myth. Seen today, Holmes's film seems naive and shrill, partly because the myths he is re-invoking are back in the foreground of the Australian sense of national character as part of a series of political constructions of the nation that seem to be shaping the eighties.

The comparison of two narratives such as these demands not only the consideration of the details of the respective representations as individual texts in different media; they also need to be considered as expressions of a particular relationship to the cultural conditions which produce them. The result, at best, is a fuller sense of what the texts *are* themselves, as well as a fuller sense of how they might have come to be that way and what function they serve for Australian culture. I would see these results as basic objectives of any comparative study of Australian film and fiction.

NOTES

1. Heinemann, Richmond, 1983.
2. 'Literature and Film' in Jean-Pierre Barricelli and Joseph Gibaldi (eds.) *Interrelations of Literature*, MLA, New York 1982, pp.278–306. The first half of this paper draws extensively on Mast's article and it is commended to any reader interested in following the arguments further.
3. Seymour Chatman, 'What Novels Can Do That Films Can't (And Vice Versa)' in W.J.T. Mitchell (ed.) *On Narrative*, University of Chicago Press, 1980, pp. 117–35.
4. p. 281.
5. 'Stars as Signs' in Tony Bennett et al (eds.) *Popular Television and Film* BFI, London, 1981, pp. 236–69.
6. See Mast, p. 292.
7. Mast, p. 299.
8. *The Savage Mind*, Weidenfeld and Nicolson, London, 1966, pp. 17–33.
9. University of Queensland Press, St Lucia, 1983, p. 13.
10. *In A Critical Condition*, Penguin, Ringwood, 1984.

11. Nelson/Cinema Papers, Melbourne, 1980, p. 125.
12. Quoted in Sue Matthews *35mm Dreams*, Penguin, Ringwood, 1984, p. 268.
13. 'Action and Adventure' in Scott Murray (ed.) *The New Australian Cinema*, pp.79–80.
14. Sydney, Currency, 1981.
15. For a short account of this see Tim Rowse, *Australian Liberalism and National Character*, Kibble, Malmsbury, 1978, pp. 239–46.

9 'Achieving' Culture in the Australian Cinema

Ian Craven

After scarcely more than a decade or so of activity, the history of the 'new' Australian cinema is already starting to coalesce into a suspiciously coherent narrative. Slowly but surely its history is assuming the symmetries and trajectories of 'classical' film structure. This history-narrative usually begins with a startling disruption of a given continuity; the establishment in 1970 of the Experimental Film Fund (EFF) and the Australian Film Development Corporation (AFDC) by the outgoing McMahon government. From here it runs, via the sub-plot of the National Film and Television School, through the melodramatic set-piece of Whitlam's election victory in 1972, to the proliferating story-lines of the State-based Corporations from about 1975, legislation against restrictive trade practices, tax-shelter investment schemes, and the explosion of the independent commercial sector. Recognizing *en route* the international success of a dozen or so features, it finds closure in a notation of decline in the early eighties and increasing co-production for television. It seems as though the party is over. A recent season of Australian movies on British television shows us, we are told, 'what has been and what might – hopefully – come again'.[1]

Valuable as they are, such neat industrial histories involve a variety of significant absences. They speak, for example, only indirectly of the new cinema as a *cultural* institution, involved in the manufacture of forms of representation that bear on social practices as well as company balance sheets. As histories of production, rather than exhibition, their tendency is to applaud individual films as cultural 'achievements' with little or no theorisation of the viewing context within which 'achieving' might have a meaning. The aim here is therefore to re-insert one or two films into definitions of culture to try to materialize the value-systems through, and against which, the Australian cinema has consistently been celebrated. In so doing I hope to map some of the options available to film-makers concerned to intervene specifically in their *national* culture, and some of the possible (and unintended) consequences of those interventions.

121

Clearly through the late sixties and early seventies many Australian film practitioners appealed, in the name of culture, for such an intervention, triggered in part by emerging film histories, and more generally by growing unease about the extent of overseas control of Australian economic, political and cultural life. In retrospect, this emergence of a new national consciousness in Australia through the seventies can be seen as part of a much wider international phenomenon. It was not only in Australia that the mass movements of the sixties led not towards a strengthened internationalist socialism, but to an array of self-confident new nationalisms. In many countries social struggle was couched increasingly in the rhetoric of nationalism. Most shades of political opinion found themselves contesting the nation, and time and again the Left in particular had to wrestle with some unexpected home truths about the grip of the nation on our imaginations. As Cairns Craig has usefully depicted the situation:

Once again – as in 1914 – the Left had to struggle with the fact that the nation, and the apparently irrational devotions both patriotic and religious that it could mobilize, was not going to wither away, and that when socialists took power the power they took was a national power, whose national dimension proved far more decisive than international class solidarity.[2]

It is arguable that the election of the Whitlam Federal government in 1972 was itself an expression of such national 'devotions'. The Australian Labour Party had campaigned on policies with distinctly nationalist overtones, and had included in their manifesto a stated commitment to the development of the national culture that was realized very quickly in the expanded operations of the Australian Council for the Arts. The film industry in particular benefitted swiftly and extensively from the institutional reforms that came after 1972, but the setting up of apparatuses such as the Film Development Corporation left the crucial question of what a national cinema might look like substantially unanswered. The Tariff Board of 1972 could only report unhelpfully that 'most producer witnesses considered that a film which exhibits both quality and craftsmenship and national characteristics is most likely to achieve international acceptance', without venturing a definition of what these 'characteristics' might be.[3] Yet if the findings were not informative, they were significant, simply assuming the necessity of an international sale for any serious attempt at national production. Apparently, the goal of the more vocal of the interested parties was the generation of a national cinema and national prestige by participation in the global economy; a curious counter-movement to the cultural homogenization of capitalist incorporation that stages its own operation as the fight for a place within that economic order, but a familiar one in the history of Australia's manufacturing sector, combining an appeal to national sentiment with pragmatic monetary self-interest. Much of the fascination of the films emerging from this confusion lies, however, in the contradictions bound together here. How can the accommodation of controlling (overseas) interests be squared with discourses on national culture? The critical question has of course its historical variant. How far has it been possible to *project* the national culture on film, given the constraining economics of the industry?

I

In a sense the question is as significant for its metaphor as its object. To speak of 'projecting' culture is to make many assumptions about its character, and about the effects of the mediating apparatus through which the projection is to take place. It is also to speak from a particular time and place. As cultural criticism repeatedly stresses, our ideas of culture do have a particular history, which involves a continuous displacement of assumption by challenge. Moreover cultural critics have always participated in this process, intervening directly to mobilize notions of culture for explicit and implicit ends. When in 1948 T.S. Eliot entered contemporary debates about the reconstruction of post-war culture, he did so quite openly to 'rescue' the term, in the hope of arresting the cultural 'decline' he saw around him. Since Eliot's intervention the word has assumed a wider and wider reference, whilst at the same time the distinction of culture's meaning – pivoting crucially for Eliot around the 'disentanglement' of culture from politics – has been posed consistently in political terms. Increasingly the boundaries of the cultural 'space' as well as the evaluation of its constituent 'elements' have become areas that most schools of social and aesthetic criticism have felt it necessary to contest.

Eliot had staged his cultural rescue mission by arguing, in *Notes Towards the Definition of Culture*, for the integration of two divergent strands of cultural theory.* The first (associated with the Matthew

---

* Clearly both strands of cultural theory have long and related histories. We might however usefully associate the former usage centrally with Matthew Arnold, whose *Culture and Anarchy* (1868) encapsulated the idea of culture as *standard*. For Arnold culture is an index of precious traditions to be defended, in the face of social and industrial revolution. So for Arnold the cultural artefact is an object within which instances of human perfection are preserved, to be served by the critic, and worked upon to release the 'universal' values they crystallize. Culture study involves:

> the study and pursuit of perfection; and that of perfection, as pursued by culture, beauty and intelligence, or in other words, sweetness and light are the main characters.[5]

The cultured subject assumes the qualities of 'sweetness and light' by pursuing the perfections of the cultural.

Arnold of *Culture and Anarchy*) centres around notions of culture as a specific *standard* of aesthetic and moral excellence, to be *aspired towards*. The second (which I would like to associate with the Raymond Williams of *Culture and Society*) sees culture as a specific set of *social practices* that are *possessed*, and lived out in everyday life. Characteristically, Eliot seeks to hold these definitions together, through his celebrated concept of the 'worthwhile'. For Eliot, put simply, culture becomes 'that which makes life worth living'.[4] The subsequent development of cultural criticism however suggests that Eliot's utopian vision of a wholly unified culture, bound together across regional, class and religious difference, was by 1948 already an anachronism. What followed were increasingly distinct articulations of the real heterogeneity of the cultural discourse. Subsequent theories stressed first the vital character of class-specific cultures (Richard Hoggart), then showed how these had been transformed through history (E.P. Thomson) and finally been appropriated in the interests of particular social groupings, as expressly ideological practices (Roland Barthes). Very different in their accent and implication, such studies shared nonetheless a certain challenging consistency, holding as they did that cultures are elaborated within a complex of necessarily *contradictory* social logics and not simply distilled through the creative, or in Eliot's sense 'religious', will of individuals or movements.[8]

To return my argument to the Australian cinema, it seems that a challenge for criticism now lies in the possibility of extending these various models and approaches in relation to the question of a

---

Within the latter definition – culture as a set of social practices – the subject need not 'pursue' the cultural since he/she is bound to live within it. Usage based on the idea of culture as *practice* finds increasingly complex definition through the twentieth century, but has found its most subtle expression in the various writings of Raymond Williams. Here:

> culture is a description of a particular way of life which expresses certain meanings and values not only in art and learning, but also in institutions and ordinary behaviour.[6]

Importantly, Williams's re-definition broadens the cultural franchise, by recognizing elements in the 'way of life' which, within Arnold's idealist definition, would probably not qualify as culture at all:

> the organization of production, the structure of the family, the structure of institutions which express and govern social relationships, the characteristic forms through which members of the society communicate.[7]

Significantly, he places this early stress on the importance of communication systems within the cultural process, and in refusing (with greater and lesser conviction) the judgemental function of Arnold's version of cultural criticism, opens up the area of *popular* culture within which, for instance, the study of the commercial cinema must presumably take place.

specifically *national* culture, to which each seems only casually to address itself. For the most part the definitions lead away from questions of the nation. The models I have associated with Arnold, in which culture becomes 'the best that has been thought and known in the world', presumably mean precisely that. Culture defines a standard of *worldly* (ie. international) value. Similarly, Raymond Williams and the cluster of critics associated with the so-called 'old left' work across national difference, concerned principally to distinguish class-based cultures. As Hoggart remarks in *The Uses of Literacy*:

If we want to capture the essence of working class life in . . . a phrase, we must say that it is the 'dense and concrete life', a life whose main stress is on the intimate, the sensory, the detailed and the personal. *This would no doubt be true of working-class groups anywhere in the world. . . .* [my emphasis][9]

It is as though unspoken associations between discussion of national culture and some wider sense of a reactionary national*ism* have tempered work on national culture within the spheres in which discussion of cultural 'value' has traditionally taken place. It is, however, significantly mainly within nations subordinated by the onset of a truly multi-national capitalism that debate about the potentially progressive value of a discrete national culture has been raised with much consistency or confidence. Since the late sixties in particular, cultural criticism at the metropolitan or economic 'centre' has tended to work over cultural formations not bracketed so much by Hoggart's ideas of working-class identity, as by some wider, even Universal, theory of ideology. In the eighties, though, the challenge for 'emerging' or 'developing' nations is still to some extent a matter of forming national identities, and the need for cultural criticisms working over their cultures is thus at least partly still to formulate a practice that can accommodate cultural elements within texts, in terms of their specifically national resonances. Only then can the discourses on the national that circulate around and through them start to be opened out. And a central part of such a practice would seem to involve the consideration of these discourses' availability to different national audiences, and some gauging of their possible effect in shaping individual and/or collective national consciousnesses.

To become available as a cultural discourse the text must clearly be re-inserted into an active context, not simply set against, and at a remove from, its 'background'.[10] Traditionally this involved the invocation of an authorial presence, with culture seen as shaping biography, the creative consciousness, the production process, and so becoming implicated as meaning in the text. Latterly, as modernist and structuralist accounts of culture have challenged such notions of authorship, so direct a chain of cultural determination has become much harder to argue. At the same time, industrialised/collaborative forms, such as cinema, have always posed the problem of contextualization in an acute form. Produced commercially for mass consumption, implicated in formula and economies of style and desire, the mediating forces between the text and the cultural have always seemed too insistent in the case of cinema to be conjured away through the invocation of an all-embracing authorial point of origin. The films of the Australian new wave are no exception in this respect. As 'properties' developed pragmatically in an institutional context in which varying (even contradictory) constraints must be met and multiple aspirations enacted, a systematic author-function can only be imposed on film texts with considerable damage to their play of meaning. Similarly, the aspiration to project a national culture must negotiate the economic, industrial, technological and ideological forces that all act upon production, inflecting and qualifying intention. It was such a recognition that led the editorial collective of *Cahiers du Cinéma* to argue that the commercial movie stands in an oblique or 'decentred' relationship with its context:

an artistic product cannot be linked to its socio-historical context according to a linear expressive, direct causality (unless one falls into a reductionist historical determinism) . . . it has a complex, mediated and decentred relationship with its context.[11]

There are suggestions here, perhaps, about how a cultural criticism needs to proceed. Following psychoanalytic criticism's radical displacement of the intending subject, the *Cahiers* editors abandon notions of the text as simply *reflective* of context, and propose a relation based on a more *metaphorical* distance from history and culture. This model sees the conscious discourses of the film as intrinsically suspect, since they must be framed in language and 'scrambled' by the work of the unconscious. As Barthes put it, in the text 'a real motive may be *inverted* into an alibi which contradicts it'.[12] The analysis suggests that just as a text can no longer be read as the deterministic expression of authorial intention, neither can it become a simple point of entry to any national consciousness, since here language is seen as productive of meanings *in itself*, and endlessly runs beyond mere instrumentation.

II

Given the extent to which structuralist criticisms have de-stabilized texts as cultural artefacts, we are perhaps fortunate in having declarations of intention to work with in approaching the new Australian cinema. Australian film-makers have been unusually prepared to state and define intentions, and have clearly often conceived of their own work in directly cultural terms. Very few Australian film-makers define their activity as simply commercial, although many state the ambition to entertain as a central part of their work. At any rate, a certain continuity of aspiration does seem to inform the work of many current Australian film-makers, which is focused in the *Statement of Aims and Intentions* issued by the South Australian Film Corporation (SAFC) in 1975.* Early in the *Statement* SAFC states its intention:

to provide opportunity for Australian artists and craftsmen to develop and express themselves within the film medium, making a positive, creative contribution to the culture, learning and industry of the nation.

Re-emphasizing more general convictions within the industry and elsewhere that representations of the Australian were deficient, SAFC's executive argued for films to 'reflect' Australian culture with 'truth and artistry, showing South Australia to Australians and the world'. Elsewhere they talk of extending 'the horizons of film by researching the effectiveness of existing techniques of production and distribution' and of 'discovering new means of visual communication' through film, so linking in a quite concrete way the pragmatic issues of economics and industry that shaped their activity, and the more directly aesthetic issues that would mould the films and thus trigger the activity of the spectator. It is perhaps the commitment to the reconstruction of that spectator, running across the less heady awareness of the day-to-day difficulty of sustaining production, that has produced films of such value to debates in and around the issue of Australian nationality, by allowing passage onscreen to the complex issues of representation and history, through forms that have avoided alienating the mass audience necessary to sustain production.

In SAFC's terms then, the thrust of the emerging cinema is conceived as a struggle towards greater industrial independence and thus greater authenticity in representations of the national culture. It is a matter of *simultaneously* producing an arresting image of the national culture for projection overseas, and an image for home consumption through which the culture can itself be propagated. Couched in these terms, the new cinema is posed as a loosely reformist impulse, less interesting here for its party-political or class resonances than for the contradictory model of culture it assumes. Fascinatingly the document echoes both Arnold (in its stress on 'truth and artistry') and Williams (a literal reference to the South Australian 'way of life') and binds them together in the conviction that films *can* be produced that will find an audience at home and abroad, and that a suitably prestigious film industry can be sustained as part of a vital film culture at grass roots level, encouraging film-making, film appreciation and research in film history. All of this

---

* Relevant sections of the SAFC *Statement* are reproduced as an Appendix at the end of this essay.

involves considerable contradictions, which the films developing out of SAFC's initiatives and others like them have often found great difficulty in containing. So, not surprisingly, many of the films produced demonstrate varying degrees of commitment to the very idea of representing a specifically national culture.

Many Australian producers have in fact defined their goal as the 'cracking' of the American market, producing low-budget imitations of successful American formula films. Others have acquiesced to different cultural formations as they have assaulted the more international markets of the Art cinema. Non-Hollywood cinemas have often sought to carve out spaces for themselves by posing their products as 'quality' art objects, and the new Australian cinema has repeatedly explored this possibility, often leading to a certain association of the films with an over-determined aestheticism typified by a film such as *Picnic at Hanging Rock* (d. Peter Weir 1975). *Picnic* in fact does seem only intermittently concerned to produce a national reference, offering its fictive interest in landscape, accents, colonial lifestyles, etc. as essentially subordinate to its central thrust, which is more focused on declaring the technical expertise and cultural credentials of its producers. Appropriately then at the level of narrative its project is to marginalize the history of European settlement in Australia within the superior determining categories of Aboriginal and geological history (the film flirts with a disturbing equivalence of these), involved in which is the desire to vault more problematical histories (and thus the contradictions they generate in the present). This ambition is signalled very early on in the film. A party of schoolgirls from Appleyard College, go to picnic at the foot of Hanging Rock on St. Valentine's day 1900. As the group first approaches the rock, their driver Ben Hussey (Martin Vaughan) and the maths mistress accompanying them, Miss McCraw (Vivean Gray) debate its antiquity:

HUSSEY: More than 500 feet high she is. Volcanic of course. Thousands of years old.

McCRAW: A million years old, Mr. Hussey, or thereabouts.

HUSSEY: Yes, that would be right. Thousands. Millions. A devil of a long time anyway, in a manner of speaking.

McCRAW: Only a million years ago. Quite a recent eruption really. The rocks all around. Mount Macedon itself, must be all of 350 million years old. . . . Quite young geologically speaking.

Miss McCraw's victory in the dating-game revises recorded history as a footnote to a pre-historical time-scale that insists on the absurdity of any would-be historical continuum the fiction may fabricate, and thus goes some way towards explaining *Picnic*'s manifest reluctance to sustain any satisfactory historical movement for its characters. Like Ben Hussey the narrative swiftly accedes to Miss McCraw's formulation of history, giving way to the speculative excesses of the *mise en scène*. From the first moment of the party's arrival at the rock the movie is more than content to proceed through a fetishistic invocation of the colours, compositions and textures of early European and Australian 'impressionist' paintings. Almost every frame invites us to consider its organization and motivation, but to celebrate an authorial intervention rather than to identify ourselves as positioned/constituted by the film. *Picnic* offers itself as an impeccable catalogue of visual pleasures displaying the sensual possibilities of the cinematic apparatus operating at a peak of intensity. As such, discourses on the cultural take a back seat, whilst the film offers itself to its audience primarily on the basis of its manifest 'quality' rather than of its positions in relation to the condition of Australian culture. It is rather a film about the state-of-the-art of commercial cinema, whose 'pornographic good taste' perfectly embodies the cultural and commercial double-thinks that underpinned the policies of its producers. Its British distributors were careful to preserve this patina. GTO Films, we are told, 'were careful not to sell it as an Australian film', but presented it more on the basis of its appeal to the supposedly universal values of mild eroticism and European art history.[13]

Picnic, then, works more in relation to the universal model of culture noted in relation to Matthew Arnold than with the ideas of culture I have associated with Williams. Appealing in the first instance to standards of aesthetic value, it takes the codes and strategies of painting, already firmly encoded within the cultural by generations of criticism, as a guarantee of its own status and aspirations. All we might note here is the quite different bases on which the film is likely to circulate within the domestic market, where its particular national reference is likely to function with more insistence than it will overseas. As a result the film is not unavailable for a *national* reading, despite its manifest attempt to transcend debate offered at that level.

III

Perhaps, nonetheless, the dominant strand of thought in the SAFC document goes back to Raymond Williams, since throughout it runs the assumption that some sort of *essential* and specific national culture does exist, only awaiting depiction. Once refurbished and re-vitalized this will secure the population as a continuous identity. Although traditionally elaborated over class-specific cultures, this model does suggest it might be extended into a consideration of national culture. Arguing in a distant but highly comparable national context, John Caughie has suggested that it 'would be the role of a national culture to provide points of identification around which individuals or groups could discover or recognize their [Australian-ness]'.[14] So initially in the Australian context the work of the nationally conscious film-maker might be defined as the process of bringing to the screen those elements of the culture that answer this need to recognize. At its simplest this is partly a process of *substitution* and *revision*, involving the presentation of elements obliterated in the suspect representations that have defined the marketable image in the past, for production interests and audiences on the other side of the world.

Given the very real difficulties involved in getting production off the ground, it's hard not to admire the work of those film-makers engaging consciously with this model of cultural struggle, but for the critic – and as Walter Benjamin and others have usefully reminded us we are all in a sense produced as critics by cinema's regime of viewing, so that our approach becomes one of 'testing' – the strategy does suggest both positive and negative values.[15] Interestingly (and here I need to stretch my definition of the cinematic slightly, to include materials produced for television . . .) some of the most positive instances of cultural revision/substitution are to be found within the developing form of the television mini-series. A series such as *The Dunera Boys* (d. Ben Lewin 1985) works over the question of Australia's cultural identity, by focusing on a particular historical moment at which the boundaries of that identity came under stress. The series details the events surrounding the internment in London of a group of 'foreign' nationals at the start of the Second World War, their transportation to Australia, and subsequent life together in an Australian prisoner of war camp. The series provides little support for the argument that burgeoning multi-nationalism will *necessarily* inhibit idiosyncratic local production. Here the production resources of both time and money that *can* accrue from international pre-sales, the employment of recognizable overseas performers and the promise of 'high' production values combine to create a discursive space in which pressing local questions of history and identity can be articulated.

The value of *The Dunera Boys* stems to some extent from the television series format itself. As a result of the sheer duration of the narrative (some five hours on its transmission in Britain) space is available precisely for the investigation of idiosyncracy. Across the span of the mini-series attitudinal positions are less liable to reduction as shorthand codings of costume, dress, accent or demeanour. Lacking cinema's voyeuristic 'pull', television drama *can* resist the unthinking reconstruction of its protagonists as elements of spectacle. In *The Dunera Boys* the reduced size of the television image impedes the disabling fetishization of the foreign as 'other' that has been such a feature of Australian cinema. What Roland Barthes once complained of as the reactionary 'deprivation' of dominant cinema's *mise en scène* seems less a feature of much recent material especially produced for television. His analysis of the 'irresponsible' representation of the foreign in *The Lost Continent* (d. Michael Carreras 1968) would be harder to argue in relation to television's typically 'restricted' visual style:

The device which produces irresponsibility is clear: colouring the world is always a means of denying it. . . . Deprived of all substance, driven back into colour, disembodied through the very glamour of the 'images', the Orient is ready for the spiriting away which the film has in store for it.[16]

Without the resources of the image to satisfy the spectator's gaze, television typically renews our attention to its image through the regenerative possibilities of the cut (especially the cut 'in' to close-up). Within television's 'regime' of viewing therefore the social world and the history to which it is subject are sometimes less easily displaced into Barthes' 'essences'. When *The Dunera Boys* represents refugees it is not as essences or 'themes of an eternal condition' but rather as subjects of a particular historical conjuncture.

The dispersal and proliferation so characteristic of television's narrative forms is exploited in *The Dunera Boys* to examine and juxtapose the terms of its own cultural analysis. Australia's 'traditional' ties to the 'mother' country are set in their class determinations (the internees' confinement extends because they have been designated as alien by senior British *and* Australian officials); the relationship between multiculturalism and the nation is scrutinized (the internees form an aggregated identity – joined eventually by their gaolers – from a variety of positions, beliefs and practices), and the effectively *intermittent* desirability of forming a fixed identity faced by the cynical exploitations of political expediency are repeatedly stressed (the series ends with the prisoners released, but immediately conscripted into the 'Allied' forces). Where *The Dunera Boys* seems more unusual however, is in its posing of these relatively familiar thematics within a wider discussion of their cultural significance, and a consciousness of the shifting definition of that term. The series works intermittently across the two models of culture I have tried to work around (the prisoners recreate the 'high' culture of Viennese café society within the camp, whilst the camera cuts rhythmically back to display the outback iconography of semi-desert and cloudless sky extending anonymously just beyond the perimeter fence), refusing any easy endorsement of a national consciousness grounded in an unthinking response to supposedly specific national signifiers such as landscape. In *The Dunera Boys*, then, Australians might uncover the historical sources of a contemporary culture that might be mobilized for new acts of recognition and the production of new identities, whilst overseas (especially British) audiences might at least be moved towards a revision of that inhibiting ensemble of

elements (Ned Kelly, Waltzing Matilda . . .) which still somehow manage to designate the Australian, so introducing difference and unsettling
identities. For everyone there is also a reminder of the elements missing
from its examination of Australian culture. As they are travelling by
train across the outback towards the prison camp, Baron von Feldstein
(Joseph Furst) and Alexander Engelhardt (Joseph Spano) have a brief
but significant exchange. Feldstein wonders about the hostile crowds
that had met them on their arrival in Sydney. 'Why were they all
white?', he asks, 'I came all this way, I wanted to see the Australians'.
Half-jokingly Engelhardt replies, 'Maybe they go black in the summer'.
In an instant the series' manifest progressiveness is thrown into a
relative, and productive, perspective.

Interestingly, sustained discourses on the origins and functions of
national consciousness of the kind I have associated with *The Dunera
Boys* seem less a feature of the Australian cinema than they did even five
years ago. As the film industry has turned, since 1980, increasingly
towards the international market, it has been television that has started
to take up the discursive spaces once occupied by films such as *Break
of Day* (d. Ken Hannam 1976) and *In Search of Anna* (d. Esben Storm
1979). A positive instance of progressive cultural revision/substitution
might be provided however by a film such as *Sunday Too Far Away*
(d. Ken Hannam 1975) which systematically details and specifies the
labour of shearing, usually elided by shorthand references to the shearer
as an abstract component of bush mythography. An identity is revised
and a tradition uncovered that can, as in *The Dunera Boys*, be mobilized
for cultural struggles in the present. Yet it is significant that this process
of specification also reveals differences and discontinuities within that
identity (eg. the discussion of whether the visiting shearer from New
South Wales is cheating or not when he leaves his clippers 'running' in
an oil-filled shoe between sheep) which work to prevent any simple
misrecognition by a mass audience, which is thus forced to gauge its
own distance from the representation and its own internal divisions and
differences. Strengthened by an awareness of regional variations, new
images of a national culture are circulated by the film, and a space on
the 'map' of world cinema is secured within which complex acts of
national identification can take place.

IV

In a country deprived for so long of local production facilities through
the 'colonization' of its distribution and exhibition systems, and the
moulding of production for an overseas market, instances such as those
provided by *The Dunera Boys* and *Sunday Too Far Away* can easily

appear as unproblematical breakthroughs. Both works clearly have a considerable value in early consciousness-raising; but both also involve significant problems when their strategies are given a wider historical dimension. Through its frank presentation of outback conditions, *Wake in Fright* (d. Ted Kotcheff 1971), for example, broke with dominant 'epic' representations of landscape familiar from films such as *The Overlanders* (d. Harry Watt 1946) and to that extent bore a potential for a progressive reading at the time of its release. But the kinds of shock-effects involved here inevitably weaken over time, and the cutting edge of the substitution is invariably blunted as the new representation becomes institutionalized through its repetition. For every *Wake in Fright* there is a *Sunstruck* (d. James Gilbert 1972) an insipid comedy starring Harry Secombe as Stanley Evans, a Welsh schoolmaster newly arrived in the outback, inevitably immersed in ritual conflict with the wildlife, and the local stock of comic stereotypes. Here, casual invocations of 'ocker' Australia are presented without even the saving excess of their manifestation in *The Adventures of Barry McKenzie* (d. Bruce Beresford 1972).

Clearly the dividing line between staging the recovery of lost traditions that can illuminate continuing struggles, and the empty celebration of cultural identities that may be nationally-specific but are ultimately confining is a very narrow one. Some critics have challenged the very possibility of remaining on the 'correct' side of the dividing line. In Britain, the celebrated *Screen* 'realism debate' of the mid-seventies focused challenges to the very notion of progressive (national?) realisms, which argued that merely substitute representations, so centred as they must be on individual experience, cannot hope to reveal the wider structural forces that shape the culture. Without re-entering that debate, what seems important here is to note that such critiques place only a slight value within acts of cultural criticism on the expression of identity, and argue instead from other definitions of culture. What polemics against progressive realism did usefully underline was the danger always implicit in the strategy of producing an idealized national identity, concretized through an effective, but limited set of iconographies and stereotypes. Raymond Williams has seen just this regressive tendency as the characteristic way of thinking about culture in the twentieth century:

the idea of a general process of intellectual, spiritual and aesthetic development was applied and effectively transferred to the works and practices which represent and sustain it.[17]

Through the process that Williams describes, a national culture, for example, would be produced as an identity detached from social and ideological formations, as something somehow *given*, as natural as the weather, or more usually in the case of thinking about Australia, as a direct consequence of the interplay with landscape. For Williams the process of 'transference' from culture as process to culture as objects is not in itself regressive; for many other commentators, avoiding such *cul-de-sacs* has required some re-definition of the idea of culture itself. Several recent schools of criticism have attempted this re-definition, arguing that culture may only fleetingly be grasped as an identity and questioning the totalizing vision of national culture as a reservoir of values simply shared across history, class, gender etc. by the subjects of a single nation. Much such work may be traced back to Roland Barthes' earliest criticism, and suggests with John Caughie that culture properly understood involves not a fixity of identity, but is:

continually in process, produced not simply out of the will of the people for self-definition, but out of the contradictions and differences of the discourses and practices that go to make it up.[18]

The implication here is that around the problem of what might constitute the 'correct' or 'appropriate' representation, lies a broader international problem of the perceived relationship between represent-ation and culture which cannot simply be constructed as a matter of expression. This is the area which Barthes opened up in *Mythologies* (1957), when he started to pose cultural formations not as expressed identities, but as hegemonic operations concerned to naturalize and universalize value-systems specific to, and supportive of, only a small section of the society as a whole. After Barthes, therefore, many cultural critics see their activity as a matter of unsettling and exposing these 'naturalizations', contesting the supra-social resonances of the cultural that I've associated with Arnold. Within this model then, the positive representation of culture must describe not a collection of national characteristics or identity traits, but the exploration of the sources and functioning of these elements as they are transformed across history. This involves in Caughie's terms, an opening out of:

the specific contradictions of the historical development of the nation, using contradictions to continuously transform a national identity which was never given, and will never be completed.[19]

Despite the associations of contradiction and transformation with progressive criticisms, and the manifest self-consciousness of so many Australian film-makers of the political dimension of cultural prod-uction, instances of a cinema opening out the issue of culture in this way seem difficult to isolate. One suspects that the reasons are practical and formal as well as directly ideological, since the stress on contradiction in particular seems to imply a substantial revision of the narrative and realist strategies of mainstream cinema. One film that has attempted such a revision however is *Newsfront* (d. Phillip Noyce 1978) which sets out to examine the forces and interests which produce, 'project' and sustain the materials through which national culture is propagated and recognized. The movie presents a sustained discussion of the importance within any act of cultural criticism of a sensitivity to the historical *transformation* of cultural elements, and the means of their production in the past, as well as to their apparent use-value in the present. *Newsfront* attempts this ambitious project through a format that is deceptively simple. The film follows the activities of two rival newsreel companies from 1948 to 1956 and charts the professional and domestic lives of their employees. Personal melodramas of familial conflict are integrated systematically with institutional struggles for authenticity and control, allowing us both an emotional identification with characters acting through the culture, and an awareness of the structural dynamics of which those lives within that culture are an expression.

This juxtaposition is maintained by the film at a number of levels, as it tries to explain the 'decentring' mechanisms which produce, but which are hidden by, articulations of culture as identity. One method involves the re-screening of 'actual' newsreel footage of the period, together with scenes showing the editing and dubbing of that material and various other fragments of 'reconstructed' documentary material supposedly shot by the cameraman within the fiction. By taking the cinematic fragments (the conquest of Everest, the anti-communist purges of the late forties, the arrival of television, the visits of Nixon) and re-integrating them into a history the film starts to de-stabilize the unimpeachability of these documents. This has the effect not only of opening up history as a discourse that is potentially changeable, but also of posing the cultural present as to a large extent fixed by the discourse-producing institutions such as the cinema. *Newsfront* therefore makes no claim to distance itself from these processes, but offers its own discursive activity for our scrutiny, deliberating and hesitating over the cultural discourses it may circulate and the positions it may offer up for identification.

Newsfront's focus is therefore on culture in-the-making and the relationship of film to the production of popular memory. As such it insists on the historical determinations of its own functioning and enacts its own diverse obligations to the needs of the present; the film insists throughout that any act of historiography, whether in print or on celluloid will have what Sylvia Lawson terms a 'patent serviceability' (i.e. that any film history 'will constitute a story which the society needs to be telling itself'[20]) as a series of tensions, disunities and abrupt shifts of time, place and mode of address. Thus developmental linear narrative is superseded by a more episodic structure which starts to depict certain unchanging contradictions (the love-hate relationship with the 'mother' country, the appeal to landscape as emblem in one of the most urbanized cultures on earth, the dubious expediency of relations with the USA, the particular blend of patriotism and socialism characteristic of the Australian radical tradition) within which the culture is lived and experienced. The result is a film which alternates between celebrating the summary fragments of a shorthand Australia (it opens with a montage of newsreel images familiar to many Australian viewers in particular) and a questioning of their adequacy and specificity by posing them against the everyday lives of its protagonists. The past emerges from this process as both a comfort and a threat, and *Newsfront* offers itself to its spectator on the same ambiguous basis.

The confidence of the film is marked throughout by its refusal simply to depict any straightforward cultural identity, as something fixed through supposedly uniform experience and enshrined in objects or attitudes. From the outset the stress is on the mix of cultural traditions that comprise modern Australia. Some of the earliest shots in the film show the arrival of ships in Sydney Harbour bringing immigrants from Europe. One of the film's central characters, Chris, (Chris Haywood) is himself a newly arrived immigrant. And throughout the film we are shown a population in flux; Geoff (Bryan Brown) will leave for England – 'the best place for an ageing radical', and Frank Maguire (Gerard Kennedy) will quit the newsreel company for the greater financial rewards of Hollywood. At points the film seems to crumble into a series of arrivals and departures, leaving the protagonists as endlessly displaced persons desperately trying to form stable identities and social formations in the face of the historical contradictions in which they are cast. Len Maguire (Bill Hunter) spends much of the film trying to reconcile professional 'ethics' with the demands of the cinema institution in which he is situated. At home his family disintegrates as his positioning within a religious order comes into conflict with deeply felt political conviction. Idealism is always compromised; the film casually informs us only sometime after the break-up of his marriage that Len has moved in with Amy (Wendy Hughes), and we are never entirely certain whether the relationship builds from conviction and mutual affections, or simply forms out of inevitability and convenience. At any rate the union offers only a momentary point of stability. Before long Amy is discovered staring at a blank television screen in the middle of the night, reduced to catatonia by the impossibility of realizing an integrated identity, caught in a web of circumstances that deprive her of any position from which to act.

In a sense Amy's fate is one which the film as a whole must struggle hard to avoid. Opening out the contradictions and dynamics of the processes shaping the culture can easily prevent any workable point of identification from forming. *Newsfront* consistently verges on depriving its audience of *any* position at all from which to read it (something which I think the film does ultimately avoid, however) as the systems of coherence that traditionally bound our experience of cinema together are broken by the systematic integration of documentary footage supposedly shot by the cameramen, actual documentary footage culled from the National Film Archive and the 'staged' events of the family melodrama. Our reward for the sense of insecurity this tends to generate is a film which starts to examine different strands of national development, and the work of the cinema in producing a sense of culture across them. From the outset, through its toyings with the figures of post-war film melodrama (the use of racked-focus in the credit sequences, the use of following shots, even its seemingly unmotivated returns from colour to black and white filmstock) the film allows us to enjoy its fascination with the cinema of the past as a bridge across the generation gap, but remains insistently aware of its constraining grip on the present. It de-constructs the 'propaganda' of Griersonian documentary cinema in a similar way, although again taking great relish from the emotional force of, say, the film of the conquest of Everest. In this way, *Newsfront* refuses its spectator the easy identifications that both cinemas used to provide, placing a consistent stress on the inadequacy of any single level of identification within the fiction. Time and again the point-of-view systems, the pattern of looks that usually works to draw us into the diegesis, is shattered by the intrusions of the newsreels. The unity of our placement in the film is so undermined in fact, that the movie as a whole seems to cry out for the voice-of-God narration that we witness Ken (John Dease), Geoff and the rest orchestrating for the newsreels. Yet at the same moment, *Newsfront* stresses the extent to which the accompaniment of such voice-over narration works to order and contain the contradictions often thrown up by the image track (the Damien Parer footage comes close to exposing these, nonetheless). The result is an uneasy mixture of discontinuities within the fiction that threaten the invisibility, and thus much of the authority, of the narrative discourse.

It is somewhat ironic, then, that *Newsfront* ends by bringing its documentary and fictional addresses together. Len's final assertive walk out of the frame, sticking to principles, refusing to sell out for the fast dollar, is cunningly transformed into a Pathe News-style montage. The final end-credit centres the Cinetone News logo on *our* screen. *Newsfront* itself, like the newsreels within it, has been a necessary fiction, one of the stories that we need to be telling ourselves at this historical moment, an act productive of culture in the present as well as an expression of the culture of the past.

V

As they stand here, the various cultural initiatives I have described seem to propose marked aesthetic shifts away from the standards of the commercial cinema (large-budget films dependent upon massive international audiences, constructed largely around spectacle, with appropriately 'high production values', etc.) which they seek to displace from domestic movie theatres. In the Australian context therefore, controlled as it still is by the major American conglomerates and private finance, we may expect to find a cinema working with either model of culture only in compromised form. The struggle towards difference (conceived either as essence or system in contradiction) is always to be balanced against the requirement of similarity forced upon Australian producers by the foreign interests defining the economics of exhibition at home, and by the need to secure an overseas (specifically American) sale for all but the lowest-budget of releases. Thus an 'Australian' cinema cannot be isolated through the tabulation of a particular set of textual strategies or elements of representation, since the impulse to build a national film industry militates against any over-determination of thematics too closely fixed by their national reference.

Until the early seventies, most even vaguely nationally conscious producers defined their response to the contradictions involved here as a matter of *balance*. The reflex, conditioned by the long experience of Australia's trade relations with Europe and North America, was to seek a balance between these different self-interests across the text. The production proceeded through the meeting and arbitration of contradictory needs at as many points as possible. What the new Australian cinema has really 'achieved' since then relates in part to this idea of balance. It might perhaps be argued that at their best the films of the new wave have contributed positively to debates through and about Australian culture precisely by breaking the terms of this industrial balancing act, opening up the films as discourses on the international determinations of cinema within dominant ideologies, and (more specifically) as commentaries on the functions of the cinema as it has operated to shape social practice and national identity for Australians over history. This achieved, the films open themselves to productive reading *through* their 'compromises' as spaces through which conflicting determinations pass, so that formal and aesthetic struggles within the films can become available as traces of the cultural struggles that surround and constitute them.

APPENDIX

Reproduced below, by kind permission, are relevant sections of a statement of *Aims and Intentions* drawn up by members of the Executive Committee of the South Australian Film Corporation in 1975.

AIMS AND INTENTIONS

Aims: To establish a viable film industry within this State;

to reflect our way of life with truth and artistry showing South Australia to Australians and the world;

to provide opportunity for Australian artists and craftsmen to develop and express themselves within the film medium, making a positive, creative contribution to the culture, learning and industry of the nation;

to extend the horizons of film by researching the effectiveness of existing techniques of production and distribution and attempting to discover new means of visual communication;

to promote and assist the distribution, exhibition and appreciation of the cinema as an art and as a vital part of education, mass media and entertainment.

Intentions: To liaise with all State Departments and private industry to promote therein effective use of film, encourage and supervise the contracted production of films most suited to their needs and the demands of the intended audiences;

to produce, through contracted film companies, our own productions aimed at high artistic merit and experimentation;

to stimulate the existing film organizations and encourage the establishment of new commercially viable companies by investing, guaranteeing loans, locating commercial investment or co-production in feature and documentary films being predominantly produced within South Australia using predominantly Australian talent. Such financial involvements to be examined closely for their commercial viability with a definite expectation of profit from such investment;

to establish effective distribution and exhibition of films within the State, throughout Australia and overseas, using other government and commercial agencies where possible. Particular emphasis will be placed on the operation of the educational documentary film library and the establishment of regional centres throughout the State. New methods of distribution and exhibition will be researched and implemented;

to foster film appreciation and circulate information. A reference library of film books, magazines and scripts will be established for specialist use. Research findings will be published and assistance given to the publication of film books. Encouragement and assistance will be given to film societies, festivals, school, university and "underground" film-makers within the State. Strong liaison will be established with educational agencies so that film-making and film appreciation will be encouraged amongst both teaching staff and students.

NOTES

1. See Brian Baxter's preview article, 'Wizards from Oz' in the *Radio Times*, 9–15 November 1985, pp.11–13.
   For a fuller version of this skeletal history see the closing chapters of Graham Shirley and Brian Adams, *Australian Cinema: The First Eighty Years*, Melbourne: Angus & Robertson and the Currency Press, 1983. esp. pp.217–278. David Stratton's *The Last New Wave*, Angus & Robertson, Melbourne, 1980. esp. pp.1–20 provides a shorter outline of the cinema during the period of the so-called film 'revival' in Australia.
2. See Cairns Craig's review article, 'Nation and History', *Cencrastus*, No. 19 (Winter 1984) pp.13–16.
3. Quoted in Graham Shirley and Brian Adams, op. cit. p. 251.
4. See T.S. Eliot's *Notes Towards the Definition of Culture*, Faber & Faber, London, 1972. esp. pp.21–34 and 50–66.
5. See Arnold's *Culture and Anarchy*, included in *Matthew Arnold: Poetry and Prose*, Rupert Hart-Davis, London, 1954. My quotation appears on p. 494.
6. See Raymond Williams, *The Long Revolution*, Penguin, Harmondsworth, 1975, p. 57.
7. Ibid., p. 58.
8. I refer here to Richard Hoggart's *The Uses of Literacy*, Pelican Harmondsworth, 1963; E.P. Thompson's *The Making of the English Working Classes*, Pelican, Harmondsworth, 1982; and Roland Barthes's essay 'Myth Today' in *Mythologies*, Paladin, London, 1976.
9. Richard Hoggart, op. cit., p. 105.
10. See Raymond Williams, *Culture and Society 1780–1950*, Pelican, Harmondsworth, 1979, p. 49.
11. See John Ford's *Young Mr Lincoln*: A Collective Text by the editors of *Cahiers du Cinema*, originally published in *Cahiers du Cinema*, No. 223, 1970. The article is usefully translated and reprinted in *Screen*, Vol. 13, No. 3 (Autumn 1972) pp.15–56, and also appears in *Screen Reader One*, S.E.F.T., London, 1977, pp. 113–51. My quotation appears on p. 115 of this reprinting.
12. I draw here on Barthes's early critiques of the orthodoxies of literary criticism represented by his work in *Critical Essays*, Northwestern University Press, Evanston, Illinois, 1972.
13. Quoted in David Stratton, op. cit. p. 73.
14. See John Caughie's essay, 'Scottish Television: What Would it Look Like?' in Colin McArthur (ed), *Scotch Reels: Scotland in Cinema and Television*, British Film Institute, London, 1982, p. 116. I am very grafeful to John Caughie for reading and commenting on sections of this essay during the course of its preparation.
15. See Walter Benjamin's essay, 'The Work of Art in the Age of Mechanical Reproduction' in *Illuminations*, Fontana, London, 1973, pp. 230–1.
16. See Roland Barthes's review essay 'The Lost Continent' in *Mythologies*, Paladin, London, 1976, pp. 94–5.
17. See Raymond Williams, *Keywords: A Vocabulary of Culture and Society*, Fontana, London, 1976, p. 80.

18. John Caughie, op. cit., p. 117.
19. Ibid., p. 117.
20. See Sylvia Lawson, 'Towards Decolonization: Some Problems and Issues for Film History in Australia', in *Film Reader*, No. 4 (Summer 1979) p. 64.

10 Post-war Australian Painting: An Interpretation

Sam Smiles

Art history, like any other discipline, has witnessed changes in methodology that reflect wider shifts in critical discourse relevant to society as a whole. It is therefore of more than historiographic interest to witness the move away from the formalist interpretations of twentieth-century art that had such currency from the 1950s to the late 1970s towards a view of art and art-practice that locates meaning not simply in the formal constituents of a work of art, but also in its wider social context of production and reception, of mediation and presentation, of function and value: all those factors that confer meaning on a work of art in a richer and more inclusive analysis than the often arid taxonomy of formalist description.

It seems likely, given this development in art history, that much of the history of twentieth-century art will need to be rewritten; hitherto forgotten or marginalized artists will have to be critically rehabilitated; aspects of avant-garde orthodoxy will need to be re-examined and assumptions about artistic progress heavily qualified. In addition, it is possible to detect two important pressures in the art world that are having a marked effect on art historical writing concerning the twentieth century; first the recognition that artists working outside the so-called mainstream areas (e.g. artists in non-European or non-North American countries, or self-trained artists within those countries) cannot by that fact alone be ignored; and second, the revival (or perhaps reselection) of figuration as a means of expressing human emotion in art, thereby recovering for art a more central and important position within society as a whole. All of these factors point to the recuperation of Australian painting from something approaching almost total neglect in this country. Indeed, given that certain aspects of Australian art-practice present themselves more nakedly than they might in a more prolific artistic culture, it may be that Australian painting and its position within Australian society could act as a paradigm for the analysis of art within Europe and the United States. In this essay I hope to deal with some of the issues concerning the development of Australian painting

143

since the Second World War, and more particularly with the discourse concerning the land, mythology and abstraction that seems to run like a connecting thread through much of the more significant work produced in the last forty years. Of course, I must stress at this point that my analysis will necessarily have a Euro-centric bias, discerning too easily a homogeneity where variety exists for Australians, linking the specific qualities of Australian painting too readily with developments in Europe and America. But perhaps there is some value in allowing outsiders to comment on the salient features of a terrain whose inhabitants (rightly) concentrate on the richness of its topography; for only an outsider can experience the surprise and the excitement of discovering what for others had been there all along.

It is something of a truism that landscape painting has dominated Australian art, and that the land itself has dominated the Australian imagination, to an extent rarely seen elsewhere. Certainly as regards painting this can be explained by the fact that the growth of an Australian school of artists coincided with an immense growth of and interest in landscape painting in England and Europe. Joseph Lycett, Conrad Martens, Eugen von Guérard and Louis Buvelot – to take four key figures working between 1800 and 1880 – encoded and so made available (i.e. 'real') their adopted land in ways precisely analogous to their European contemporaries. But in just the same way as there was no one particular mode for portraying all landscapes in England or France or Germany, so in Australia we witness a variety of procedures employed to address a variety of Australian landscapes; some of these landscapes proved amenable to representation, some recalcitrant, and these latter sometimes helped to 'force' stylistic innovation on artists. What is significant in this process, however, is that by at least the 1880s the 'separateness' of the Australian visual environment from anything witnessed in Europe was being seen as its *key* quality, so that notions of 'typical' Australian and European landscapes and landscape painting procedures could be contrasted in the interests of an identity not simply for Australian artists, but for the country as a whole. (That this interpretation of landscape painting falsifies the situation holding between Australian and European art and landscape and begs important questions concerning representation, naturalism and realism is irrelevant here.)

The formation of the Heidelberg School in the 1880s under Tom Roberts and Arthur Streeton, their choice of motif and handling, their insistence on the 'Australianness' of their imagery, may be seen as the crystallization of landscape as a national symbol; and their success in this endeavour is witnessed by the continuation of such imagery into the first three decades of the twentieth century. As Basil Burdett wrote in 1929:

Whatever may be the final judgement upon the works of this initial fifty years of Australian landscape painting, there can never be any doubt as to the reality of its accomplishment in revealing to Australians the landscape of their country and providing them with formulas and conventions by which they might perceive it in terms of beauty, where once they had seen it with the eyes of indifference, of apathy, even of distaste.[1]

Given such a cultural, almost ideological, loading, landscape painting came to assume an importance quite different from its position in Europe, where formal manipulation of the motif did not construct a body of beliefs about the land (and by implication the state and its inhabitants) in anything like as strong a way. And equally, given the importance of this attitude to landscape painting, it is less surprising that modernist art practice, in European terms at any rate, was sporadic and unpopular in Australia until after the Second World War. For the European development through Fauvism to Cubism and Abstraction had been a progressive devaluation of specific qualities associated with the visible world and the elevation of pictorial qualities in place of anecdotal ones. True, German Expressionist tendencies in the 1910s and Surrealism in the 1920s and 1930s did in fact move back from an excessive concentration on form at the expense of subject matter (and, as indices of an alternative tradition, were of very great importance for Australian artists in the 1950s), but Modernism was so closely identified with France in the early part of the century, that it is doubtful whether the first Australian modernists could have looked to any other centre. It makes sense, indeed, to say that artists like Ronald Wakelin, Grace Cossington-Smith and Roy de Maistre are important less for their pioneering response to European modernist tendencies than for the very partiality of their achievement and the frustration of their careers. (De Maistre left Australia for good in 1923.)

When a successful modernist art practice emerged in Australia after the second world war it was, perhaps inevitably, heavily involved with landscape imagery; and, like contemporary developments in the United States, was able to encompass different areas of experience from the European model precisely because the leadership of European art had been disrupted by the war. That disruption – in the sense of breaking a continuity as well as in the physical dispersion of European avant-garde artists – called the old cultural hegemony of Europe into question. The Australian artist of the 1940s and 1950s had one crucial advantage over the previous generation: modernism itself had altered its definition to something more elastic and pluralist. In that moment, before the new hegemony of American art practice began to dictate the terms of post-war culture, the new Australian art was born. In these altered circumstances it was possible for the first time to marry old concerns about landscape and national identity with a technique that was aggressively modern yet independent of European exempla.

The new landscape imagery that was produced in these years dealt with a land of extremes, of menacing forests, arid wilderness, Aboriginal otherness; replacing the qualified pastoralism of the Heidelberg School and their twentieth-century inheritors with a vision of geographical desolation that often stands as an emblem for spiritual desolation as well. These post-war landscapes are less an image of potential – the possibility of the bush being settled or at least understood – than a repository for abandoned hopes and the stark refutation of optimism. Drysdale's small holders scratch a harsh and meagre existence from a landscape shorn of promise; Nolan's Kelly or Mrs. Fraser act out their archaic dramas against an uncaring background; while Boyd and Tucker delve deep below the visible surface of the Australian landscape to find there the demons and forces of evil that had been exorcised from Europe. This was no straightforward reworking by modernist artists of Heidelberg imagery; it was the deliberate selection and presentation of a new vision.

In this production of the 'archetypal' or 'essential' Australia these artists, and others like Noel Counihan and Lawrence Daws, chose to locate the otherness of Australia less in particular qualities of light and space than in its capacity for mythic presentation as a place of primitive imaginings, heroic gestures, symbolic activities – all that human potential unavailable to old world countries buried under the civilization of centuries. These pictures thus link crucially with currents of thought – Nihilism and Existentialism especially – common to many artists working in the same period in Europe and the United States. But whereas American Abstract Expressionists had returned to the primacy of myth by emptying their canvasses of literal meanings, Australian artists preferred to paint the emptiness itself, the hollow inside of a continent whose civilized litoral masks the terrors of primal existence. This concentration on myth and archetype needs some further examination, for it is not the least remarkable thing about this generation of Australian painters that, although working on broadly similar lines to the Abstract Expressionists in their attitudes to painting as a social activity, their means (especially their retention of figuration at a time when most artists world-wide were overwhelmed by Abstract Expressionist practice) and their achievement represent an alternative to the procession of 'isms' beginning to stem from America. An alternative that is coming to assume greater and greater importance as our viewpoint lengthens.

American Abstract Expressionists, having ingested something of the Surrealists' belief in the psychic functioning of the art object, were prone to the use of mythical or archetypal titles for their work in the early 1940s, some of them retaining this direct appeal to commonly-held beliefs until well into the 1950s. Well-known examples of this tendency include Jackson Pollock's *The She-Wolf* and *Pasiphae* (both 1943) and *Totem I* (1944), Adolph Gottlieb's *The Rape of Persephone* (1943) and *The Seer* (1950), Mark Rothko's *Syrian Bull* (1943) and *Entombment* (1946), Barnett Newman's *Vir Heroicus Sublimus* (1951) and *Ulysses* (1952) and Willem de Kooning's *Excavation* (1950). The reasons for this strategy, both of work (private myth expressed via the painted surface) and of presentation (public myth shared via an ambiguous painted surface), were clearly announced by the participating artists, and have been the subject of much recent analysis.[2] In essence it seems that many Abstract Expressionists were concerned to locate their work in a non-partisan context, such that notions of national style or political adherence became irrelevant. (That such a stance speaks volumes about their own relationship to nationality and politics need not detain us here.) The most direct way to cut through specific meanings in art was to appeal to levels of understanding that transcended such localized readings of the art work. As Barnett Newman claimed in 1948:

We are reasserting man's natural desire for the exalted, for a concern with our relationship to the absolute emotions. . . . We are creating images whose reality is self evident and which are devoid of the props and crutches that evoke associations with outmoded images, both sublime and beautiful. We are freeing ourselves of the impediments of memory, association, nostalgia, legend, myth, or what have you, that have been the devices of Western European painting.[3]

Thus Myth, in the general sense of humankind's tendency towards the creation and elaboration of myths, could be used to short-circuit the power of the particular localized myth ossified into restrictive systems of belief.

Australian painters, in stark contrast, used myth in quite different ways. Here the very specificity of imagery effected a vigorous relationship to the Australian landscape and Australian history; its discoverers, settlers and citizens are placed in various relations to the landscape (usually uneasy or precarious ones it should be noted), relations that are further reinforced by the paint-handling itself: quite literally incorporating the figures into the landscape. Unlike their American contemporaries Australian painters rarely offered easy (or seemingly easy) identifications with classical myth or European culture; the context was resolutely Australian and demanded knowledge of that society and its history for an adequate reading. Although careful scrutiny of the pictures might reveal similarities between Australian and European experience and myth, such features had to be achieved by the viewer rather than absorbed without effort as part of a well-understood 'common heritage'. Equally, even in pictures with ostensible non-

Australian subject matter, such as Arthur Boyd's *Nebuchadnezzar* series, the location of the subject in a landscape whose essential topography lies outside European experience wrenches that subject out of its familiar context to reclaim it for new cultural uses. Paradoxically, this incorporation of myth into the Australian landscape does not act as a bridge between old and new world cultures, but asserts their separation at the moment of closest proximity; for whereas an Australian viewer may witness this use of landscape with something of the equanimity we imagine to have been the case in the reception of topographically 'incorrect' mythical or religious landscapes in the Renaissance, for a European such appropriations of old world culture can never seem 'natural' or 'unproblematic' unless a supreme effort is made to understand the landscape itself.

The transition from Euro-centric modernism to Australian myth-making is nowhere better exemplified than in the career of Sidney Nolan in the 1940s. In an important recent article[4] Ian Burn has demonstrated the complexity of Nolan's reaction to modernism in the early 1940s, especially in the Wimmera landscapes, where a specific critique of both European modernist practice and the tradition of Australian landscape painting was developed. Yet, if Nolan's assertion of contemporary Australia in such landscape imagery represents a radical revision of the landscape tradition, it is difficult to see his investigations of Ned Kelly, Mrs Fraser and Burke and Wills as anything other than a retreat from such complexities to a form of painting that would henceforth incorporate myth as a constituent element and so reinforce cultural stereotypes at the expense of the less glamorous Australia of the Wimmera paintings. It is as though Nolan had decided to abandon the contemporary situation – the mechanization of farming, better communications and transport – in favour of the continuity underlying the received version of Australian culture; a continuity that demanded the re-invocation of Australian icons for each generation. Drysdale's paintings of the early 1940s had demonstrated the vitality of imagery that had its origins in the nineteenth century literary tradition (e.g. *The Drover's Wife*) although its realization in paint partook of a modernist aesthetic. Now Nolan, as it were, leap-frogged over him to reclaim the founding and settlement myths – a sort of white Dreamtime – for that same aesthetic. And although these later paintings still offer a complex critique of European and American modernism this element is less present to spectators by the very potency of their imagery. Nolan's subject matter pre-determines the reception of these pictures to such an extent that no really satisfactory account of their formal invention has yet been offered; neither has there appeared an adequate treatment of their place within post-war painting world-wide. For example, to call the figures in the Kelly series grotesque, primitive or clumsy is but a partial description that depends entirely on the figurative strength of these images; seen in terms of pure form (the characteristic analysis applied to American or European painting) these same figures function as areas of flat, virtually unmodulated pigment contrasted with the variegated surface of the rest of the painting: a procedure that reminds one of Hans Hofmann's insertion of rectangular slabs of colour within a variegated colour-field. (*The Camp* (1946) is probably the most dramatic example of these formal relations, but they are vital for the tension seen also in *Glenrowan* (1945), *Glenrowan* (1946) and *Mrs Reardon at Glenrowan* (1946).) The sophisticated use of naive painting practice has been one of the recurrent features of twentieth-century art (and Nolan is on record concerning his liking for the paintings of Rousseau), but given the cultural context of Australian painting finding its voice *apart* from 'mainstream' modernism – a quest much bound up with post-war confidence, and economic strength – Nolan's use of a mock-naive style develops his critique of modernism from the measured detachment of the Wimmera paintings into a self-ironic, sardonic commentary on modernism and the image of Australia. (A comparison with de Kooning's *Woman II* (1952) may help to elucidate this element within Nolan's early painting practice. Both painters incorporate a 'primitive' figuration, but de Kooning's melding of naive and learned elements is held together by a sophisticated overall facture as opposed to Nolan's deliberately crude *contrast* in handling and his use of an almost anti-art style.)

It is, however, precisely this masking of sophistication by an aggressive mock-naivity that gives Nolan's work of the 1940s and early 1950s such importance for the development of much subsequent Australian painting. His achievement might be characterized as having legitimized a modernist approach to art by presenting it as intrinsically home-grown (and thus free of the taint of European modernism) and also supremely capable of portraying the essential Australian myths in all their complexity and abiguity. And, at the risk of over-emphasizing Nolan's importance, it is possible to see much of the work produced in the 1940s and 1950s as exploiting the same rich seam. Whether working out of 'figurative' Melbourne (Nolan, Tucker, Boyd, Pugh) or 'abstract' Sydney (Olsen, Passmore) a tendency developed in which imagery was pushed towards non-specific, multi-layered meaning, while abstraction was invested with figurative connotations – a declaration of 'both/and' as opposed to the 'either/or' that dominated painting practice in Europe and the United States. It is unclear whether this amplitude of approach came about in response to the need for myth-making pictures or whether such investigations were the result of a multi-valent practice; but it resulted in a body of work that stands in an oblique relation to much that was going on outside Australia, both in terms of its formal

manipulation and its subject matter. Much of this latter was concerned
with the mythic portrayal of Australia, a tendency best represented in
the paintings of Albert Tucker and Arthur Boyd but including also such
crucial works as Jon Molvig's *Ballad of A Dead Stockman* series, the
landscapes of Lawrence Daws, Ian Fairweather's hermetic images and
the graphic memory traces of John Olsen. These artists did not
constitute a group, they shared no manifesto, they span a wide range of
approach and attitude; yet a comparison between the two most seemingly opposed artists, Olsen and Boyd, reveals their common concern
with the articulation of non-literal meaning through imagery. Thus
Olsen's tendency towards expressionist *brio* is qualified by a need to
hint at memory and association via discrete areas of symbolic or
figurative reference; whereas Boyd's images, which at first seem to be
clearly defined, often lose this coherence under a welter of paint,
enmeshing the figures in a force field of purposeful yet barely represent-
ational thrusts and counter-thrusts, thereby gaining an enriching ambiguity.

     In all of these artists two key features seem to characterize their work.
First, a critique of the abstraction/figuration split that exercized the
art-world of Europe and the United States; a critique that resulted in
paintings that insist both on their purely formal means and on their
objectification outside the canvas in experience and emotion. Second, a
concern with public meanings in art (usually expressed by what I have
called Australian myths) that located their act practice within fictive or
actual notions of nationhood and culture, thus precipitating an Australian identity out of the undifferentiated flux of universal myth. Yet with
the signal exception of Peter Booth, it seems that this mode of practice
should be associated with that generation of Australian painters born in
the 1920s and coming to prominence in the immediate post-war era.
The pattern of Australian painting since then has been more hetero-
geneous in aims and methods, more open to American influence, less
concerned with producing a rider to the consensus of world art. The
reasons for these changes have a lot to do with the growing internationalism of the art market itself and the need to develop a product
that could attain financial reward outside Australia, whose market for
art must of necessity be comparatively small, given the total population.
In this regard it is significant that Nolan's generation formed their styles
at a time when the war restricted art sales to Australia alone, and that
most of them felt impelled to emigrate temporarily or permanently from
the late 1940s onwards. But, market forces apart, it may be that this
change in approach has much to do with the changes in Australian
society and culture that have taken place since the war. With increased
material confidence and a Pacific sphere of influence, with the rapid
increase in urbanization and the development of efficient commu-

Plate 1: Rock engraving is one of the oldest art forms in Australia. This engraving site at Mootwingee is already showing signs of deterioration resulting from fracturing of the rock face.

Plate 2: Kakadu National Park has some fine examples of the x-ray style of rock painting. This painting is a representation of one of the mythological beings.

Plate 3: Stencil art at Carnarvon Gorge. The scratches in the rock surface (centre left) are evidence of an abortive attempt to remove part of the art face for a souvenir.

Plate 4: This boardwalk at Carnarvon Gorge is an extensive structure designed to enhance the visitor's view of the art while keeping them away from the art face.

Plate 5: Sidney Nolan. The Camp 1946 (Enamel on composition board 89.5 × 121.5 cm). Art Gallery of New South Wales.

Plate 6: Arthur Boyd. Nebuchadnezzar on fire falling over a waterfall *c.* 1968–71 (oil on canvas 183.5 × 175.9 cm). Gift of Catherine Palmer. Art Gallery of New South Wales.

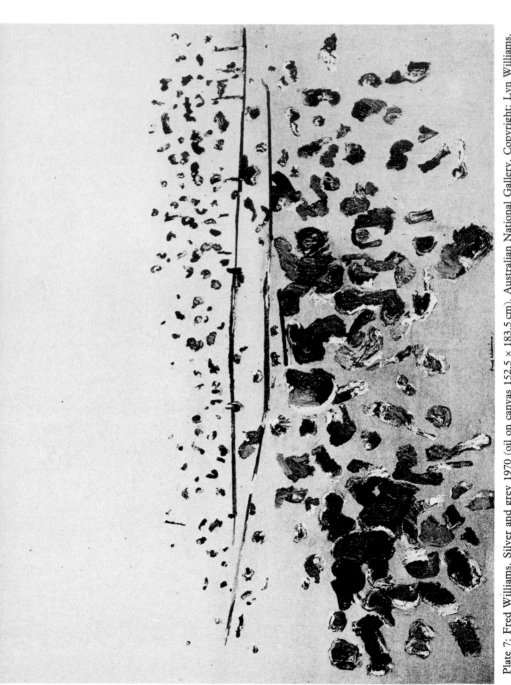

Plate 7: Fred Williams. Silver and grey 1970 (oil on canvas 152.5 × 183.5 cm). Australian National Gallery. Copyright: Lyn Williams.

nications, with new immigrants reconstituting the image of Australians from British descent to something less closely defined, with all these factors a new self-determined identity for Australia has developed. And with this new identity the need has disappeared or weakened for a Dead Stockman, a Kelly or an Australian Nebuchadnezzar, investing with mythic overtones feelings about the society and the land. A landscape of menace and difficulty, shot through with expressionist excess and heroic potential, has become a fragile environment needing protection; the role model function of the heroic pioneer or outlaw has been replaced by urban-rooted values; the land, in short, has been stripped of its potential to function as the stage for scenes of mystery and human endeavour. Only in Australian film does the old menace, alienness and weirdness of the land survive.

In the landscapes of Fred Williams it is possible to detect that pivotal movement from mythic presentation to a less charged response; although as I shall argue, it would be an oversimplification to see Williams's landscapes as devoid of emotion or expressive selectivity of vision. Like Olsen, his work lies poised between the poles of abstraction and representation, but whereas Olsen pushes landscape imagery into a frantic recovery of oneiric fantasy and memory, Williams's paintings are presented with such stability that his often violent paint handling is locked into a composition of utter stasis: the painterly gesture diminished through repetition and scale. Williams's pictorial strategy is thus analogous to the evacuation of the Australian landscape's heroic qualities and is also reminiscent of the cool irony displayed in the Minimalist canvasses that called into question the histrionic excesses of Abstract Expressionism, working with repetition or a uniform colour-field to concentrate on the painted surface rather than any emblematic or iconic quality the imagery might possess. Yet, in the same way as aspects of Nolan's practice seem to have offered an alternative to American developments, so Williams's paintings gain much of their impact by fusing concerns that were deemed antagonistic across the Pacific. Even at their most abstract Williams's pictures are deeply involved with place and the response to place, and so continue the central debate in Australian painting concerning attitudes to the land. Even at their most naturalistic the intellectual concerns of the artist-as-composer dictate the organization of form with a lucidity of presentation every bit as refined as the most rigorous post-painterly abstraction. Furthermore Williams's attitude to place, his preferred landscape type, his response to natural phenomena must be emphasized as placing his art firmly within the tradition of mythic presentation. For, although his landscapes lack the heroic dimensions found in his immediate predecessors, they are manifestly concerned with portraying the 'otherness' of landscape, its intractability, range, scale and monotony in contrast to the malleable tight-knit, varieform cities it invests. Whether identified with a title or not, Williams's generalizing art gives his pictures an air of being about the quintessence of Australian landscape. His typical subject-matter is shown from an aspect that insists on the irrelevance of topography compared with the scale of the scene in view; we are presented with framed portions of a landscape that we know extends far beyond the confines of the canvas, as though only through this piecemeal portrayal and a rigorous discipline in its organization can we comprehend any of it at all. Whereas Nolan had used the landscape to act out heroic dramas, Williams's paintings locate heroism in the act of perception, in the human intelligence bringing under control a landscape quite foreign to human culture.

The histories of post-war painting in Europe and America are in the process of a major revision. The triumphal parade of -ism after -ism, further refining and re-refining the means of abstraction from the 1940s to the 1960s, the nonconformist gestures of Pop Art, Minimalism and Conceptual Art – all of these critical tags and labels are now open to considerable scrutiny; a scrutiny largely instigated by the alternative tradition implied in the widespread return to figuration that has emerged from the mid 1970s. Western art critics now speak glibly of the 'crisis' in art, the 'failure' of modernism and the 'bankruptcy' of avant-garde practice – united one and all by a feeling that art empty of human content and bound up only with itself and the art market was and is doomed to sterility. Art styles and artists that failed to satisfy the critical discourse developed out of one form of modernist practice are being reclaimed from obscurity in Europe and America to serve the needs of the new pluralist histories. Many critics are presently demanding that artists paint pictures imbued with meaning, open to a wide acceptance and public understanding, located in shared experience and common knowledge. Such writers would do well to examine the history of Australian painting since the war.

NOTES

1. In *Australia Landscape Painters of Today*, Art In Australia Ltd, Sydney, 1929; quoted in Ian Burn *Popular Melbourne Landscape Painting Between the Wars*, Bendigo Art Gallery, 1982.
2. See in particular Serge Guilbaut *How New York Stole the Idea of Modern Art*, University of Chicago Press, 1983.
3. Barnett Newman 'The Sublime Is Now' in *The Ides of Art, Six Opinions on What is Sublime in Art?* Tiger's Eye (New York), No. 6, December 15, 1948, p. 53.
4. Ian Burn 'Landscape and Life, Nolan and the Australian tradition', *The Age Monthly Review*, August 1984, pp. 18–21.

11 Surprise, Surprise: Australia and the Visual Arts 1980–1985

David Bromfield

In 1980 the visual arts in Australia seemed to be on the edge of a depression. The Whitlam years had given a great boost to visual arts of all kinds. They had brought the first artists' grants from the newly-formed Visual Arts Board of the Australia Council, and marked the awareness of the role of the visual arts in the Australian community as a whole. The chief beneficiaries of this new pattern of support were established artists in the traditional media, particularly painters. However, State and Federal funds also encouraged the growth of a whole range of 'alternative' art practices which had played their part in the changes in Australian culture during the 1970s. Above all, there had been a major initiative in setting up a series of well-funded courses in Fine Art throughout Australia which had acted as a major new form of patronage.

By 1980 however, Government funding had declined. Individuals and institutions were feeling the pinch. Only the most established of commercial galleries, such as Barry Stern and Macquarie in Sydney, Tolarno in Melbourne and Ray Hughes in Brisbane could be sure of a survival based on the selling power of their most famous artists. Corporate patronage, too, seemed at a low ebb. One might have concluded that, after a brief period of self-assertion, Australian artists and the art scene were returning to their traditional role of second-hand dealers for art ideas and styles from elsewhere. Yet during the next five years, the very opposite was to happen. Australian artists were to cease looking to achievement in the overseas art world as the only way to develop their careers. An Australian art audience was to develop which had a much more subtle appreciation of the achievements of Australian artists both past and present. The work of Daniel Thomas, the Curator of the Australian Collection at the Australian National Gallery (which opened in 1982) was to play a leading role in this development.*

---

* Daniel Thomas is now Director of the Art Gallery of South Australia, Adelaide.

Access to major international exhibitions had always been very difficult for Australians. The Art Gallery Directors' Council, which had been formed with the aim of remedying this situation, collapsed after one great success, *The Revolutionary Decades* in 1980, an exhibition of Art of the French Revolution coordinated by Virginia Spate. This brought early nineteenth-century painting to Australia for the first time. The National Gallery was to set itself the task of remedying this situation with notable success. However, in 1980 the best of art, traditional and contemporary, could only be seen overseas and Australians had no option but to travel.

At this time it was still common for painters to see their future only in New York. A panel convened in 1980 by *Art and Australia*, which was then the only visual arts magazine in the country, agreed in general that the break-up of international Modernism was somehow permitting Australians to develop diverse forms of visual arts. Nonetheless, the idea of a 'mainstream' art centred on New York was a very powerful one in Australia. In 1981 the high priest of the mainstream, Clement Greenberg, was listened to respectfully by Paul Taylor when he suggested that:

One big disadvantage you have in this country might be remoteness, though I am not so sure of that – but you do not have enough people here and somehow that's important.... I'm talking about the whole country. You don't have enough millionaires either – neither absolutely nor proportionately.[1]

Rudi Fuchs, the leading European curator of contemporary art, voiced similar sentiments in 1982 at the Sydney Biennale. He gave an address which concluded with the assertion that the centre of Western culture would always remain in Europe. Australia, he thought, was about as far away from things as you could get and Australian artists had better face up to this. By 1982 though, these attitudes were not acceptable to most of his audience and he faced a vigorous barrage of questions. The very idea of a specific centre for contemporary culture was no longer acceptable.

The early 1980s have seen a series of major international retrospective exhibitions in Australia, including Kandinsky, Picasso and Phillip Guston. They have also seen the development of an independent Australian art with a large body of work and unique stylistic concerns, vocabulary and imagery. As in many other areas, the clichés of Australian imagery have gone along with the dependence of Australian styles on overseas models. A new art practice has arisen which speaks directly to contemporary Australian experience. There isn't a single kangaroo or dead sheep in sight. In 1984, exhibitions such as *An Australian Accent* at PS1 in New York, and *Anzart* at the Edinburgh Festival, were successful on their own terms rather than on those of international curatorial fashion. Australians have found the money and commitment to bring this about despite hard times, and they appear to be willing to continue doing so. Moreover, unlike many of their European and American colleagues, Australian artists still think of art as a positive way to spend their time. Many are prepared to work for less than a minimum income in order to produce first-rate art. The Australian community shares these values. A 1985 study of attitudes to the arts in New South Wales by Professor David Throsby, an economist from Macquarie University, suggests that the public would welcome a two- or threefold increase in the current government subsidy for the arts.[2]

The policies and institutions begun by the Whitlam government in 1973 have been allowed to mature in the intervening years. In particular, Australians have found that it is possible to justify arts subsidy in terms of the market return on investment and not simply in terms of human values or prestige. The arts, and especially the visual arts, have been part of a shrewd coming-of-age, a deliberate questioning of much of the narrow, consumerist materialism which still dominated public thinking in the 1970s.

Many earlier Australian art institutions were founded on stern Ruskinian principles of beauty as moral improvement. This has never sorted very well with much in the Australian temperament and culture. The new interest in the visual arts in Australia marks a change in these attitudes to art which may at first appear paradoxical. Ways are being found to fulfil a growing need for involvement with the arts which do not entail preaching or snobbery. According to Andrea Hull of the Australia Council, more than 700,000 people attended an art exhibition of some kind in New South Wales in 1984, while only 150,000 attended cricket matches. One could not imagine a more impressive index of changing values.

The opening of the National Gallery in Canberra in 1982 was the major institutional event of the period. The Gallery had been long in the planning. In 1965 the Menzies government had made a commitment to a National Gallery, but the major step was in 1973 when Gough Whitlam laid the foundation plaque for the building and simultaneously supported a number of controversial purchases, including Jackson Pollock's *Blue Poles*, now amongst the most important works in the collection. The Fraser government continued support, and by 1982 the Gallery and its collection were ready for the Queen to open. The most important achievement of the National Gallery is undoubtedly the Australian Collection, where for the first time Australians were able to see the painting, sculpture and decorative arts of Australia as a developing unity. These rooms in the Gallery reflect Daniel Thomas's detached, independent assessment of Australian art and showed it to be a much finer achievement on its own terms than many had believed. This contrasted strongly with the overall organizing principle of the Gallery, which was still dedicated to mainstream values and to a blinkered view of the possible relations of Australian art to international art. The visitor was intended to reach the Australian Gallery only after having progressed through the works of mainstream Modernism displayed in triumphal sequence in the main gallery, where there was no Australian work at all. I was involved briefly in the controversy over this, and suggested that Nolan's *Ned Kelly Series* might well form a pendant for *Blue Poles* as they were coeval, and that such a contrast would emphasize the independent values in Australian art. Shortly after, the Nolans were indeed moved into the main hall and in general the National Gallery has shown increasing willingness to abandon the role of missionary for the mainstream, and to become instead a multiple resource which stresses the many available relationships of Australian art to western International art, Aboriginal art and to the arts of the Pacific and Indian Ocean countries.[3] This change is significant for contemporary art both as a sign of the new ethos, but more especially because of the importance of the National Gallery in shaping the expectations of the audience for the arts.

Other major events in art institutions during the 1980s included the opening of the magnificent State Art Gallery in Queensland in 1982, and recently the commitment of the Government of New South Wales to dedicate the marvellous Customs and Excise building at Circular Quay in Sydney to the Power Institute collection of contemporary art. In the last few years, there have also been a large number of regional galleries and museums built across Australia to provide for the demands of those Australians who do not live in one of the six capital cities. A similar growth has occurred in alternative art spaces such as Praxis in Western Australia or Art Space in Sydney. These largely public-funded organizations have provided a relatively secure exhibition circuit for new and young artists, and for aesthetic experiment of all kinds. In the last five years, then, the presence and availability of the visual arts in Australia has grown beyond all expectation. Individual artists have extended their roles to meet many of the new needs, working as muralists, community artists and experimenting with new media. Unfortunately, it is only in the last year or so that adequate ways of supporting these new roles have been found.

A long-running attempt to recover the broader historical basis of Australian art from oblivion culminated in the early 1980s. Apart from the National Collection of Australian art in Canberra, there were a number of scholarly exhibitions such as the *Eugen von Guérard* exhibition of 1980 and most recently a retrospective of the work of the Sydney artist *Passmore* (1985). These exhibitions, and innumerable publications, have fleshed out the public picture of the history of Australian art. Von Guérard is now recognized as much more than a second-rate German Romantic, and the sight of Victor Passmore's earlier works has given particular definition to his role in the development of Sydney abstract paintings in the 1960s.

One specially important achievement is the recovery of a radical tradition in the visual arts that had been virtually annihilated during the Menzies years. This tradition linked the idea of an independent Australian identity to experimental and modernist art, surrealism in alliance with optimistic socialism, and has once more become a vital element in Australian cultural debate. The initial recovery was made by feminist artists and writers who were looking for a base to work in the community as artists in the 1970s. More recently, exhibitions such as Charles Merewether's *Art and Social Commitment* (1984) and to a lesser extent *Aspects of Australian Figurative Painting* 1942–1962 by Christine Dixon and Terry Smith (1984) have shown the importance of this tradition for the formation of Australian visual art after 1945. Books such as Richard Haese's *Rebels and Precursors* (1981) have added to this picture. It is ultimately from this radical tradition that current Australian artists draw their ability to negotiate Post Modernism so successfully.

Even in something so 'orthodox' as painting, a new feeling of freedom has appeared. Most public Australian painting had defined its possibilities through the relationship between the experience of the Australian landscape as a metaphor for Australian history and social relations, and whatever 'style' of painting was seen to be dominant in Europe and America at the time. The deaths of two major Australian landscape painters who resisted this signalled the passing of this definition as the abiding truth of Australian art. Russell Drysdale, who died in 1981, had given the definitive image to Australian landscape painting and to an Australian society which depended on the landscape. The other tragic death was that of Fred Williams in 1982. Williams was the first Australian painter to 'naturalize' Modernism. At the time of his early death he had escaped all references to the Modernist canon he had studied so thoroughly in Britain in the fifties and was the first Australian painter whose vision was fully emancipated. Unlike other painters of his generation, he succeeded in resisting the pressure to become superficial; the demand that he should find a new single reference point in American heroic abstraction of the sixties and seventies. His example was of major importance to middle generation and younger Australian painters, particularly those working in and around Melbourne. Some, such as Geoffrey Makin, have continued to work with the landscape. Others such as Victor Majzner have moved into a very complex emotional figuration which depended, in part, on Williams's example. He had an acute appreciation of the resonances between technique and response to the image within the European way of making a painting. The general rejection of pure abstraction that came with Post Modern art around 1980 was no revelation to Australians, but the superficiality of the new International art has been regarded with great suspicion by many of them. It could be argued that the effect of Post Modernism was to authenticate much in Australian art that had been repressed by the dominance of previous international trends. Despite a debate on the 'death of painting', it had never been seriously under threat here as a major means of expression, and neither had the relevance of imagery. Even an abstractionist like Fred Cress had always asserted the value of the image and the emotional content in his work, and in the 1980s this has been emphasized. In a sense, Australian painters have been able to negotiate the end of Modernism and the new pluralism of styles far better than their British colleagues as the resources to do so had always existed in the context of Australian art. Looked at from the outside, the progress of a young painter like Jenny Watson might seem like the old familiar story of the Emperor's clothes. Watson began her public career as a photo-realist, but in the 1980s she began to produce work of a simple gestural kind leading to the paintings she showed in the 1984 Sydney Biennale.

It would be a serious error to read Watson's work, and the work of other 'New Wave' painters from Melbourne (or Australia as a whole), as Australia's version of the New Expressionism or of any other style on the international curatorial agenda. These artists have distanced themselves from these international movements in a way that shows their own roots and richness. One only has to compare the vapid metaphysical generalities and Hollywood historicism of the images of horses by the British painter Christopher Lebrun with Watson's immediate and funny horse paintings, to see what has happened. For artists here, many 'Western' problems are ceasing to have any relevance. Young Australian artists have developed an incisive and direct attitude to their art which is rarely found elsewhere.

In Sydney, the relationship of artists to the freedoms of Post Modernism are more diffuse but just as liberating as in Melbourne. A principal beneficiary of the new sensibility has been Keith Looby, who has been a constant irritant to international art curators. Looby has always attempted to develop an Australian imagery which would stand the highest test of aesthetic standards and resist any reading out of its Australian context. As a result, he has been rewarded with great private success but public and institutional indifference. His failure to win the Archibald Prize, the prestigious annual prize for portrait painting at the Art Gallery of New South Wales, has been greeted with general disbelief and controversy. Looby's point in entering every year was that establishment exhibitions, and public tastes and attitudes to the arts as part of Australian life, do matter. In 1984 he won the contest with a painting of his long-term friend Max Gillies, the actor, impersonating Prime Minister Bob Hawke as he does regularly at a Sydney nightclub, and on his satirical television show 'The Gillies Report'.

The series of paintings of which this was one was shown at the Roslyn Oxley Gallery. Since it began in 1982, the Oxley Gallery has been well-known as the home of much of the new art in Sydney and Looby's work seemed at home in the space. Terence Maloon, the art critic of the *Sydney Morning Herald*, wrote that after twenty years Looby seemed to have been vindicated in his role as the conscientious objector of Australian Modernism.[4] According to Maloon, this vindication was due to the appearance in Australia of a touring exhibition of the work of Phillip Guston. Whilst it is true that both Looby and Guston paint large tragic human figures in heavy paint, Looby has always worked figuratively and would not lightly accept the proposition that his work shares Guston's concern for the tragedy of American abstraction. It is more a case of success after many years of determination.

Looby's vindication was part of the reassessment of the attitudes expressed by Bernard Smith in 1959, when he and his artist friends founded the 'Antipodeans'. Smith argued in 'The Antipodean Manifesto' that the easy imitation and assimilation of international abstraction would lead to a loss of vitality in Australian art and advocated a new native figuration.[5] Talking in Perth in early 1985, he gave an account of the way in which a promising independent Australian art was diverted into a subdivision of international Modernism. The art of the 1980s has proved much more independent; more awake to the dangers that Smith identified. Current attempts to read Australian art as an outback Post Modern appear to be failing. This is because many middle generation artists have found it necessary to resist international pressures in order to respond adequately to their own concerns. They keep close control over the ways in which their work is presented. The impact of Post Modern sentiment on Australian art has largely been to make the maintenance of a separate identity much easier. The idea of a decentred culture consisting of vernacular styles has been most important in this respect.

Many Australian artists have been able to make use of this new freedom of means offered by Post Modernism. They include the artists represented in *An Australian Accent*, an exhibition organized by Australian art patron John Kaldor and Daniel Thomas. Mike Parr, Ken Unsworth and Immants Tillers have each been active in diversifying the possibilities for Australian art. (There is no time in this brief article to trace their individual development beyond late Modernism.) Parr had been a distinguished performance artist from the early 1970s. His latest work consists of a series of complex drawings in which various modes of autistic relation to one's emotions and the environment are given a symbolic description by means of contrasting drawing styles.[6] The two other artists whose work was exhibited in this show have a similar breadth of concern from the physical 'making' of the work to myth, and the foundations of personality and human relations. *An Australian Accent* was an exhibition which marked the recognition of this broad range of human concerns in Australian art at a time when such range appears to be beyond the capacities of most western countries. Parr's work has always concerned itself with human identity and action. One of his most notorious early pieces made use of the fact that he has only one arm. He had a false arm made for his other shoulder, full of fake blood, and then chopped it off in front of a bewildered and uncomprehending audience. His recent work consists of a series of large charcoal self-portraits. It makes use of a variety of drawing styles, ranging from the tightly controlled and illusionistic, through various planar projections of the same image, to the most incoherent of gestures, which barely represent anything at all. All these works have to do with the boundaries and codes which we establish as acceptable representations of the human condition and which themselves betoken acceptable behaviour. His great interest in various forms of psychology, in particular the group consciousness theories of Jung, has had a marked effect on his meditations as to how the person is defined in Australian culture. If one compares Parr's work with Gilbert and George, whose art lays claim to a similar range of concerns, Parr emerges as more open to the whole of the human condition. Like many Australian artists working in experimental areas, he often seems to have more to say than his European counterparts and, I believe, says it more excitingly. This was seen most strikingly in two recent exhibitions at the Art Gallery of Western Australia. The Australian artists working in a contemporary mode in the *Pleasure of the Gaze* exhibition, seemed far more energetic and relevant than many of the big name artists who were part of the great *British Show* which had appeared here earlier this year. Richard Dunn and Julie Brown, two Sydney artists in this exhibition, offered subtle meditations on the construction of the person through history and the media.

None of this specifically Australian success has stopped the endless march of the international curators into the country hoping to find a tailor-made Australian art which they can fit into their international cultural schema. These visitors are mostly American. They are very attracted to the dead desert centre of the country, about which they romanticize at length, and they usually invent an idea of Australian art as primitive, an art born out of the absence of European culture. This tactic was first used by Bryan Robertson, the English curator, who organized the exhibition at the Whitechapel Gallery, London, in 1961 which included Nolan, Boyd, Juniper and many other important figures.[7]

Nowadays, however, Australian artists are more sophisticated and are learning to live with the problem, and to present themselves and their work outside the frame of this overseas-centred internationalism. They are themselves more international, often travelling a great deal. This has enabled them to resist prepackaging and the narrowing of the range of their work which goes with it. An artist such as Dale Franks, for instance, is as fully international as any European, yet his base remains Australia. Franks's work was included in the 1984 exhibition assembled by Diane Waldmann for the Guggenheim in New York, *Australian – Visions*. Over the years the Guggenheim and Waldmann have conducted one of the most imperious and imperial of New York art circuses, and typically the exhibition misread Australian art into a New York context. Franks in particular suffered badly from this, but he was able to arrange his own New York exhibition out of reach of Waldmann's reading of Australia.

Previous generations of Australian expatriates never had this opportunity to become self-confident and knowledgeable about international art as their work developed. For them it was a great mirage compounded of coloured illustrations and theoretical rhetoric. When they went overseas, they went to make a career. Significantly, several important Australian artists who did that in the late sixties and seventies, have returned to Australia in the early 1980s. These include Michael Johnson, Robert Jacks and Colin Lanceley. The independent self-esteem which Australian artists have felt in the 1980s was supported by the sudden appearance of a whole range of new art magazines. These include *Arts National* from Brisbane, *Praxis M* from Perth and most importantly *Art Network* edited in Sydney and *Art and Text* in Melbourne. *Art and Text* was the creation of one man, Paul Taylor, who wished to produce a journal in which current theoretical issues affecting the visual arts could be discussed in depth. Taylor deliberately resisted the notion that an art magazine should, in general, consist of monographs on individual artists and colour plates. This format had been that of *Art and Australia*, which was unable to cope unaided with the diversity of the Australian art scene by 1981. Originally *Art and Text* was pluralistic in its choice of writers, and at times opened up some very exciting debate. More recently, it has tended to reflect a limited international perspective rather than develop the local critical debate in depth. This may be because it has an international circulation. *Art Network* has almost the opposite problems to *Art and Text*. It was founded, idealistically, as a collective with a brief to report on art and the art world across Australia. It does this successfully, but it lacks the resources of *Art and Australia* in terms of colour or a ready coffee-table audience. Despite this, it has been able to produce some good writing and in many ways gives a much broader perspective on Australian art than any other magazine. In any case there is now a critical debate in depth in Australian art criticism, and critical writing is developing at a very rapid pace.

In such a short space it has only been possible to sketch a brief outline of the enormous excitement currently to be found in the Australian visual arts. Much to their surprise, and for the first time in history, Australians have recognized the excellence of their artists and are giving them full support. One may soon have to fly to Sydney, Perth or Melbourne to see the best in contemporary visual art.

NOTES

1. See Paul Taylor, 'Clement Greenberg and Post Modernism – an Interview', *Art in Australia*, Sydney, Vol. 18, No. 2, 1980, p. 139.
   The same issue (p. 133) contains a very interesting survey, 'The Australian art scene in the 1970s', and also (p. 158) an article in which Von Guerard and the Hudson School are compared as equals.
2. C.D. Throsby (Chairman), 'The Artist in Australia Today', *Report of the Committee for the Individual Artist Enquiry*, Australia Council, c. 1983.
3. See my article 'Never mind the Quality', in the *National Times*, 10–16 October, 1982.
4. Maloon, Terence, 'Looby: throwing gauntlets like confetti', *Sydney Morning Herald*, 8 December 1984, p. 46.
5. Smith's essay, first published in 1959, is reprinted in his collection *The Antipodean Manifesto, Essays in Art and History*, OUP, Melbourne, 1976, pp. 165–7. For the context see Gary Catalano, *The Years of Hope: Australian Art and Art Criticism 1959–1968*, OUP, Melbourne, 1981, pp. 203–5 and passim.
6. See the exhibition catalogue *An Australian Accent*, written by Daniel Thomas and John Kaldor, Sydney, 1984.
7. For an account of this from the receiving end, see Bernard Smith, 'The Truth about the Antipodeans', in *Praxis*, Perth, No 8, Autumn 1985.

12 Aboriginal Rock Art: 'Threatened Species' of the Visual Arts in Australia

F. Gale and J. Jacobs

In traditional Aboriginal society the visual arts were not reserved for the talented, educated or wealthy few, as they tend to be in European Australia. In the Aboriginal world art belonged to everyone and children were brought up to appreciate the various art forms as an integral part of their lives.

Religious belief and practice provided the essential inspiration for all artistic expression, and it is difficult to appreciate Aboriginal art unless it is seen within the context of people intimately related to their land and its spiritual and creative essence. Aboriginal religion was a very sophisticated system of beliefs and its expression could be seen in a variety of artistic modes. This does not mean that all art is directly concerned with religious phenomena. The more mundane activities of food hunting and gathering are also depicted frequently, but even the primarily domestic art must be viewed from the perspective of a people expressing their intimate relationship with the land and with each other, as well as with the essentially spiritual as well as material basis of those relationships.

The Art Forms

The visual arts found many forms of expression in Aboriginal society, reflecting the materials and art surfaces available in the local environment as well as the lifestyles and beliefs of the people.[1] Drawings in the sand and ceremonial paintings on the body were of particular importance in Central Australia and the desert areas where bare earth encouraged sand or earth drawings, and where elaborate ceremonial dance rituals were carried out requiring considerable body paintings. These forms of visual expression, although very important at the time of their execution, are ephemeral in nature and cannot be viewed after the events which lead to their creation.

Other forms of art with a similarly long-standing historic tradition are more permanent. Some, like the engravings and paintings drawn on rock walls and flat rock surfaces, have survived for many thousands of years. Ochre pigment used in rock paintings was found in an excavation in Arnhem Land and dated to 19,000 years, and circumstantial evidence suggests that wall markings in Koonalda Cave on the Nullarbor Plain could be up to 24,000 years old.

Engraving is a loose term used to describe the marking of rocks by pecking, carving, abrading or pounding so as to produce pictures and designs with indentation as opposed to those produced by the application of paint. Engraving is possibly the oldest and certainly the most permanent of the art forms which can be viewed today (Plate 1). The distribution of engraved stones stretches across Australia from Port Hedland in the Pilbara region of Western Australia through sites such as the Cleland Hills and Ewaninga in Central Australia to Red Gorge in the Flinders Ranges and Olary outcrops such as at Panaramitee and Teetulpa in South Australia, and eastwards into western New South Wales to well-known sites such as Mootwingee. There are also areas of engravings in northern Queensland at places like Laura, in sandstone exposures in the Hawkesbury area around Sydney and in Tasmania at Mt Cameron West, as well as at several isolated sites across the continent. This particular art form depends upon the availability of suitable engraving surfaces and as such its distribution appears to be determined more by rock formations than by cultural factors. The actual style of art, however, varies considerably from one site to another.

Rock painting involves a completely different technique from that of rock engraving. Paintings can be found in most areas of Australia where rock shelters enabled the paint to be applied and protected. Painting is more widespread than engraving and was still being practised throughout Australia at the time of European settlement. As far as can be determined rock engraving ceased as an art form at some earlier date. Although Aboriginal people appeared to paint in most areas where suitable rock walls or shelters exist, the most extensive and elaborate paintings are to be found in northern Australia stretching from the Kimberleys in Western Australia across the Arnhem Land region of the Northern Territory to Cape York Peninsula in Queensland. Caves and rock shelters in Central Australia also contain a profusion of paintings, although they are not as varied or elaborate as those in the north. In southern and eastern Australia paintings appear to be much more simplified in both style and extent and the majority of examples have been lost or defaced since the Aboriginal people were driven from these southern lands some 150 or so years ago. In northern Australia, however, rock painting remained a vital form of artistic expression until very recent times (Plate 2). It now appears to have ceased as westernization has penetrated to all groups of people and even tradi-

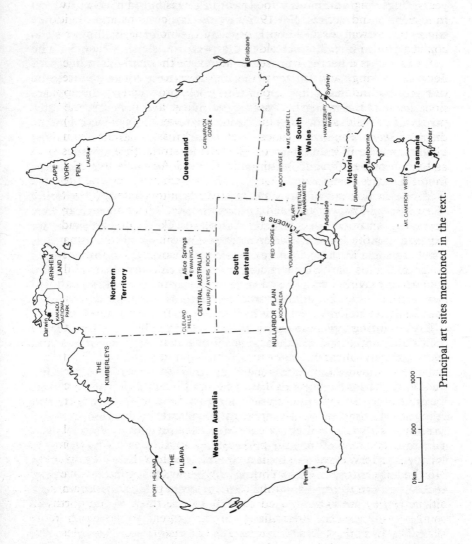

Principal art sites mentioned in the text.

tionally oriented Aborigines have been encouraged to transfer their painting skills to other mediums.

Paintings vary enormously in style and technique according to local conditions and practices. For example, in Carnarvon Gorge the sandstone surfaces encouraged application by means of stencilling, that is blowing paint on to the rock around a prepared stencil (Plate 3). The result is quite different from that achieved by direct painting with finger, stick or brush. In stencil art the dominant colour tends to be white or ochre depending upon the rock, but when surfaces are smoother and paint can be applied by more direct means a greater variety of colours can be used including charcoal and yellow. Pigments were extracted from many sources but red ochre was viewed as the most important form of paint and extensive trade routes were developed to make this pigment available to painters living considerable distances from the ochre mines.

More recent forms of art, such as sculpturing in wood and painting on bark sheets, appear to have replaced the once continuous art of rock engraving and painting. Wood sculpture and bark paintings are confined mainly to northern Australia and their development has enabled people in these areas to transfer their designs to forms which are portable and can be constructed at mission or camp sites away from the former rock shelters. The newer surfaces are also more amenable to new techniques and equipment and are saleable items for an economy with limited economic viability in western terms. And more recently still Aboriginal people, especially in Central Australia, have transferred their skills and designs to canvas, masonite and other transportable and marketable art surfaces.

The very development of these alternative forms of art, using traditionally based designs in new styles and using different mediums, illustrates the cultural strength of Aboriginal art and the flexibility and ingenuity of the artists. New forms of artistic expression are also emerging with the application of older designs and styles to woven materials by way of printing, tie dying and batik. But with the emergence of these new and more adaptable surfaces there is real danger that the long history of rock painting will be neglected and lost forever. If the rock art is not maintained and protected Australia will lose a unique artistic heritage.

Art Endangered

The rock art tradition is not only as old, and probably older, than the well known prehistoric art of Europe, it also represents a continuous process right up to the present day. The rock walls thus reflect some 20,000 years of changing environments and art styles. A magnificent record of the history of art! But this invaluable record is under serious threat from both environmental and human factors. Recently considerable attention has been given to environmental agents which cause deterioration of the rock art surfaces. The impact of mud-building insects, feral and wild animals, water, mineral deposits and other agents has been well documented and considerable headway made in understanding ways of halting or slowing deterioration resulting from them.[2] The direct concern of the present authors is not with these environmental factors but with the impact of humans, specifically tourists, on the art.

Much of the rock art in Australia has for many years been protected from visitors by its location in remote and isolated areas. In days gone by such art sites would be visited only occasionally by the lone stockman or art enthusiast. No so today. Areas once protected by distance are now receiving large numbers of visitors. Improved roads, four-wheel-drive vehicles, the opening of camping grounds, motels and other facilities in remote areas have all led to a rapid upsurge in the number of people visiting some of the most magnificent art sites in Australia and, indeed, the world. Now tourists are not only able to gain easy access to such areas but are being encouraged to do so by the promotion of remote areas as exciting tourist destinations. Art sites are consequently being exposed to a massive scale of visitor pressure previously unknown.

Kakadu National Park in the Northern Territory, for example, has witnessed a substantial increase in the number of visitors since its dedication in 1979. The Park is an area of great natural beauty, rich in sub-tropical flora and fauna, and in addition contains some of the finest examples of Aboriginal rock painting in Australia. In October 1982 the Park was accepted on to the World Heritage list by UNESCO. It is to be expected that an area of such outstanding natural and cultural heritage should attract the interest of tourists, and indeed the Park has been heavily promoted as a tourist destination. Improved roads and visitor facilities have added to the appeal of the area. In the first year of the Park's operation (1979) it is estimated that some 20,000 people visited the region. By 1985 in excess of 95,000 visitors came to the Park. The majority of these visitors go to at least one of the art sites in the area.

Just as outstanding is the growth of visitor numbers at Uluru National Park (Ayers Rock) in Central Australia. The main attraction for visitors who go to this Park is undoubtedly the great monolith of Ayers Rock itself. Although the Aboriginal paintings in various caves and shelters at the base of the rock are not the main reason people go to the area, the majority of visitors do include at least a cursory visit to some of the art sites during their tour of the Rock. The once remote Ayers Rock is now accessible by way of high-grade roads or by air. It has always been heavily promoted as a tourist attraction and its value as a resource for the tourist industry has recently been confirmed by the building of the $160 million Yulara tourist centre approximately 15 km from the Rock. In 1958/59, the earliest year for which visitor numbers are available, only 2,296 people visited the Rock. By 1984/85 this had increased to 94,000 and it is projected that by the year 1994/95 the Rock will attract an astounding 281,000 visitors (figures calculated by Peak, Marwick and Mitchell Services, Tourist Industry Consultants).

At both Kakadu and Uluru the art is showing signs of deterioration. Both areas have had sporadic problems with vandals putting graffiti on art surfaces. More persistent is the damage resulting from visitors touching the art either accidentally by brushing against it, or deliberately fingering it, usually out of sheer curiosity. High visitor levels have also created problems with ground dust which is kicked up by visitors on to the art face, as well as the devegetation of areas in the immediate vicinity of an art site, with the consequent effects of increasing dust levels in the air. The removal of vegetation also tends to expose once shaded art to direct sunlight. In the smaller, confined galleries there are also problems arising from rapid changes in temperature and humidity as people crowd into the shelters to see the art.

Rock Art Management

This pressure is of great concern to those wishing to conserve Australia's heritage of Aboriginal rock art and as a result numerous attempts have been made to manage or control visitor pressure. The management responses have thus far been varied, ranging from complete inaction in areas where the art is seen as doomed, to the installation of complex built structures designed to keep visitors away from the art surfaces. At Kakadu, for example, Park management has introduced a wide range of mechanisms for controlling visitor pressure. In order to contain the impact of tourists on the art of the region the management, along with the traditional Aboriginal owners of the area, decided to encourage tourists to visit two already popular sites while discouraging them from going to other sites. Access to the selected sites was improved and the areas publicized in Park brochures. In contrast, access to other art sites was discouraged by camouflaging or fencing off old tracks or, in some cases, installing signs warning visitors not to enter.

At the two sites selected by the Kakadu Park management for tourist use numerous efforts have been made to limit the damaging effects of visitor pressure. Movement of visitors at the sites has been controlled by the introduction of high-quality access routes, car-parking areas and walking trails. Visitors arc kept away from direct contact with the art but are able to approach within reasonable viewing distance. This has been achieved by fencing, boardwalks, and signs warning that fines apply to those who damage the art. In order to maximize the enjoyment and interest of the tourists' visit to these sites considerable effort has gone into providing interpretive material which deals with the age of the art, the techniques used by the artists, the cultural significance of the art and so on. The visitor centre of Kakadu National Park Headquarters has an audio-visual display dealing with the art which is complemented by brochures and the on-site interpretive signs. By providing this information, and thereby increasing the visitor's understanding of art, it is hoped that visitors will view the art with greater respect and as a result will be less inclined to behave in a way which places the art at risk. A study of visitor behaviour at the Kakadu art sites prior to and after the introduction of these controls showed that they were very successful in reducing the amount of behaviour known to place the art directly or indirectly at risk.[3]

With all of the built controls installed at Kakadu considerable care has been taken with materials and design to ensure that the structures are sympathetic to the environment and do not intrude on the general tone of the area. Although environmental suitability must be a major consideration in design, management must also acknowledge that these structures are to be used by tourists. This is not always the case. For example, a timber boardwalk and fence constructed in front of one of the sites at Kakadu to keep both feral buffalo and visitors back from the art has had some design problems in terms of visitor requirements. The fence has successfully kept buffalo from rubbing their backs on the art walls but the boardwalk is so placed that it is difficult to take uninterrupted photographs of the art. This type of design oversight can cause frustration amongst visitors and encourage them to disregard the fencing and render it ineffective as a control mechanism.

At Carnarvon Gorge, where boardwalk controls were initially developed in Aboriginal art areas, particular care was taken to ensure that the structures not only met the needs of management to keep people away from the art but did not, in doing so, interfere with or detract from the visitor's experience of the area. For example, the boardwalks are built in local timber well suited to conditions in the area (Plate 4). Further, the layout of the boardwalk and its distance from the art is such that visitors are always able to have an uninterrupted view for photography. This sort of design consideration is absolutely crucial, especially as taking photographs is now such an integral part of the touring experience.

Very few areas in Australia have undertaken such comprehensive management programmes as are now evident at Kakadu or Carnarvon Gorge. At Uluru, for example, little has been done to deal with the pressures arising from the large and increasing number of visitors. A visitor centre has been constructed as part of the Yulara development but the effectiveness of interpretive material located some fifteen kilometres from the art itself is questionable. Rangers from Uluru Park have been conducting daily tours of one area of art. These tours are both popular and instructive. However, because of limited staffing levels, these ranger tours are offered only once a day and cover only one group of art sites. During the peak season the tours can attract up to one hundred people. The interpretive value of these tours must then be weighed against the enormous and unusual pressures arising from having large numbers visit often small and confined rock art sites.

In southern areas of Australia where the art areas are often more accessible, and closer to population centres, visitor levels have been high for a much longer period of time than in the more remote areas discussed to date. Many of these southern art sites have suffered enormous damage from visitors and their propensity to add graffiti to the art surfaces. This pressure has encouraged dramatic management responses in some areas. In the Flinders Ranges of South Australia and the Grampians of Victoria entrances of caves and shelters containing rock art have been caged from floor to ceiling by steel grills. This may be an effective way of keeping visitors away from rock art surfaces, but the caging is unsightly and rarely engenders a positive response from visitors to either the art or Aboriginal culture. For the majority of visitors it is frustrating and disappointing to have the view so horrendously obstructed. Such measures may in fact now be outdated. Much of the damage in evidence at these sites is the result of past rather than current patterns of vandalism. Changes in the scale and nature of the visitor population mean that it is not always appropriate to gauge the impact of visitor presence by the evidence left behind from past visitor patterns. The effectiveness of more subtle management strategies now operating elsewhere in Australia suggest that less obtrusive measures may now be effective as well as preferable.

The long-term success of any management strategy designed to reduce the impact of visitors depends in essence on encouraging visitors to accept that such measures are necessary and must be obeyed. This, in turn, depends largely on the attitude of visitors towards Aboriginal rock art. While Australians today appear to be more willing to accept the need to preserve European heritage items to which they can strongly relate there is not the same commitment to Aboriginal rock art. At present the majority of visitors see Aboriginal rock art as primitive and unsophisticated, and as peripheral to their experience of Australia. It is seen as having little or no aesthetic appeal and certainly no direct cultural relevance. The majority of visitors rarely go to a remote area specifically to view the Aboriginal art. Rather, they are seeking exposure to the Australian environment and Aboriginal rock art is an unexpected extra, rarely understood or appreciated for its intrinsic or historic value.

Changing this attitude is an important step in ensuring the long-term conservation of rock art. In many ways the management measures themselves operate to alter tourist attitudes. Interpretive signs providing accurate information increase visitor understanding of the cultural value of the art. Signs warning of fines associated with the deliberate damaging of the art establish a sense of the art's value, as do obtrusive management measures such as fencing. Once these protective mechanisms are installed it becomes clearly apparent to the visitor that they are looking at something of value. However, it is crucial that the management controls add to, rather than detract from, the visitor's experience and appreciation of the art.

Conclusion

The significant role which the visual arts play in Aboriginal culture is evident not only from the long history and central position in Aboriginal life but also from the amazing ability and desire of the artists to see their work adapted to new forms. Bark paintings are very popular amongst tourists and Aboriginal designs and motifs are now reproduced in a variety of different ways from simple prints of table mats to elaborate ornaments. But it is equally important that the extensive artistic history exhibited on rock walls is appreciated, and not destroyed or lost through ignorance and neglect.

In France, for example, where the prehistoric rock art is seen as part of the cultural roots of modern French culture, enormous measures have been undertaken to try and preserve that art. But in Australia there is much less concern with the preservation of Aboriginal rock art. Most Australians recognize their cultural roots as being based in Europe and they do not perceive Aboriginal art as intrinsic to the development of modern day Australian culture. For the majority of non-Aboriginal Australians Aboriginal culture is viewed as peripheral to an Australian experience and its visual representation is not even recognized as art – let alone as a unique world heritage. Australians will need to re-examine their artistic concerns and their identity with this country if this valuable treasure is to survive for future generations (both Aboriginal and non-Aboriginal) as well as overseas visitors to appreciate, study and enjoy.

NOTES

1. See, for overview of Aboriginal rock art in Australia: Edwards, Robert (1979), *Australian Aboriginal Art: The Art of the Alligator River Region, Northern Territory*, Australian Institute of Aboriginal Studies, Canberra; and Isaacs, Jennifer (1984), *Australia's Living Heritage: Arts of the Dreaming*, Lansdowne Press, Sydney.

2. See, for overview: Rosenfeldt, Andree (1985), *Rock Art Conservation in Australia*, Australian Heritage Commission, Special Australian Heritage Publication Series No. 2, Australian Govt. Publishing Service, Canberra.
3. Our research into visitor pressure on rock art has involved field surveys at both Kakadu and Uluru National Parks. For details of the research methodology and results see: Gale, G.F. (1985), 'Monitoring Visitor Behaviour at Rock Art Sites', *Rock Art Research*, Archaeological Publications, Melbourne, Vol. 2, No. 2; and Gale, G.F. and Jacobs, J.M. (1986), 'Identifying High-Risk Visitors at Aboriginal Art Sites', *Rock Art Research*, Archaeological Publications, Melbourne, Vol. 3, No. 1.

ACKNOWLEDGEMENTS

These studies were undertaken with initial support from the Academy of the Social Sciences, the Australian Institute of Aboriginal Studies and the Northern Territory Conservation Commission. This pilot work was followed up with assistance from the Australian National Parks and Wildlife Service for work at Kakadu where Dan Gillespie and Hilary Sullivan gave considerable support. The work at Uluru was made possible by a grant from the Australian Heritage Commission and the on-site assistance of Derek Roff and Hilary Tabrett. Thanks to Josephine Flood and the Australian Heritage Commission it has been possible to employ Jane Jacobs to take a major responsibility for the collection of data and also to analyse the material from both sets of surveys.

Index

173

Notes on Contributors

Delys Bird has been a member of the School of English, Western Australian Institute of Technology, Perth for the last five years. She is at present on secondment to the Faculty of Arts, University of Western Australia, where she is the co-ordinator of a new programme of postgraduate study, an MPhil in Women's Studies and Australian Studies. Her major teaching, research and publishing interests derive from these broad areas. She is completing a doctoral thesis on narrative structures in Australian women's fiction.

David Bromfield is Director of the Centre for Fine Arts at the University of Western Australia.

Bruce Clunies Ross is an Associate Professor in the Department of English at the University of Copenhagen. He was born in Adelaide, educated at the University there, and later at Balliol College, Oxford. He has written on various aspects of Australian literature and music, and is currently editing the musical essays of the Australian composer, Percy Grainger.

Ian Craven lectures in Film and Television Studies at the University of Glasgow, and is a member of the John Logie Baird Centre for Research in Television and Film. He is currently preparing a study of the South Australian Film Corporation.

Fay Gale is Professor of Geography at the University of Adelaide and a Fellow of the Academy of Social Sciences in Australia. She has worked in a wide spectrum of research dealing with Aboriginal issues, the latest being the protection of Aboriginal art. Her publications include: *Settlement and Encounter* (editor), *Woman's role in Aboriginal Society* (editor), *Urban Aborigines, Race Relations in Australia, Poverty Among Aboriginal Families in Adelaide, We are Bosses Ourselves* (editor), *Adelaide Aborigines: a case study of urban life 1966–1981.*

Don Grant teaches Australian Studies and Literature and is a Principal Lecturer at the Western Australian Institute of Technology where he also is Director of the Institute's Centre for Australian Studies. He is Western Australian and Federal President of the Fellowship of Australian Writers and President of the Australian Studies Association (AUSTA).

Sneja Gunew teaches literature and women's studies courses at Deakin University, Victoria, an institution which specialises in producing off-campus correspondence material. She has published in both areas and is currently preparing a book on migrant writing in Australia.

Jane Jacobs is a Research Associate in the Department of Geography, University of Adelaide. She is a graduate of the University and her postgraduate studies dealt with the politics of Aboriginal land rights action in a rural town of South Australia. She has undertaken numerous consultancies in the field of Aboriginal affairs for both private and government bodies. For the past two years she has worked with Professor Gale on the protection of Aboriginal art.

Peter Quartermaine teaches Commonwealth arts in the School of English at the University of Exeter. A graduate in English literature and philosophy, he taught for a year in Calcutta before initiating Exeter's Commonwealth programme in the mid 1960s, since when he has published three previous books on Australian arts (*Gundagai Album*, Canberra 1976; *Readings in Australian Arts*, Exeter 1978; *Jeffrey Smart*, Melbourne 1983). With David Lowenthal he is convenor of an international conference on Australian Landscapes at Exeter in 1987.

Henry Reynolds is Associate Professor of History at the James Cook University of North Queensland, Townsville.

Werner Senn is Professor of English literature at the University of Bern. He has published books on Elizabethan drama and on Joseph Conrad and articles on Robert Greene, Herman Melville, Patrick White, Randolph Stow as well as on problems of narrative fiction. In his teaching he includes Australian literature and other areas of Commonwealth writing. He also was the convenor of the 1984 conference on 'War: Australia's Literary Response' held in Bern.

Sam Smiles is Senior Lecturer, School of Arts Research, Exeter College of Art and Design. He studied philosophy and art history at Cambridge and – apart from a two year period of fascinating tedium in an advertising agency – has been teaching the history of art at various institutions ever since. Forthcoming publications include an article on Turner in Devon for the Australian National University and a short study of Sidney Nolan for Marshall Cavendish.

Graeme Turner is a Senior Lecturer in Communications at the Queensland Institute of Technology in Brisbane. He has published on Australian literature, film, television, and is an editor of the *Australian Journal of Cultural Studies*. His book on Australian film and fiction from which this material is partly drawn, *National Fictions: Literature, Film and the Construction of Australian Narrative*, is to be published by Allen & Unwin in 1986. He is co-author of another book on Australian popular culture, *Myths of Oz: Readings in Australian Popular Culture* (with John Fiske and Robert Hodge), to be published in 1987.